AMERICAN MEDIA

AMERICAN MEDIA

The Wilson Quarterly Reader

Edited by

PHILIP S. COOK
DOUGLAS GOMERY
LAWRENCE W. LICHTY

THE WILSON CENTER PRESS   WASHINGTON, DC

The Wilson Center Press
Smithsonian Institution Building
1000 Jefferson Drive, S.W.
Washington, D.C. 20560 U.S.A.

Distributed by arrangement with
UPA, Inc.
4720 Boston Way
Lanham, Maryland 20706

Still photographs from "The Creature from the Black Lagoon" and "The Cabinet of Dr. Caligari" reproduced courtesy of The Museum of Modern Art/Film Stills Archive.

Drawing (p. 122) by Lee Lorenz from *Real Men Don't Eat Quiche* (Pocket Books). © Lee Lorenz.

Storyboards from "Raiders of the Lost Ark" © Lucasfilm Ltd. All rights reserved. Courtesy of Lucasfilm Ltd.

Still photograph from "The Beginning or the End" © 1947 Loew's Incorporated. Ren. 1974 Metro-Goldwyn-Mayer Inc.

Advertisements for Ford Motor Company and Camel cigarettes courtesy of Collection of Advertising History, Archives Center, National Museum of American History.

Printed in the United States of America.
♾ Printed on acid-free paper.

Library of Congress Cataloging-in-Publication Data

American media.
Bibliography: p.
1. Mass media—United States. 2. United States—Popular culture.
I. Cook, Philip S. II. Gomery, Douglas. III. Lichty, Lawrence Wilson.
IV. Wilson quarterly.
P92U5A49   1988   302.2'34'0973   88–20885
ISBN 0–943875–10–2 (alk. paper)
ISBN 0–943875–09–9 (pbk. : alk. paper)

9 8 7 6 5 4 3 2

THE WILSON CENTER is the "living memorial" of the United States of America to the nation's twenty-eighth president, Woodrow Wilson.

The U.S. Congress established the Center in 1968 as an international institute for advanced study, "symbolizing and strengthening the fruitful relationship between the world of learning and the world of public affairs." The Center opened in 1970 under its own presidentially appointed board of directors.

Each year The Wilson Center holds open international competitions to select approximately fifty residential fellows to conduct advanced research, write books, and contribute to seminars, conferences, and discussions with other scholars, public officials, journalists, and business and labor leaders.

Research at The Wilson Center ranges across the entire spectrum of the humanities and social sciences. Staff and fellows employ comparative, multidisciplinary approaches. The process of discovery that operates at The Wilson Center frequently illuminates new understandings of the world in which we live, an expanded awareness of history, choices, and future consequences.

Results of the Center's research activity are disseminated internationally through the book and monograph publishing program of its Press, and with co-publishers as appropriate; and through *The Wilson Quarterly*, a scholarly journal published five times a year. Additional dissemination in the United States includes monthly *Meeting Reports*, providing summaries of formal seminars and conferences; and Radio DIALOGUE, a weekly FM series of half-hour programs.

In all its activities, The Wilson Center is a nonprofit, nonpartisan organization, supported financially by annual congressional appropriation, and by the contributions of foundations, corporations, and individuals. The Center seeks diversity of scholarly enterprise and points of view. Conclusions or opinions expressed in Center publications and programs are those of the authors and speakers and do not necessarily reflect the views of other staff members, fellows, trustees of the Center, advisory groups, or any individuals or organizations that provide financial support to the Center.

CONTENTS

FOREWORD

It used to be—during what those of us who are over sixty think of as the golden age of television and the press—that being fair, complete, in good taste, and as close to the truth as we could get was an end in itself.

But this changed with the recent rise of intense competition in the media, especially among the major broadcast organizations. It was no longer enough just to be fair, complete, tasteful, and truthful. We had to win.

We all became so busy competing, selling our "product," and giving our viewers or readers exactly what our focus groups told us they wanted that we lost sight of why we are part of the only private enterprise singled out by the Constitution for protection under the First Amendment.

The news media are singled out not so they can make money or win ratings or sell soap or entertain. They are singled out for protection so they can *seek* the truth and report what is as close to the truth as journalists can get.

No journalist believes that the press and television have a divine right to disseminate knowingly what is not the truth. But every time we in the media forget why the Constitution protects us, and every time we do not get as close to the truth as we can, we erode our special position in American society.

Most Americans seem to be ambivalent about the media because they expect so much and rely so heavily on the nation's press and television.

They want the media to be informative but not one-sided.

They want the media to be responsible but not ponderous.

They want the media to be entertaining but not frivolous.

They want the media to be aggressive but not without compassion.

And they want the media to be absolutely up-to-date and totally free from error.

Openness toward such often contradictory demands, and the criticisms they imply, is incumbent upon the media today.

I can think of no better way to stimulate rational examination of the media than by the perusal of this book, *American Media: The Wilson Quarterly Reader*.

American Media's breadth is useful; its facts persuasive; its writing vigorous, and its approach peppery. Its contributors range beyond the analysis of journalism to explain the evolution of advertising and of film and video entertainment, which are also part of "the media."

I enjoyed the sections on newspapers, the movie business, and advertising. But I am in awe of the section on television, the field I know best. In awe of its evenhandedness, its completeness, and the richness of its information.

As *American Media* makes clear, the press and television have become, in reality, a fourth branch of government, favored further by virtual immunity from external checks and balances.

Just as the American media have a special implicit responsibility under the Constitution to keep officeholders honest and to serve as a brake on excesses of governmental power, they have an equal obligation to remain honest, fair, and civil, and to curb their own inclinations toward excess.

Nothing will help the media maintain that delicate balance more effectively than informed opinion and lively discourse—exactly what this well-wrought book is likely to encourage.

Roger Mudd
Congressional Correspondent
MacNeil/Lehrer Newshour

PREFACE

Since *The Wilson Quarterly* first appeared in autumn of 1976 as a "national review of ideas and information," the magazine has published articles and essays on subjects that range from the American Revolution, American agriculture, and Antarctica, to the Vatican, Venezuela, and Vietnam. Between those alphabetical poles has been a rich mélange of material selected to satisfy *WQ*'s mission: "to bring the world of scholars and specialists to the intelligent lay reader [and] to provide an authoritative overview of current ideas and research on matters of public policy and general intellectual interest."

The *Quarterly* was launched by The Woodrow Wilson International Center for Scholars as a self-supporting venture. The Center also publishes Wilson Center Press books and various special reports, and supports preparation of a series of *Scholars' Guides* designed to help researchers in specific fields, from Soviet studies to film and video, find their way through the vast archival riches of the nation's capital. Soon to be added to this list is a *Scholars' Guide* to news media collections in the Washington, D.C., area to be prepared by The Wilson Center's Media Studies Project and published by Smithsonian Institution Press.

All this is part of The Wilson Center's special mission as the nation's "living memorial" to the twenty-eighth president of the United States. Congress established the Center in 1968 as an international institute for advanced study, "symbolizing and strengthening the fruitful relation between the world of learning and the world of public affairs." The Center opened in 1970 under its own presidentially appointed board of trustees, headed by former Vice-President Hubert H. Humphrey.

xi

Chosen in annual worldwide competitions, some fifty Fellows at the Center carry out advanced research, write books, and join in seminars and discussion with other scholars, public officials, journalists, and business and labor leaders. Often they contribute to the *Quarterly*.

The magazine, unlike many others, was intended to have a long shelf life, and surveys indicate that a substantial number of *WQ* readers save back issues for ready reference. This does not obviate the need for an occasional collection of *WQ* articles that have a natural affinity for one another. Hence this anthology of essays entitled *American Media: The Wilson Quarterly Reader*.

Peter Braestrup
Editor, *The Wilson Quarterly*

INTRODUCTION

The media profoundly influence both our vision of ourselves and our view of the world around us, often in ways that are surprising and subtle. Within the pages of *American Media: The Wilson Quarterly Reader,* both the serious student and the interested observer of the communications media will discover provocative ideas and fresh insights. Organized under the general headings of "Literacy," "Newspapers," "Movies," "Television," and "Advertising," the articles have been substantially revised and updated to reflect current developments. Major additions have been made to the "Background Books" sections of the *Reader,* and the appendixes contain charts and statistical information that will be especially useful to communications students. Throughout the book, we have attempted to examine those elements of communications that have been particularly significant in the last several years.

The *Reader* does not provide a complete primer on the media. The treatment of advertising is somewhat limited, and the newsmagazines and their changing impact on the American scene are not mentioned. Nevertheless, these essays, written by noted authorities in their respective fields, make a major contribution to understanding the media they examine.

We begin, logically enough, with literacy and the written word. "Reading maketh a full man," Francis Bacon declared in 1597, "and writing an exact man." His aphorism, penned a century and a half after Gutenberg's creation of the printing press, expressed the West's revived faith in the awesome power of literacy—to elevate the human mind, to uplift the citizenry, to spur progress. Today, many Americans, awash in memos and junk mail, take the written word for granted. Yet, perhaps 27 million of their countrymen are "functionally illiterate"; they must strain to decipher the warning label on a bottle of aspirin. In many other places reading and writing remain uncommon, the printed word a mystery. Illiteracy afflicts more than 90 percent of the people in some Third World countries. Indeed, of humankind's 3,000 spoken languages, only some 78 are written. The introduction to our "cluster" on literacy traces the development of writing in ancient times. In the essays that follow, Steven Lagerfeld describes the impact of literacy in the West, and David Harman examines the uneven state of reading and writing in the United States today.

The next grouping of articles falls under the general heading of "Newspapers." When *The Wilson Quarterly* first focused on "The News Media" in 1982, media researchers could agree on little except that it was a time of rapid transition for the multibillion-dollar "news business." A process of consolidation was under way that resulted in a decline in the number of large, independent daily papers and the creation of powerful newspaper chains, some of which also controlled important broadcast properties. At the same time, other more subtle changes were taking place that tended to increase the power and influence of the press and the role of individual journalists, even as newspaper circulation and readership remained ominously static despite a growing population. Younger Americans, it appeared, were losing the newspaper-reading habit.

These and other matters are explored by Leo Bogart and James Boylan. A.E. Dick Howard looks at the development of First Amendment doctrine, and Arthur Asa Berger examines that peculiar expression of popular culture known as "the comics."

For good or ill, American movies project a powerful image throughout the world. No form of expression conveys more vividly the hopes, dreams, fears, and preoccupations that ripple through the American psyche. Film making is both an art form and big business. Today's movies, seen on the screen, on TV, and lately on videocassettes, reach an immense audience. In the process, they reinforce our myths, launch silly fads, introduce new words to our vocabulary, and provide countless role models both ridiculous and sublime. In our cluster on the movies in America, Douglas Gomery explains how Hollywood works; Noël Carroll argues that current film fare is more escapist than ever; and David Bordwell appraises the dilemmas of the cinematic avant-garde. In the first of two accompanying articles, Frank D. McConnell asserts that, "We are not alone because we speak to one another—and nowhere at a deeper level than through the mythology of film." Finally, Nathan Reingold discusses the birth pains of one of Hollywood's first attempts at docudrama, MGM's *The Beginning or the End,* a 1947 film about the making of the first atomic bomb. It is a curious tale that helps explain why art, at least in Hollywood, has such trouble holding a mirror up to life.

Watching television is the one thing that virtually all Americans do; and if the experts are right, they will be doing more of it every year for some time to come. This is reason enough for the *Media Reader* to include a cluster of articles on "Television in America."

Television has become a focus of much scholarly inquiry. Does television shape voting patterns or sway public opinion? Has it fostered a decline in literacy among the young? Is it a spur to violence, to sexism, to promiscuity? In these articles, Lawrence Lichty explains how TV acquired its present character; Steven Lagerfeld looks at the docudramatists who have turned history into soap opera and thus created serious problems for educators who seek to teach history as truth; and Joel Swerdlow discusses how television affects the way we view the world, our neighbors, and ourselves. In additional articles, Lichty challenges the widely held belief that TV is the chief source of news for most Americans; Stuart Brotman weighs the probable impact of cable TV and other new technologies; and Stuart Shorenstein and Lorna Veraldi look at public television's uncertain future.

T.J. Jackson Lears provides the finale as he describes the development of advertising in America from the earliest painted brick walls and billboards to the "psychological" techniques now used to promote politicians as well as to sell cars, perfume, and low-calorie beer. Advertising touches all our media in one way or another, providing the sustaining revenues for publishers and broadcasters and allowing artists, photographers, and writers to explore new forms of expression. It is fitting that this tour of the media horizons ends with a discussion of the industry that remains, like so many of our current media, preoccupied with manufacturing illusions.

This book is intended both for students of the media and communications arts and for the general reader. It does not presume any special knowledge on the part of those who choose to explore its contents. Indeed, wherever possible and appropriate, the editors have included supplementary material in both text and graphic form to provide the reader with basic background information.

The editors wish to express their gratitude to the authors of these essays for their willingness to review and update their original work, often under rather intense deadline pressure. They also wish to ac-

knowledge the advice and tireless assistance of many people connected
with The Wilson Center, most especially Lisa Campbell, executive
assistant to *Wilson Quarterly* editor Peter Braestrup, *WQ*'s senior
researcher Virginia Cornett, and Shaun Murphy, director of The Wilson Center Press, who was extraordinarily patient in the face of
repeatedly missed deadlines.

Philip S. Cook, Douglas Gomery, Lawrence W. Lichty

LITERACY AND POPULAR CULTURE

Chapter 1

FROM STICKS AND BONES: AN INTRODUCTION TO LITERACY

Early in 1835 Henry Creswicke Rawlinson, a young British army officer and amateur orientalist, stood in the shadow of a fabled mountain near the town of Bisotun, in what is now western Iran. His superiors in London had sent him to Persia to reorganize the army of the shah; his passion for the history of ancient civilizations had brought him to the mountain.

Far above him, carved into a vertical expanse of rock 60 feet long and 23 feet high, loomed a huge bas-relief of nine men in chains being led before a king. Beneath the tableau were hundreds of lines of cuneiform inscriptions, their meaning lost to history. Rawlinson was determined to unlock their secret.

Just copying the inscriptions into his notebook cost him years of grueling labor: crawling from toehold to toehold in the hot sunlight, dangling from ropes suspended 500 feet above the desert floor, perching on flimsy ladders lodged on narrow outcroppings of stone. When he was done, he had copies of a single inscription written in what proved to be three ancient tongues—Old Persian, Elamite, and Babylonian–Assyrian. Rawlinson already had some knowledge of Old Persian; he thought he would be able to use a translation of the Persian inscription to crack Elamite and Babylonian–Assyrian.

Even so, it took him another ten years of toil to decipher the Persian cuneiform—the bas-relief, he discovered, celebrated the victories of King Darius of Persia during the sixth century B.C. Four more

Reprinted from the Spring 1986 issue of *The Wilson Quarterly*.

years passed before he made sense of Babylonian–Assyrian. He never did decode Elamite (the language of a people who lived in what is now southwestern Iran), and indeed it was only in 1890 that scholars managed to decipher parts of it. Some of its secrets remain hidden to this day.

But Rawlinson's achievement was monumental. He opened the world of ancient Mesopotamia to a nineteenth-century Europe newly curious about the "lost" civilizations of the past.

Rawlinson was not alone in his passion for decoding the scripts of the ancients, but the information that he and other nineteenth-century Europeans gleaned provided little more than a tantalizing glimpse of the cultures that produced the earliest writing. Not only did translation remain a daunting task, but written records were (and are) few; and the interpretation of other artifacts required painstaking scholarship. Only during the last fifty years has scholars' knowledge of the ancients deepened enough to allow them to draw firm conclusions about the role of writing in the rise of early civilizations.

Some scripts—the so-called Linear A and the Phaistos Disc from Crete—still defy translators. Nevertheless, from those that have been deciphered, researchers now know that the birth of civilization and the development of writing were intertwined.

Writing alone does not explain the greatness of ancient Egypt, China, or Greece. But writing always accompanied the flowering of civilizations. As the University of Chicago's Ignace J. Gelb, one of the scholars who pioneered the twentieth-century study of ancient scripts, put it in 1952: "Writing exists only in a civilization and a civilization cannot exist without writing."

In recent years archaeologists and linguists have gone beyond the old "uniformitarian" view that early writing did little more than extend the political rule of reigning elites. Instead, researchers such as C.C. Lamberg-Karlovsky of Harvard's Peabody Museum now argue that the effects of the early scripts were far more varied and complex, subtly influencing commerce, the arts, and farming, as well as government.

Picture Writing and Early Man

Human use of graphic symbols dates back at least to the late Stone Age (between 25,000 and 12,000 B.C.), when the people of prehistoric Europe painted vivid pictures of the deer, bison, and other animals that they hunted. The paintings were in part the expression of an animistic faith: Prehistoric man hoped that he could influence the hunt by symbolizing his prey. This notion that symbols can affect the life of what is represented has endured. To this day, for example, certain groups in India have no word for the cobra, a threat in everyday life, because they fear that creating the word may conjure up the thing itself.

A new array of symbols was added to the old as prehistoric humans increasingly took to settled farming and livestock herding after about 8000 B.C. One reason was the need to keep accounts. By the late Stone Age, it had become common practice to notch sticks and bones to record the passing of days and months and the number of animals claimed in the hunt. With the development of sedentary village life, the emphasis changed to recording the number of sheep or goats in a flock or the amount of grain held in storage. Often, easily counted tokens were used. As the new way of life increased the importance of private property, incised or painted marks and various kinds of stamps appeared as a way of marking one's possessions. Always prey to the vicissitudes of nature, farmers created symbols for the supernatural forces that governed rainfall, fertility, earth, and water.

The Emergence of Symbols: Sumerian Cuneiform

Not all the new farming cultures used symbols for all these categories, but the practice was widespread, particularly in the Near East, Egypt, southeastern Europe, the Indo–Iranian borderlands, and probably northern China. These were the places where the earliest civilizations took root.

The first was probably Sumeria, which emerged in ancient Mesopotamia beginning around 3200 B.C. At the heart of the Sumerian world were its cities, strategically positioned where tributaries flowed into the great Tigris and Euphrates rivers. These waterways, augmented by canals, fed the cities' outlying fields of wheat, barley, and oats. But Mesopotamia was in the end a desert land flanked by the mountains of the Iranian Plateau and the arid wastes of the Arabian deserts, and the Sumerians were beset by unpredictable cycles of drought and plenty.

The precariousness of their existence, compounded by the scarcity of stone, metal, and wood within their realm, made the Sumerians the ancient world's premier traders. Notched sticks and other devices were no longer sophisticated enough for keeping records of rates of exchange, past transactions, and inventories. Thus, after a period of evolution, Sumerian cuneiform writing made its appearance around 3100 B.C. (*Cunei* were the wedge-shaped marks that the Sumerians incised in soft clay tablets, which were then baked.)

But another concern spurred the creation of cuneiform, one that led the Sumerians to make an enduring contribution to civilization itself. Vulnerable to nature, to enemies near and far, and to turmoil in their own cities, the Sumerians realized that they would never survive without a formal system of regulation and control. Their solution was to create a system of laws.

Sumerian philosophers were aware that nature itself seemed to be controlled by laws of regularity: sunrise, sunset; dry season, wet season; death and rebirth. In addition, there seemed to be "functional" laws: birds flew, plows plowed, soldiers fought. Violation of these laws created disorder. Beginning about 2600 B.C., the Sumerians promulgated a series of very specific written laws that are preserved in the code of the Babylonian King Hammurabi (1792–50 B.C.), the successor to the Sumerian kings. The Code of Hammurabi touched on nearly every realm of human activity, specifying, for example, the rights of women and war veterans, the responsibilities of city architects, and the legal rights of slaves.

At first, literacy was probably confined to Sumerian temple scribes, but it seems likely that aristocrats and merchants also learned to read and write. The Sumerians established schools with regular hours and a full complement of teachers and teachers' assistants, offering instruction that went well beyond writing, to geography, astronomy, law, ethics, and perhaps other languages. A culturally sophisticated people, the Sumerians used writing not only for practical purposes, but also for narrative histories and commentaries on the human condition.

The exigencies of existence led some to profound speculation on the meaning of life itself expressed in such Sumerian writings as the *Epic of Gilgamesh,* in which a hero–king vainly seeks immortality. Such writings survive—and will probably turn out to be the largest cache of surviving documents of any of the ancient civilizations—because they were written on virtually imperishable clay tablets.

Egyptian "Sacred Writing": Hieroglyphics

If the Sumerian world view was pervaded by pessimism, a sense of helplessness in the face of nature's unpredictability, the Egyptians, living some 1,000 miles to the west in the fertile Nile River valley, were generally optimistic. Long before the first great Pyramids were built, the Egyptians believed that death was simply another form of existence, not an end, and thus that a person's name was a label for all time. By the time King Narmer unified ancient Egypt around 3100 B.C., kings and nobles were concerned that their names be represented not only by artifacts left in their tombs, as in the past, but by writing. "Thy name shall endure" is one of Egypt's most ancient epithets.

As the Pharaohs consolidated the Egyptian state, implanting the fundamental belief that the Pharaohs themselves were gods, Egyptian writing became almost entirely a priestly function. It was not that the scribes were priests, but that their writing served priestly, as well as secular, purposes. Because much of the writing that survives has to do with religion, the script is called hieroglyphics (sacred writing).[1] The Egyptians referred to it as "God's writing." This formal script of "beauty, dignity, and above all, permanence," as British ethnologist Albertine Guar described it, was part of the symbolism that held Egypt together.

Egypt's scribes also developed two cursive forms of writing (hieratic and, later, an even more abbreviated form called demotic), usually brushed onto papyrus, that were used as a kind of shorthand in the day-to-day business of an empire.

By creating a system of signs with specific meanings, the Egyptians made ordinary messages, religious statements, and the Pharaohs' directives as readily understood in the southern reaches of their empire in the Sudan as on the shores of the Mediterranean. Without writing, it is doubtful that the Egypt of the Pharaohs would have endured over the centuries. Yet, because the Egyptians restricted literacy to a scribal class, hieroglyphic writing perished with the old Egypt some four centuries after the birth of Christ.

The Chinese Ideograph

In China religious beliefs nurtured early writing, just as they had in Egypt. Almost as far back as settled life can be traced in China, the Chinese were conscious of their social relationships. Each individual's identity was linked to his or her social class, extended family, and, quite likely, lineage. Systematic Chinese "ideographic" writing in which each word is represented by a pictorial sign was probably created during northern China's Shang dynasty during the second millennium B.C. Ideographs were commonly used to record names, lineage, and ownership; but one of their most important uses was in "oracle writing." It was unthinkable to embark on an important endeavor without first seeking guidance from the ancestral gods. Shang kings and nobles consulted them through diviners, who drilled holes in animal shoulder bones or turtle shells and then heated them over a fire. The resulting cracks were read as divine statements and recorded by scribes on the bone or shell.

Chinese writing had existed before the Shang dynasty; but it took the invention of a series of indicators, much like determinatives in Egyptian hieroglyphics, to make the system more efficient. Essentially, these indicators—over 200 in number—told readers how to distinguish the meaning of words that share the same ideograph and pronunciation. The indicators were developed after the Shang dynasty, but they were rooted in the picture-writing concept.

Chinese ideographic writing may seem cumbersome to Westerners, but it had (and has) one great strength: A word might be pronounced differently in Shantung, the birthplace of Confucius, than in Kansu to the west, but it was always "spelled" the same way, using the same ideogram.[2] Written Chinese thus united a dispersed people who spoke several different dialects.

Other societies besides those of Sumeria, Egypt, and China invented their own forms of writing: By 1400 B.C., for example, the merchant princes of Crete and Mycenae were using Linear B to create commercial and governmental archives. Across the Atlantic, the Maya were using glyphs by the fifth century and the Aztecs were using a form of picture writing nine or so centuries later. But in the Old World, with the exception of Chinese ideographs, virtually all of the writing systems that had survived slowly died out after the invention of a markedly more efficient writing system, the alphabet.

Introduction of Vowels: The Phoenician and Greek Alphabets

Scholars generally credit the creation of the alphabet to the Phoenicians, the merchant seamen of the eastern Mediterranean, who had in turn derived some of *their* signs from Egyptian hieroglyphs. The Greeks then adopted the Phoenician system's consonants and added the crucial missing element: vowels. Greek, like all the Indo–European languages that came after it, changed the meaning of words by changing vowels. (In English, for example, "man" becomes "men.") An alphabet made learning to read and write breathtakingly simple. Instead of using hundreds or even thousands of symbols, each standing for a specific object, word, or idea, the alphabet equated a scant handful of signs with the sounds of speech.

The Greek alphabet may have been in the making before the time of Homer (who probably lived during the ninth or eighth century B.C.). Already in love with rhetoric and the spoken word, the Greeks became a highly literate people. A grave insult among ordinary Athenians of the fifth century B.C. was to say of a man, "He can't read, he can't swim."

"Cadmus, the legendary inventor of the alphabet, is said to have sown the dragon's teeth that raised a crop of warriors," writes Long Island University's Robert Pattison. "On Greek soil, the alphabet, once established, also bore a mighty crop." The results are still with us: the comedies of Aristophanes, the histories of Herodotus and Thucydides, and the philosophy of Aristotle.

The alphabet proved to be at least as precious a legacy as the Greeks' great works of intellect and art. In Italy new alphabets—amalgamations of borrowed Greek letters and indigenous signs—sprang up like weeds in a garden. Latin writing was a hybrid of Greek, Etruscan, and native letters, adapted to the Latin language, and, finally, refined to only twenty-three signs. Like the Greeks before them, the Romans prized literacy. At least as early as the first century B.C., they pressed reading and writing on their citizens, helping to create an empire unified by its cultural beliefs and by Rome's ability to have its written proclamations understood from the British Isles to North Africa. Polybius, who recorded the rise of Rome in the second century B.C., writes that the army required literacy even of its lowliest soldiers. The gift of writing was so widespread that one of its curses was also common. On the walls of Pompeii and other towns, ordinary Romans freely scrawled graffiti, misspellings and all.

The writings of Virgil, Cicero, and Seneca, republican ideals, and the elements of Roman law are among the literate Romans' legacy to the West.

The spread of alphabetic systems beyond these early beginnings is a long and complex story. The Latin alphabet became the basis of the writing systems of modern Western Europe, while some of the alphabets of Eastern Europe and Russia were derived from Greek letters. By the fourth century, Greek letters had also supplanted hieroglyphs in Egypt. The generally vowel-less alphabet of Aramaic, an early Semitic language common in the Levant as early as 1300 B.C., became the basis of several alphabets in India, far to the east. Arabic and Hebrew also owe much of their written character to Aramaic.

Nonliterate Cultures: Progress without Literacy

All of the ancient civilizations that created scripts, including those that lacked an alphabet, also developed a sense of themselves as superior to nonliterate cultures. Yet many societies thrived without writing: the "chieftainships" of Polynesia, the Ashanti and other tribal kingdoms of West Africa, and the Indians of America's Pacific Northwest. In most cases, they developed symbols such as the totem pole or the designs used in painting pottery that served their purposes. The Inca of what is now Peru used a pendant of knotted cords called a *quipu* to keep an accurate census, assess taxes, and record trading transactions. Over the course of three centuries, the Inca managed to build a sizable empire, marked by elaborately terraced farms and an extensive network of well-engineered roads, which they lost only when the Spanish *conquistadores* destroyed it in 1532.

Yet writing clearly made a vast difference. The history of writing and the cultures that developed it is a romance of immense significance. The invention of writing was probably the most significant step in human cultural evolution. Aside from its daily utility, writing has preserved long-dead tongues and the record of ancient institutions. It has preserved the history of humanity's triumphs and failures. It has made possible the rapid sharing of new knowledge. Above all, it is magical in its ability to bring the past alive and to allow us to imagine the future.

NOTES

1. Egyptian hieroglyphs make up a so-called logo-syllabic system that has three elements: ideograms that are pictures of the things referred to; phonograms that stand for consonants (there are no vowels in Egyptian writing); and determinatives that clarify the meaning of the glyphs.

2. Some 50,000 ideographs exist in written Chinese, but only about 3,500 are in everyday use.

Chapter 2

THE READING REVOLUTION

by Steven Lagerfeld

Writing "will implant forgetfulness in [men's] souls; they will cease to exercise memory because they rely on that which is written." Thus Plato (speaking through a character in one of his dialogues) questioned the value of literacy some four centuries after the Greeks began adopting the alphabet. Only knowledge gained through spirited debate, Plato argued, "is written in the soul of the learner."

Of course, the ultimate reply to Plato is that his doubts about literacy are known to us only because he committed them to writing. Yet, in one form or another, Plato's reservations have preoccupied thinkers through the ages. Do reading and writing transform human consciousness? How so? Is literacy best left in the hands of the few, or is *mass* literacy better? Will widespread literacy ensure social and economic progress? Never in the past were the answers to all these questions self-evident, and some remain, in one form or another, subjects of scholarly debate.

Despite the invention of the alphabet, which vastly simplified the task of learning to read and write, the spread of literacy was far from inevitable. The leaders of Greece and Rome had chosen to promote reading and writing among their citizens. For many centuries, their successors in the West did not.

Latin as an Elitist Language

Interestingly, the early Christians sided with Plato. Christ is said to have written only once—in the dust, as if to signify the transience

11

of the written word. His disciples did not commit his teachings to writing until some thirty to sixty years after his death, preferring that the Word be transmitted orally, kept alive on the tongues of men. Yet Church leaders soon recognized that a holy book would be needed to keep the faith intact. (The Gospels and Old Testament had already been written.) Amid the cacophony of Europe's hundreds of languages and dialects, few of them written, only the old imperial language of Latin could be read as easily in the British Isles as in Holland or Italy.

Reluctantly, the Church adopted Latin as its official language. The *literati* of the Middle Ages—mostly priests, along with a handful of nobles and merchants—reserved the ability to read and write for themselves, in part because they believed that it gave them power over the souls of commoners. (Not only in Europe: In medieval India, for example, only the Brahmin, or "twice born," were permitted to read the sacred Veda.) Indeed, a mystical quality was attached to the written word; in Middle English, the word *grammar* referred to occult lore; in medieval Britain, those accused of murder who could read from the Latin Bible were automatically spared the hangman's noose.

But the truth was that from the fall of the Roman Empire until the fourteenth or fifteenth century, even most of the highborn cared little for literacy. "Letters are removed from manliness," a group of German Goths told Queen Amalasuntha of sixth-century Italy, "teaching . . . results for the most part in a cowardly and submissive spirit." Among the notable illiterates of the era were William the Conqueror and Charlemagne, whose clerics did their reading and writing for them. It was the Church, with its legions of literate men, that organized and spearheaded the Crusades. It was the Church that provided Western Europe with a semblance of cultural unity.

The common folk did not begrudge the *literati* their monopoly on letters. Reading and writing, quite simply, were unnecessary luxuries for the peasant farmers of the Middle Ages. Knowledge passed by word of mouth from father to son, from mother to daughter. As late as the seventeenth century, English country squire Nicholas Breton noted, farmers could "learn to plough and harrow, sow and reap, plant and prune, thresh and fan, winnow and grind, brew and bake, and all without book."

Imagining today what daily life was like in such an oral society is as difficult as putting oneself in the place of a blind man. Say a word and a literate person will immediately see it spelled in his or her mind's eye: It is the written word that has form, substance, and meaning, that produces the mind's order. But in an oral world, the written word is ephemeral. In the courtrooms of twelfth-century England and France, written deeds and bills of sale counted for less in resolving legal disputes than human witnesses who, according to St. Louis University's Walter Ong, "were alive and . . . could defend their statements; writing was [viewed as] dead marks on a dead surface."

Even among the literate of the Middle Ages, old ways lingered. Reading more often meant speaking aloud (or sotto voce) than thinking in solitude. In the scriptoria of the monasteries, one monk would read from the pages of the Bible while his fellows labored over their rote transcriptions; in the classrooms of medieval universities, professors recited to their students from the few available texts. (Books were so lightly regarded that old writings were commonly rubbed out when paper and vellum were scarce so that the monks could continue their copying.) Writing was no different. Few medieval authors, observes Ong, wrote with quill in hand, painstakingly building their arguments word by word, brick by brick, a house of logic. Rather, most dictated their thoughts aloud to scribes.

The Power of Reading

Reading (or writing) in silence, internalizing words, is an experience of a very different kind. "To engage the written word," notes New York University's Neil Postman, "means to follow a line of thought. . . . It means to uncover lies, confusions, and overgeneralizations, to detect abuses of logic and common sense. It also means to weigh ideas, to compare and contrast assertions, to connect one generalization to another."

Europe during the Middle Ages was not completely without literacy, but it shared some characteristics with the unlettered Third World tribes that contemporary scholars have studied. Such oral societies, says Ong,

> must invest great energy in saying over and over again what has been learned arduously over the ages. This need establishes a highly traditionalist or conservative set of mind that with good reason inhibits intellectual experimentation. . . . By storing knowledge outside the mind, writing and, even more, print downgrade the figures of the wise old man and the wise old woman, repeaters of the past, in favor of younger discoverers of something new.

Italian City-States and the Birth of Secular Scholarship

In Europe, the first discoverers of the new appeared in fourteenth-century Venice, Florence, and other wealthy Italian city-states. Owing to their energetic merchant princes, who bartered and bargained throughout the Mediterranean, these cities had grown large and affluent by European standards of the day. They also harbored distinguished scholarly communities, which the merchant princes favored with ancient Greek and Roman texts retrieved mostly from libraries in Egypt and the Arab world. Urbanization, prosperity, and the rediscovery of ancient works nourished a new skeptical and secular outlook on life, the early Italian Renaissance. Still, the revival might never have spread so quickly beyond Italy without two other developments.

The Printing Press and the Protestant Reformation

The first was Johannes Gutenberg's invention of the printing press during the 1440s and 1450s; it stands alongside the creation of the alphabet some 2,500 years earlier as a landmark in the long history of the rise of literacy. As in the case of the alphabet, however, human choice was needed to transform a technical invention into a revolutionary device. Within decades of Gutenberg's discovery, Europe felt the first stirrings of the Protestant Reformation, led by Martin Luther (1483–1546). Luther was at first dismayed when the printing press made his famous Ninety-five Theses, nailed to the door of a church in the tiny German village of Wittenberg in 1517, the news of all Europe. But during the ensuing years, he broadened his challenge to the Catholic Church, calling for a more direct relationship between man and his Maker. He insisted that the faithful be able to read God's word themselves, and in their own "vulgar" languages, not in the Church's Latin. For him, Gutenberg's press was a weapon; printing was "God's highest and extremest act of grace, whereby the business of the Gospel is driven forward."

Printers responded to the new market with an outpouring of Bibles, Books of Days, and other holy works. Religious fervor propelled book sales and literacy rates to unprecedented levels in Protestant lands—Scandinavia, the German states, Holland, and Britain.

One of the most dramatic transformations occurred in seventeenth-century Sweden, where a Lutheran home-teaching movement swept the countryside. Once a year in Sweden's small towns and villages, pastors assembled their flocks for public tests of reading and writing: Anyone who failed was forbidden to marry or take communion. Though lacking public schools, Sweden achieved near-universal literacy by the beginning of the eighteenth century, even before most other Protestant lands.

There is no telling what would have come of Gutenberg's invention without Luther's crusade. In China, an alchemist named Pi Sheng had designed a system of movable type during the eleventh century, well before Gutenberg's time. It contributed to the flowering of literature during the later Sung dynasty and to the rise of the powerful Chinese civil service. China outstripped the rest of the world in book production until the end of the eighteenth century. But China's Confucian-trained scholars and bureaucrats restricted education to the elite, and it was virtually impossible for commoners to learn the tens of thousands of characters of the Chinese language at home. As a result, more than 70 percent of the Chinese population remained mired in illiteracy at the beginning of the twentieth century.[1]

Books and the Rise of Learning

Even before literacy reached Europe's common man, the printing press had an enormous effect on the life of the mind. At first, notes the University of Michigan's Elizabeth Eisenstein, the foremost historian of the printing revolution, printers churned out (apart from holy books) countless reproductions of ancient tracts on astrology and alchemy, fragments of "magia and cabala"—a "vast backlog of occult lore." But eventually, more illuminating works were put into print. The spread of reading and books alarmed some of the powerful. Pope Paul V, for example, banned Copernicus's *On the Revolutions of the Celestial Spheres* from Catholic-run presses in 1616.

Printing did for intellectual life what the invention of money thousands of years earlier had done for trade and commerce, spurring an explosive growth in the exchange of information and ideas. Now the astronomers and physicians and philosophers of sixteenth-century Europe had at their fingertips in book form all the accumulated wisdom of the ancients. When the great works of the past were placed side by side, writes Eisenstein, "contradictions became more visible, divergent traditions more difficult to reconcile. The transmission of received opinion could not proceed smoothly once Arabists were set against Galenists or Aristotelians against Ptolemaists."

The creation of a market for books also helped writers and thinkers free themselves from the whims of aristocratic patrons. New arguments and discoveries, treatises on theology and philosophy, poetry, fiction, works of outrageous fantasy, all shot through the ranks of the educated like jolts of electricity. The results were momentous. It was the age of Erasmus and Bacon, Shakespeare and Cervantes, Galileo and Leonardo. By 1704, when Jonathan Swift published *The Battle of the Books,* contending that the ancients were superior in wisdom and learning to modern men, he was fighting, as far as the small, educated sector of the English public was concerned, a rearguard action.

Gradually, books made their way into the hands of the common folk.[2] The ability to read and write spread slowly through Europe during the seventeenth and eighteenth centuries, partly through education. Frederick III, later the first King of Prussia, ordered farmers' children "to school, at least for two hours in the morning" in 1698. But, as in seventeenth-century Sweden, most commoners learned from their literate acquaintances or from primers like preacher Valentin Ickelsamer's *A German grammar—from which one might learn to read for oneself* (1534).

Modern historians have been able to reckon early literacy rates only by digging through parish records, diaries, and deeds, counting people who signed with their names as literate, those who made an X as illiterate. By the end of the eighteenth century, printing and the spread of schooling had produced relatively high rates of literacy, at least in Protestant countries. The Swiss were 80 percent literate by 1850 (thanks to widespread public education), as were 80 percent of the Prussians, and 50 percent of the English. Catholic Italy and Spain, by contrast, suffered much lower rates of literacy—20 percent and 25 percent, respectively. Tsarist Russia, with a vast population of impoverished serfs who "did not see any material benefit" in becoming literate, as a nineteenth-century Russian priest remarked, still remained 80 percent illiterate at the turn of the twentieth century.

Everywhere, the notion of literacy for all remained a distant dream. The well-to-do were more literate than the poor, city dwellers more literate than farmers. Men, from France to China, were far more likely to learn their letters than were their wives and sisters. Sweden's highly literate women were among the most fortunate in Europe, where literacy rates for women ranged variously from 20 percent in Italy and Spain to 55 percent in England by the middle of the nineteenth century.

Often literacy was a gift that unlocked in an individual an enormous potential that in times past would have remained dormant. Historian Margaret Spufford tells the story of Thomas Tryon, son of a poor seventeenth-century Oxfordshire plasterer, who left school at the age of six having "scarcely learnt to distinguish my letters." At thirteen, he learned to read from fellow shepherds; later he paid an itinerant teacher to teach him to write (tuition: one sheep). He moved to London, where he spent his wages on books; and before long he was writing them. There were six in all, including *A New Method of Education,* as well as *Averroes' Letter to Pythagoras* and *The Good Housewife Made a Doctor.* For most people, however, limitations of social class, circumstance, and native ability tempered the impact of reading and writing. When they took an interest in the printed word, Europe's common folk favored "how-to" pamphlets offering instruction in carpentry or farming or home medicine.

Today it is an article of faith around the world that the appearance of such a rapidly growing, educated reading public (however prosaic its reading) was one of the essential ingredients in sparking the Industrial Revolution. During the 1960s, sociologist C. Arnold Anderson and economist Mary Jean Bowman, both of the University of Chicago, concluded that a national literacy rate of 40 percent is the bare minimum needed to achieve such an industrial "take-off." England during the 1750s had reached the "40-percent threshold."

Yet, as other scholars have since discovered, industrialization had an unexpected effect: In England, the literacy rate stagnated or fell (as it did in France) as factory owners hired young workers away from schools at the age of six or seven. The rate did not turn up again until the 1880s.

Nor did factory owners need great numbers of workers who could read and write. A few agreed with reformers such as Canadian educator Charles Clarke that literacy "has lightened the toil of the laborer [and] increased his productive ability." But as British historian Michael Sanderson writes, the new jobs—furnaceman, cotton cleaner, and weaver—in the Yorkshire and Lancashire mills and factories "required even *less* literacy and education than the old ones (wood- and metal-working, for example)." Once a worker learned to operate a loom or a blast furnace, Sanderson argues, he (or in the cotton mills, she) needed to learn no more. A "knack" for things mechanical was more important than book learning.

There is no doubt that the printing press and the book, and the rise of literacy that followed, set the stage for Europe's modernization. They made possible new technology—James Watt's steam engine

(1769), Sir Henry Bessemer's converter (1856)—and the educated managers, engineers, and technicians needed to run large factories and distribution networks. Whether *mass* literacy was needed remains an open question.

The "Terrible Spectre of a Literate Working Class"

Indeed, many of the well-to-do of the mid-nineteenth century plainly feared it. In England, as reformers waxed eloquent about the education of the workers, many of the gentry saw instead "the terrible spectre of a literate, politically minded working class," as Cambridge historian J.H. Plumb put it. Sir Joseph Banks, president of the Royal Society in England in 1807, feared that literacy would teach the poor to "despise their lot in life." Instead of burying their noses in harmless popular novels, he fretted, literate English and Scottish workers were reading "seditious pamphlets [and] vicious books."

Equally worrisome was the rise of a popular press frequently given to political agitation. During the French Revolution, an event that terrified Europe's aristocrats (and other Europeans as well), the Parisian press had become, in the words of one French observer, "simply a machine of war," educating what the Paris *Globe* called "a new generation . . . smitten with liberty, eager for glory." By 1820 the introduction of new technology slashed the cost of newsprint and sent circulation skyrocketing. Newspapers proliferated in London and the major cities of Europe and the United States, with some claiming up to 30,000 readers. In 1865 Paris's *Petit Journal* was turning out 250,000 copies a day. Years earlier, a little-known journalist named Karl Marx had remarked upon the usefulness of newspapers in forging "party spirit" among the workers.

Despite conservatives' fears of mass literacy, most educated Westerners by the end of the nineteenth century had come to believe that it was the first step on the road to greater progress. Certainly, higher rates of literacy (along with widespread public education) eased the transition to industrial innovation in the United States and Canada. Teaching reading and writing seemed to be the key, as one writer put it, "to instruct[ing] a man how to live and move in the world as befits a civilized being." By the 1930s state-supported schooling had made near-universal literacy a reality in the West.

Today, the scene of the struggle to achieve basic literacy has shifted to the Third World, where nations such as Ethiopia (with a

7 percent literacy rate) and Pakistan (16 percent) have set their sights on the "40-percent threshold." Their leaders are convinced that mass literacy will secure what the Iraqi government once called "the political, economic, and social progression of the country." Maybe so. Yet, as the Cuban example shows, a literate population alone is not enough to ensure economic progress or political liberty. Shah Mohammad Reza Pahlavi of Iran, who made literacy a keystone of his modernization efforts, was toppled in 1979 by Ayatollah Ruhollah Khomeini, an old man who, from his exile in France, stirred the passions of his zealous followers back home with rousing polemics—tape recorded on audiocassettes.

THE THIRD WORLD'S WAR ON ILLITERACY

"Can there be a more moving spectacle than . . .this tall old man with his white beard, his tremulous voice, his unsteady limbs, as he slowly lifts a long bamboo pointer toward the blackboard, and with difficulty tries to pick out the letters on it?"

Such scenes, from French schoolteacher Gerard Tongas's account of a mid-1950s literacy campaign in communist North Vietnam, have been repeated thousands of times in the Third World. With high hopes for spurring economic development, promoting national unity, or indoctrinating the "masses"—and at great expense—dozens of governments have launched efforts to eradicate adult illiteracy.

Progress worldwide has been slow but steady. In 1985, according to the United Nations Educational, Scientific, and Cultural Organization (UNESCO), 27.7 percent of the world's adults were illiterate, down from 32.9 percent in 1970.

The greatest fanfare has accompanied the all-out drives against illiteracy mounted by many communist regimes. In 1961, Fidel Castro sent "an army" of 100,000 literacy *brigadistas* into the hinterlands and later announced to international acclaim that they had taught some 700,000 Cubans to read and write. Cuba now claims a literacy rate of 96 percent; Vietnam, 85 percent; and Nicaragua, after a similar "war," 87 percent. Yet the North Vietnamese campaign, Tongas says, "merely consisted of teaching the illiterate masses to recite twenty or so slogans ['Long live President Ho!'] and to copy them more or less legibly." The old man with the pointer, like most of his countrymen and women, never really learned to read and write for himself. The Cuban story is similar.

Few noncommunist leaders have claimed results as impressive as Castro does. Even in the West, teaching *adults* to read and write is difficult. The chief obstacle: persuading men and women who have lived into their middle years without literacy that a heavy investment of time and effort will pay off. Most Third World adult literacy campaigns, writes Abdun Noor of the World Bank, "have been uneconomic with a high dropout rate and a high incidence of relapses to illiteracy."

Noor is skeptical of splashy, centrally directed campaigns. Churches and other local organizations are generally best suited to doing the job, he says, and textbooks that teach people practical skills (such as animal husbandry) are the most effective tools. Brazil, Uganda, and Tanzania are among the nations where such localized efforts have worked.

Few specialists predict that more than a minority of the world's 800 million adult illiterates will ever learn to read and write. The best hope may lie with the next generation. Even Africa, with its estimated 60 percent illiteracy rate, now enrolls 78 percent of its children in elementary schools. Asia and Latin America, with far less illiteracy, boast even higher rates of school enrollment.

Literacy alone may not deliver economic progress, enlightened minds, or any of the other benefits that it seems to promise to the Third World; but without it such gains will remain forever out of reach.

For all that, no nation that hopes to tap the potential of its people can achieve very much without widespread literacy. Lacking the ability to read and write, the farmer most likely will continue to tend his crops just as his father's father did; his children will not dare to imagine what it is like to build a bridge or write an essay; democracy will make as much sense as the theory of relativity.

Even if it is not a magic recipe for personal or national progress, literacy is an essential ingredient. Oddly enough, among the few people who now question that reality are some of the Western scholars who study literacy and related subjects. Literary "deconstructionists," such as Jacques Derrida, view language as a kind of prison that constricts human thought. But at least they acknowledge the power of the written word. Others almost seem not to. In the United States, a few education specialists have argued that spoken "black English" ought to be taught in the schools. Among anthropologists, one sometimes finds a certain sentimentality about oral societies—their unsullied traditions, their lively communal storytelling, their free exchange of local news and gossip. But perhaps more frightening is the fact that academic and other specialists who are trying to enhance literacy tend to expound their views in a style so obtuse and jargon-ridden that it makes even Washington's barely literate regulation writers seem like exquisite prose artists.

If understanding our politics, our science, or simply one another is the ultimate purpose of achieving literacy, the West still has far to go. Instead of more reading and writing, we seem to have talk, talk, and more talk. The television set, the radio, the telephone, and our addiction to never-ending rounds of conferences and meetings, all produce a continuous, deafening chatter. We have seized the computer, with its great potential to extend the empire of the written word—through word processing, computer networks, and desk-top publishing—and made it yet another instrument of our limitless capacity for blather. It is not, as some apocalyptic critics of television have suggested, that we have fallen from some vaunted Golden Age of literacy. We are still groping our way toward it.

NOTES

1. The Arab world reluctantly adopted the press 300 to 400 years after Gutenberg, preferring instead the magnificent calligraphy and miniature paintings that flourished in books of the fourteenth, fifteenth, and sixteenth centuries. Today literacy remains spotty throughout the Muslim Middle East, ranging from under 10 percent in countries such as Yemen and Qatar to nearly 30 percent in Saudi Arabia.

2. Books were much cheaper than hand-illuminated manuscripts, but they still came dearly. In sixteenth-century France, for example, the cheapest New Testament cost the equivalent of the whole day's wages for a journeyman carpenter. Still, the popular market for books throughout Europe was huge. A prodigious 22,000 titles rolled off English presses between 1641 and 1662, about one book or pamphlet for every 42 readers.

Chapter 3

KEEPING UP IN AMERICA

by David Harman

"Learn them to read the Scriptures, and be conversant therein," the Reverend John Cotton urged his Boston parishioners in a 1656 homily on child rearing. "Reading brings much benefit to little children."

"Benefit" was an understatement. In the harsh moral universe of Cotton's New England Puritans, ignorance was no excuse for sin: A child who died young, as many did, could expect no mercy in the hereafter merely because he or she had not been able to read the Bible. Massachusetts's colonial authorities had already acted on the fear that parents were not doing enough to protect their children from the "old deluder Satan." In 1647, nine years before Cotton's sermon, they required every township of fifty families or more to provide a teacher for the young.

Satan may be, in this sense, behind us, but the challenge of making Americans literate is not. Almost any adult born in America today can read well enough to satisfy John Cotton; but the preacher set a simple standard. His flock did not need to ponder the meaning of a ballot referendum, or the requirements of a help-wanted advertisement, or the operating instructions for a microwave oven—all frequently written by people who may be only semiliterate themselves.

"The ability to understand an unfamiliar text, rather than simply declaim a familiar one," as researchers Daniel P. and Lauren B. Resnick put it, is today's new standard of literacy. That kind of functional literacy may seem almost quaint in an age of telephones and TV news, and of computers (with languages of their own) and color-

23

coded cash register keys that make counting or reading almost unnecessary for teen-age clerks at fast-food restaurants. Time after time in
the past literacy has seemed, for a brief historical moment, redun-
dant—a luxury, not needed by ordinary folk.

Yet those Americans who could not read and write, then as now,
became the servants of those who could; they were sometimes de-
prived of prosperity and liberty, always of autonomy and knowledge.
What will become of today's students who fail to become fluent in the
English tongue? Even those who achieve technological literacy, stak-
ing their futures on a narrow mastery of FORTRAN or UNIX or some
other computer language, will be at a disadvantage. Eventually, predicts Robert Pattison of Long Island University, they will wind up
working for "English majors from Berkeley and Harvard."

It has been said that we live in an Information Age. The information that is important is not bits and bytes, but ideas and knowledge
conveyed in clear English. All this requires a more sophisticated level
of literacy. The worker of the future, warns the National Academy of
Sciences, must be "able and willing to learn throughout a lifetime."
By that new standard, America probably has nearly half the proportion
of illiterates among its population that it did in Cotton's time.

Literacy in Early America

Traditional literacy spread rapidly in seventeenth- and eighteenth-
century America, mostly through church-run schools and through
informal education—parents teaching their children, masters teaching
their apprentices. But it is unclear just how literate colonial America
was. As Americans have been painfully reminded in recent years,
schooling and literacy are not always synonymous. And in the days
before the Revolution, American schoolchildren probably spent, at
most, three years in the classroom.

By counting the number of men who could sign their name to
deeds and other public documents as literate (literacy for women was
deemed irrelevant in most of the colonies; for slaves, dangerous),
historians have reckoned that literacy in America rose from about 60
percent among the first white male colonists to about 75 percent by
1800. That figure masks a great deal of diversity. City-dwellers were
more literate than country folk; Northerners more likely to read and
write than Southerners and Westerners; and the well-to-do better
schooled than the poor. Ninety percent of New Englanders could sign
their own names by the time the U.S. Constitution was ratified; yet the

U.S. Army found in 1800 that only 58 percent of its recruits, drawn from the lower strata of the population, were literate.

And then one must ask *how* literate? The evidence is contradictory. The farmers, blacksmiths, tanners, and shopkeepers of colonial America did not need or possess a very sophisticated understanding of written material. For the vast majority, literacy probably meant reading the Bible, almanacs, and, occasionally, newspapers, but without necessarily being able to make inferences from their reading or to decipher more complicated texts. Historian Carl F. Kaestle of the University of Wisconsin–Madison estimates that perhaps 20 percent of adult male Americans were "sophisticated readers" by the 1760s.

Lawrence A. Cremin of Columbia University takes a more generous view. Thomas Paine's *Common Sense,* he notes, "sold a hundred thousand copies within three months of its appearance [in 1776] and possibly as many as a half million in all. That means one-fifth of the colonial population bought it and a half or more probably read it or heard it read aloud."

About one thing there is no doubt. From the start, Americans, for various reasons, *valued* the ability to read and write. "A people who mean to be their own governors," James Madison declared, "must arm themselves with the power knowledge gives. A popular government without popular information or the means of acquiring it, is but a prologue to a farce or a tragedy, or perhaps both." One Ohio newspaper offered a more mundane rationale in 1839, a variant on the "read to win" theme that nowadays draws thousands of Americans into Evelyn Wood speed-reading courses. A young man who delayed marrying by five years, its editor calculated, would gain 7,300 hours of "mental application," including reading, that would advance his material fortunes later in life. But moral and religious uplift remained the strongest impulse behind the spread of literacy well into the nineteenth century. As William H. McGuffey warned the young readers of his *Newly Revised Eclectic Second Reader* (1853), "The boys and girls who can not read . . . will never know whether they are on the right road [in life] or the wrong one."

The Impact of Industrialization and Immigration on Public Education

Almost by accident, America's industrialization during the nineteenth century helped boost literacy rates. Employers in the United States, as in Europe, preferred to hire factory workers who could read and write: These skills were not always needed on the job, but businessmen believed, not unlike John Cotton, that graduates were superior in "moral character" to their unschooled and unlettered peers. Advocates of public education such as Horace Mann of Massachusetts emphasized primary-school graduates' "greater docility and quickness in applying themselves to work" in arguing for an expansion of schooling. Mann and his allies had their way in part because the growth of densely populated cities and factory towns in New England during the 1830s and 1840s made mass schooling more economical.[1]

In 1840, when the U.S. Census Bureau first asked adults whether they were literate, all but 9 percent said "Yes." By 1860 only 7 percent admitted to illiteracy.

The U.S. Army's records tell another story: They show 35 percent illiteracy among recruits in 1840, declining to 7 percent only in 1880. Schooling was showing its effects, or so it seemed. It was the U.S. Army that delivered the first shock to the believers in a literate America. By 1917, when the United States mobilized for World War I, the Army had a new way to test the competence of draftees and recruits: standardized intelligence tests, developed by psychologist Robert Yerkes. Yerkes was astonished to find that 30 percent of the young men, while ostensibly literate, could not read well enough to understand his Alpha test form. Public reaction was muted by the fact that many of the near-illiterates were Southern blacks, hence ill-schooled; but the stage had been set in America for a new definition of literacy.

Already the old "bare-bones" notion of literacy as a matter of knowing your ABCs and the Bible had been stretched. At Ellis Island, more and more immigrants were arriving from the poor countries of southern Europe, illiterate in their own languages, not to mention English. More than ever, the newcomers were also unfamiliar with the workings of democracy. Only then did the nation's political leaders begin to view the Founding Fathers' call for an informed citizenry, literate in English, as a social imperative. "There is not room in this country for hyphenated Americanism," former President Theodore Roosevelt warned in 1915. And steel magnate Andrew Carnegie (1835–1919), convinced that free libraries were "the best agencies for improving the masses of the people," dipped into his vast fortune to help create 2,500 new public libraries.

President Herbert C. Hoover launched a U.S. Advisory Committee on National Illiteracy in 1929 to study and publicize the problem; but, like Hoover himself, it was swamped by the Great Depression.

And with "one-third of a nation" ill-fed and ill-clad, more pressing matters filled Franklin D. Roosevelt's New Deal agenda. It took another world war to bring illiteracy back to the forefront. Early in 1941, before Pearl Harbor, the Army declared that it would reject draftees who failed a fourth grade equivalency test; within a year 433,000 men otherwise fit for duty were still in civvies thanks to the test. In the summer of 1942, the Army relented, deciding that any illiterate who could understand spoken English and follow basic oral instructions was good enough to wear khakis and serve under the flag.

Debating Phonics and "Look–Say" in the Fifties

After World War II attention shifted to children's ability to read and write. Rudolf Flesch, an émigré writer and education specialist, designed the first modern "readability" formulas that made it possible to gauge the level of reading ability required by children's textbooks. By measuring the length of words and sentences, Flesh could determine whether they were written for comprehension at a fourth-, fifth-, or sixth-grade level. In 1955, he authored *Why Johnny Can't Read,* a best seller that sparked a debate between advocates of instruction in phonics ("sounding out" words letter-by-letter) and the prevailing "look–say" method (recognizing whole words) that continues today.[2] Look–say not only sounded Chinese but required students to learn English (by memorizing whole words) as if it were Chinese. "Do you know," Flesch declared, "that the teaching of reading never was a problem anywhere in the world until the United States switched to the present method?"

Functional Illiteracy among Adults

Only during the past two decades has *adult* illiteracy aroused sustained public concern in peacetime. "Adult literacy seems to present an ever-growing challenge," writes Harvard's Jeanne S. Chall, "greater perhaps than the acknowledged challenge of literacy among those still in school."

The U.S. Department of Education estimates that the number of *functional* illiterates grows by 2.3 million every year: some 1.3 million legal and illegal immigrants, and 1 million high school dropouts and "pushouts," who leave school with inadequate reading and writing skills.

All told, as many as 27 million Americans over age sixteen—nearly 15 percent of the adult population—may be functionally illiterate today.[3] Another 45 million are "marginally competent," reading below the twelfth-grade level. To varying degrees, all are handicapped as citizens, parents, and workers.

More than a decade ago, the U.S. Senate's Select Committee on Equal Educational Opportunity put the cost of such slippage to the U.S. economy—in reduced labor productivity, trimmed tax revenues, higher social welfare outlays—at $237 billion annually. (Today the burden of illiteracy in terms of unemployment and welfare benefits alone is about $12 billion.) The costs Americans pay in terms of the nation's politics and civic life are not measurable.

Defining Illiteracy in Twentieth-Century America

What does it mean to be "functionally illiterate"? The term is elusive. The number of people who simply cannot read and write today is infinitesimal: The United States is about as literate in these terms as Ivory Soap is pure. Going by the standards of 1840, this represents a smashing success.

READING, WRITING, AND . . . TELEVISION

Next to sleeping and working, watching television is the most popular American activity. The average American household turns on the "boob tube" for nearly seven hours every day, and children are the chief audience. In 1982 the National Institute of Mental Health estimated that high school seniors had spent more time in front of the television (15,000 hours) than in the classroom (11,000 hours).

Does passively watching television affect the ability of children to learn to read and write? The National Assessment of Educational Progress (NAEP) reports that children who watch up to two hours of television per day score *above* average on reading tests; but *six* or more hours of television watching is "consistently and strongly related to lower reading proficiency."

Television, however, may not actually be responsible for bad reading skills. "Poor readers," the NAEP says, "may simply choose to watch more television."

Jerome and Dorothy Singer, both Yale psychologists, argue that television viewing *does* have a negative effect. Children who watch TV for 20 to 35 hours a week, they assert, simply have little time to read. Moreover, the TV screen "holds viewer attention by piling up novelty through shifts of scene, content, mixtures of visual movement, music, sound effects, and speech." Bombarded daily by this "cluttered stimulus field," children lose the ability to reflect, relax, and focus their attention.

Other scholars disagree. Educator Susan E. Neuman of Eastern Connecticut State College argues that television is a red herring. In her view it does not displace reading; it displaces other forms of entertainment. Watching television is just one of many factors—whether a child's parent reads to him or her, the child's personality, intelligence, schooling, and socioeconomic status—that affect reading ability.

The specialists are also divided over the much-touted merits of "educational" television. Public television's *Sesame Street* employs jokes, stories, rhymes, and puppets to make learning to read more fun. Some studies suggest that *Sesame Street* helps teach its 10 million preschool viewers to recognize numbers, letters, and words—at home, without fear of failure or embarrassment. The Singers, however, find that *Sesame Street* does more harm than good. Each sixty-minute show, they say, includes up to thirty-five unrelated scenes. The result: "short attention spans." *Sesame Street* watchers are bored by classroom work and the "relatively calm, bland environment of most public schools."

For all that, children may be better off watching public television's *Sesame Street* or *Reading Rainbow* than *Dynasty* or the *A–Team*. Yet watching seven hours a day of any kind of TV does not strike most researchers as a recipe for intellectual growth among the young.

However, the old standards no longer apply. The 1840 sort of literacy does not suffice to master the details of contemporary American life. Just filling out federal income tax forms, for example, requires a twelfth-grade education. And, if individuals are to prosper, literacy means more than just getting by. "If we are literate in twentieth-century America," writes Harvard's Patricia Albjerg Graham, "we expand the ways in which we can learn, understand, and appreciate the world around us. [Literacy permits] us to become more autonomous individuals, less circumscribed by the conditions of social class, sex, and ethnicity into which we are born." On a practical level, getting ahead in the world of work, whether that world is an insurance company's clerical office or an oil company's executive suite, requires a high level of literacy.

Most specialists agree that an eighth-grade reading ability is the minimum level of functional literacy. Seventeen states now require students to pass an eighth-grade competency test to qualify for a high school diploma. This is a modest standard: the *New York Times, Time,* and *Newsweek* are written at a tenth- to twelfth-grade level. Jeanne Chall cites the case of a notice she received from the New England Telephone Company. In short sentences, it told customers how to determine whether malfunctions originated in the equipment or the telephone line. Yet, according to Chall's readability formula, a ninth- or tenth-grade level of reading ability was needed to understand the notice. "For about 30 to 40 percent [of the customers] it might as well have been written in Greek or Latin."

Pegging functional literacy to an eighth-grade reading ability leaves many ambiguities. Specialists are not certain, for example, whether the skills that an eighth grader needs to pass a competency test are the same as those that a worker needs on the job. More troublesome is that most estimates of functional illiteracy are based on data on the number of years of schooling adults have completed, not on actual tests of their abilities, and, as educators well know, merely completing the eighth grade does not mean performing thereafter at that level. According to the National Assessment of Educational Progress (NAEP), only 60 percent of today's thirteen-year-olds (mostly in the eighth grade) possess even "intermediate" reading skills.

One major study does roughly confirm the estimate of 27 million functional illiterates. After testing 7,500 adults on their ability to accomplish everyday tasks—reading the label of an aspirin bottle, following the directions for cooking a TV dinner, and writing a check— University of Texas researchers in 1975 put the number of functional illiterates nationwide at 23 million.

The majority of these people are poor and/or black or Hispanic, and residents of the rural South or of Northern cities. The University of Texas researchers found that 44 percent of the blacks they tested and 16 percent of the whites were functionally illiterate. "Eighty-five percent of juveniles who come before the courts are functionally illiterate," writes Jonathan Kozol. "Half the heads of households classified below the poverty line by federal standards cannot read an eighth-grade book. Over one-third of mothers who receive support from welfare are functionally illiterate. Of eight million unemployed adults, four to six million lack the skills to be retrained for high-tech jobs."

A large number of the nation's functional illiterates are high school dropouts. Among adults over twenty-five, nearly 17 percent of blacks and 31 percent of Hispanics left school before the eighth grade. Millions more stayed in school a few more years but never reached an eighth-grade reading level. In ten Southern states, more than 40 percent of the adult population, white and black, are dropouts. Happily, overall dropout rates (now about 25 percent) have been falling fast during recent decades; but they remain high among blacks and Hispanics in city schools, auguring ill for the future progress of these minorities.

Functional illiteracy tends to be passed from generation to generation—illiterate parents cannot read to their children, help them with their homework, or introduce them to the world of books. The NAEP reports that youngsters whose parents failed to complete high school are nearly twice as likely as their peers to be functionally illiterate.

Reflecting on the U.S. Army's experience with illiterates, an American educator once wrote: "An overwhelming majority of these soldiers had entered school, attended the primary grades where reading is taught, and had been taught to read. Yet, when as adults they were examined, they were unable to read readily such simple material as that of a daily newspaper." The educator was May Ayres Burgess, writing in 1921 about the Army's experience with the Alpha tests for draftees during World War I. Complaints like hers had been heard before in American history, and they are being repeated today.

America's Schools: Getting Bad Grades

In 1986, as we have noted, most of the nation's 2.3 million new adult functional illiterates are either immigrants or dropouts. But that is not to say that the schools are blameless. According to the NAEP, one million children between the ages of twelve and seventeen now read below a fourth-grade level. Among minority groups, the problems are more severe: 41 percent of black seventeen-year-olds (and 8 percent of their white peers) are functionally illiterate; hence they are not likely to escape from the underclass.

There are signs everywhere that such data understate the extent of the problem, that many more youths—white, black, and Hispanic—do not read well enough to make their own way in American society. Of nearly 1,400 colleges and universities surveyed recently, 84 percent had found it necessary to create remedial reading, writing, and math programs. Big Business spends billions of dollars every year on "job training," often merely a euphemism for "bonehead" English courses. The American Telephone and Telegraph Company bankrolls $6 million worth of remedial education for 14,000 employees. The Polaroid Corporation teaches engineers bound for management positions how to read nontechnical material. "They never learned to scan. They don't know you can read a newspaper differently from a book or that you can read just parts of a book," said a company official.

Mastering the technique of reading is no guarantee of understand-

---

CHEATING AMERICA'S YOUTH

At each June graduation, nearly 1 million functionally illiterate youths receive high school diplomas. Among their classmates are hundreds of thousands of "marginally competent" readers, unable to comprehend their own twelfth-grade textbooks.

What has gone wrong in American education? The dozens of studies that have been published since Washington sounded the alarm against a "rising tide of mediocrity" in *A Nation at Risk* (1983) agree that television, student drug abuse, and weakened families have all contributed to declining academic achievement. But the most important influence on students' performance is still what goes on inside the classroom. (See "Teaching in America," *The Wilson Quarterly*, New Year's, 1984.) And the evidence here is sobering.

Time, one of the most precious commodities in the schools, is often scarce and poorly used. In *A Place Called School* (1983), John I. Goodlad of the University of California, Los Angeles, reports that some schools cram all real teaching into a mere 18.5 hours per week. (In contrast, longer hours and shorter vacations give Japanese students the equivalent of four extra years of instruction by the time they leave high school.)

In elementary schools, American students spend nearly one-third of their class time on writing exercises—but that often means merely filling in the blanks in workbooks. And as students move on to high school, the class time they devote to writing falls by 50 percent.

Even more disheartening is Goodlad's discovery that "reading [occupies] about six percent of class time at the elementary level," a mere two percent in high school. Students do even less at home. High school sophomores average four hours of homework per week; their Japanese counterparts two hours *every night.*

When students do read in class, they use "dumbed down" textbooks— stripped, says Bill Honig, California's Superintendent of Public Instruction, "of any distinguishing content, style, or point of view" by publishers adhering to rigid "readability" formulas. Honig recalls that a local school district he once headed was forced to buy junior high school history books for fifth-graders "because the reading levels of the [standard fifth grade] series were pitched so low."

Honig contends that the "reformers" of the 1960s deserve much of the blame. In the name of "relevant" education, they added classes like Marriage

Simulation and Baja Whalewatch to the curriculum and eased academic requirements. By the late 1970s nearly one-half of the nation's high school students were enrolled in lax "general track" programs, up from just 10 percent a decade earlier.

Honig and other analysts see the slight upturn in students' scores on standardized tests in recent years as a sign that America's public schools have begun a turnaround. But Honig also warns that the damage done to literacy and general learning during two decades of turmoil in the schools will not quickly be undone.

---

ing the substance of what is read. That requires *cultural* literacy. Most high school seniors can probably "decode" *Time,* but one wonders how much of it they understand. *What Do Our 17-Year-Olds Know?* (1987), a study sponsored by the National Endowment for the Humanities (NEH) found that one-half of the students did not recognize the names of Josef Stalin or Patrick Henry. More than a quarter could not point to Great Britain, France, or West Germany, *on a map of Europe.* The NEH did not ask its young subjects whether they knew who Mikhail S. Gorbachev and Margaret Thatcher were, but chances are that the answers would have been discouraging. Daily newspaper circulation has remained stagnant at about 62 million copies since 1970, as the nation's population has grown. At least one-fourth of America's 87 million households appear to go without a newspaper.

More Books but Less Reading

American book publishers are selling more books per capita than ever before—output totals 3.5 million copies daily—but if Jane Fonda's best-selling *Workout Book* is any guide, not many of these exercise the mind very much. The book trade's biggest sellers overall—the Gothic novels and mysteries and romances sold in drugstores and supermarkets—are mostly written at a seventh- or eighth-grade level. Even with this wide selection of light fare, 29 percent of all sixteen- to twenty-one-year-olds, according to a survey by the Book Industry Study Group, say that they do not read books at all.

Along with functional illiterates, such "aliterates" do manage to scrape by. Most are gainfully employed, active members of society, even if their lives are complicated or their futures dimmed. *Glamour* magazine recently reported the case of a successful twenty-nine-year-old female real estate broker hampered by an eighth-grade level reading ability. "I'm constantly with customers who use words that go over my head. I often have to ask them to expand on what they just said. If I can't manipulate them into saying things in words I understand, I'm lost." Her fiancé helped her read letters and contracts.

"You have to be careful not to get into situations where it would leak out or be with people that would—ah—make it show," said an illiterate Vermont farmer. "You always try to act intelligent, act like you knew everything. . . . If somebody give you something to read, you make believe you read it and you must make out like you knew everything that there was on there . . . and most of the time you could. It's kinda like show biz."

Adult Basic Education and Literacy Programs

"Illiterates become the greatest actors in the world," noted Arthur Colby, president of Literacy Volunteers of America. Colby's organization is one of many around the country that try to help functional illiterates. But widespread literacy training for civilian adults is a relatively new phenomenon. President Lyndon B. Johnson, calling functional illiteracy "a national tragedy," got Washington involved when he launched the Adult Basic Education (ABE) program in 1964 as part of his Great Society. Today Washington spends about $100 million (matched by $200 million from the states) for several kinds of ABE programs: adult elementary and high school equivalency classes, as well as English-as-a-second-language instruction. All told, ABE enrolls 2.6 million adults annually.

In 1970 Commissioner of Education James E. Allen, Jr., launched an ambitious national "Right-to-Read" effort for illiterates of all ages, but Allen was fired for his public opposition to President Richard Nixon's 1970 incursion into Cambodia; his education "moonshot for the '70s" never really got off the launch pad. In a September 7, 1983, speech marking International Literacy Day, President Reagan called for "a united effort" to eliminate adult functional illiteracy in America. Yet, thus far Washington has not chipped in much more money for the effort.

The private sector sponsors hundreds of literacy programs. Literacy Volunteers of America (founded in 1962) and Laubach Literacy International (1930) are the two biggest charitable efforts aimed at adult illiterates. They enroll 75,000 students annually. Community colleges, local public libraries, churches, community-based education and development organizations (with a mixture of private and government support), corporations, and labor unions do substantial work in the field. All told, private and public literacy efforts spend less than $1 billion annually (versus $90 billion for higher education) and reach 4.5 to 6 million people.

Although perhaps one-fifth of America's adult illiterates enroll in these programs every year (not counting those who need help to climb from an eighth- to a twelfth-grade level), many will have to stay in for several years to learn to read and write effectively. Dropout rates are often very high—over 50 percent in some classes. And among graduates, there is a disturbing tendency to lapse back into illiteracy as the ability to read and write atrophies from disuse once classes end.

What works? The American military has the longest experience with combating adult illiteracy, and even it has found no magic formulas. The switch to an all-volunteer Army made the search more desperate: From 10 percent in 1975, the proportion of functionally illiterate recruits jumped to 31 percent in 1981. (By 1985, thanks in part to high civilian unemployment that improved the quality of recruits, the rate dropped back to 9 percent.) The Army has achieved its greatest success with efforts like Project FLIT (Functional Literacy Training)—an intensive six-week course using operating manuals and other written material that soldiers actually need in the line of duty.

The same kind of approach seems to work best in the civilian world. Recently, a New York City Teamsters Union local sponsored a ten-week literacy course for card-carrying municipal exterminators. It focused on teaching the students what they needed to know to pass a certification exam and function in their jobs. Perhaps as important, the teachers were exterminators themselves, peers of the students. The result: few dropouts and a 100 percent success rate on the test for the graduates.

Unfortunately, the Teamsters example is the exception rather than the rule. The government's ABE programs and many others typically use middle-class instructors and rather abstract texts. Lower-class students who see few links between what is being taught (using texts like *Memories of East Utica*) and what they consider important (writing resumes and comparing life insurance policies, for example) often grow discouraged and drop out. Adds McGill University's Rose-Marie Weber, "Teachers [in adult literacy courses] often complain about the students' apparent lack of motivation, their negative attitudes toward learning, and their failure to recognize the long-term value of literacy skills."

Weber's observation suggests why the "all-out literacy war" that some specialists advocate would be unrealistic. Literacy is not just a simple mechanical skill that people can learn and stow away. It is almost a way of life, requiring constant exercise and the acquisition of new knowledge. The x-ray technician or computer repairperson who knows how to read but ignores newspapers and books and turns on the television set when he or she gets home is not going to achieve or sustain a high level of literacy.

Every generation seems to face its own obstacles to literacy. For the Puritans, one barrier was simply the cost and difficulty of reading by candlelight; for nineteenth-century Americans, the temptation to leave school to go to work. Today, we lack neither light nor leisure, and the "need to read" is stronger than ever. At the very least, every citizen ought to be able to learn *how* to read and to acquire the knowledge to know *what* he is reading.

Improving the quality of U.S. public education is an obvious (albeit expensive) first step: There is no logical reason why tax-supported high schools in America should produce graduates who cannot read and write at a twelfth-grade level. Continuing to do so merely consigns another generation of youths, especially low-income youths, to the bottom rungs of the economic ladder. Federal backing for successful local, "community-based" literacy efforts for adults, like those of the Teamsters, San Antonio's Barrio Education Project, and the Bronx Educational Services Program, is also needed. Yet many realities of modern life—the increasing influx of unlettered immigrants, the rising literacy standards, and television's continuing competition with the printed word for Americans' attention—suggest that functional illiteracy in America can be curbed but not eradicated. The illiterate, like the poor, will always be with us.

NOTES

1. As before, Massachusetts led the way. It had established the first common schools in 1647, but it was not until 1800 that the state allowed local school districts to levy taxes. Most of the existing states followed suit by the time of the Civil War. Compulsory attendance was slower in coming. Massachusetts was the pioneer again, requiring as early as 1852 that parents send their children to school; more than fifty years passed before Mississippi made compulsory education universal. Because schooling was coeducational, the male-female literacy gap quickly closed.

2. A dissatisfied Flesch published *Why Johnny Still Can't Read* in 1981, charging that educators are still ignoring phonics. But most U.S. schools today use a mixture of phonics and look-say instruction.

3. Opinion is by no means unanimous. In *Illiterate America* (1985), teacher-activist Jonathan Kozol endorses an eighth-grade standard but estimates that 60 million adults fail to meet it. Jeanne Chall argues that a twelfth-grade level is the minimum acceptable standard. Some 72 million adults fall below it.

Background Books

LITERACY AND POPULAR CULTURE

"The first and the greatest of European poets," as Greek historian H.D.F. Kitto called Homer in *The Greeks* (Penguin, 1951, cloth; 1984, paper), may not have been the creative genius that most Western academics long assumed him to be. In 1923 classicist Milman Parry, whose work appears in *The Making of Homeric Verse: The Collected Papers of Milman Parry* (Oxford, 1971; Ayer, 1980), edited by Adam Parry and Richard M. Dorson, shocked his fellow scholars by arguing that the *Iliad* and *Odyssey* had been orally composed and recited by wandering bards for several generations before being written.

For at least a century, scholars of ancient writing have split hairs over such questions as whether Homer was the sole author of his epics and whether the alphabet spread from a single source or was independently invented in several places. Among the notable works in this tradition are archaeologist Ignace J. Gelb's *A Study of Writing* (University of Chicago, 1952, cloth; 1963, paper), linguist David Diringer's *The Alphabet: A Key to the History of Mankind* (Hutchinson, 1948), and the more readable *A History of Writing* (Scribner's, 1984) by the British Library's Albertine Gaur.

Parry and A.B. Lord, the student who continued Parry's work in *Singer of Tales* (Harvard, 1960, cloth; 1981, paper), may have solved what historians call "the Homeric question," but they also opened the door to a controversy among anthropologists, psychologists, linguists, and classicists.

Was the transformation of the Greek mind between the time of Homer's verse and that of Aristotle's logic *caused* by writing? Does literacy in the modern world change the way people *think*?

In *Preface to Plato* (Harvard, 1963, 1982) and *The Greek Concept of Justice* (Harvard, 1978), noted classicist Eric A. Havelock answers in the affirmative. The nonliterate mind, according to Havelock, relies on concrete images, rhythmic patterns, and narrative. To put Euclid's abstract notion of an equilateral triangle in "Homeric dress," one would have to say something like: "The triangle stood firm in battle, astride and posed on equal legs." Only someone endowed with the abstract, analytic skills bestowed by literacy could have created the Platonic dialogues.

"Concrete" thought is not the only characteristic attributed to nonliterates. Soviet psychologist A.R. Luria, whose landmark study of Russian peasants during the 1930s, *Cognitive Development* (Harvard, 1976, cloth and paper), has only recently been published in the West, adds that language shapes perception. People who lack separate *words* for "blue" and "green," for example, may confuse those colors.

Likewise, Luria's peasants could not classify objects like a hammer, a saw, and an ax as tools or respond correctly to questions of logic. To the syllogism "In the Far North . . . all bears are white. Novaya Zemlya is in the Far North. . . . What color are the bears?" a peasant replied: "I don't know. Each locality has its own animals."

Language scholar Walter J. Ong, in *Orality and Literacy: The Technologizing of the Word* (Methuen, 1982), and anthropologists in *Literacy in Traditional Societies* (Cambridge, 1968), edited by Cambridge University's Jack Goody, offer other examples from medieval Europe, Africa, and India. Goody and Ian Watt of Stanford University, for instance, write that the Eskimos of Alaska or the Tiv of Nigeria "do not recognize any contradiction between what they say now and what they said 50 years ago" because they lack written records. Myth and history for the nonliterate thus "merge into one."

On the other hand, psychologist Jean Piaget, in *The Development of Thought: Equilibration of Cognitive Structures* (Viking, 1977), and anthropologist Claude Levi-Strauss, in *The Savage Mind* (University of Chicago, 1967), argue that there are few, if any, differences between the cognitive or intellectual abilities of literate and nonliterate people.

Nonliterate villagers in Africa, North America, or Asia, Levi-Strauss contends, have their own sophisticated systems of classification and logic that do not depend on writing. The Navaho of old, for example, could identify more than 500 species of desert plants off the top of their heads—a feat that any literate person would be hard-pressed to equal. "The use of more or less abstract terms," says Levi-Strauss, "is a function not of greater or lesser intellectual capacity, but of differences in the interests . . . of particular social groups."

Psychologists Sylvia Scribner and Michael Cole make much the same argument in *The Psychology of Literacy* (Harvard, 1981), a report of their seven-year study among the Vai of Liberia. The two researchers found that nonliterate and literate but self-taught Vai performed equally well on most tests of cognitive ability. Only Vai educated in Western-style schools surpassed their fellows in what Scribner and Cole call "logical functions."

The notion that simply learning the ABCs is not enough would not have surprised the organizers of a major effort, sponsored by Northern Protestant churches and abolitionist societies, to "teach & civilize" illiterate freedmen after the Civil War. Historian Robert C. Morris, in *Reading, 'Riting, and Reconstruction* (University of Chicago, 1976, 1982) describes what W.E.B. DuBois called "the crusade for the New England schoolma'am."

To the dismay of some white Southerners, the Yankee teachers taught more than 7,000 young blacks in Dixie everything from reading and arithmetic to "John Brown's Body." The schoolma'ams were successful in attracting many of their students to the Republican banner and, during the 1870s and 1880s, helped found many of the South's black high schools and colleges.

Today, as Third World governments struggle to make their citizens literate and U.S. colleges and corporations push remedial writing programs, academic specialists in the West continue to debate the impact of literacy on the human condition.

The printed word, of course, is not the only means of human expression and communication. Art and music, both sublime and mundane, also serve to convey our sense of ourselves and the world in which we live. Film, television, even advertising, must be included among the vital channels through which messages and ideas are spread amongst a mass audience of people who may not even be aware that they have been targeted. Taken together, these disparate media of mass communication produce a vibrant, restless, ever-changing image of our society that we collectively refer to as "popular" or "mass" culture.

Books on "popular" or "mass" culture are nearly as numerous as the formula novels, movies, TV shows, comic strips, popular songs, "pop" paintings, and other manifestations of twentieth-century life with which they deal. Some are excellent studies. Others are themselves a kind of "pop" scholarship; these are written according to formula, aimed at the college campus. Sometimes they make good reading, but too often they are no more nourishing than spun-sugar candy.

Moreover, few broad theoretical studies of the United States' constantly refurbished, repackaged, and recycled mythology are available. Hence, academic specialists often recommend French structuralist Roland Barthes's *Mythologies* (Hill & Wang, 1972, cloth and paper). Barthes argues that popular or mass culture does not simply arise out of a community. He sees it as imposed by the Right on the rest of society. His ideological critique covers recent films and literature, wrestling matches, and the already outdated art of the striptease.

Popular culture's best ethnography (defined by the *American Heritage Dictionary* as "the social anthropology of primitive tribes") to date may be that offered by Tom Wolfe in *The Pump House Gang* (Farrar, 1968, cloth; Bantam, 1969, paper). The people who attract his interest are not passive audiences but members of the media-incited communities that grow up around popular culture fads or celebrities.

In this collection Wolfe writes vividly about the rituals and codes of *Playboy* creator Hugh Hefner's followers, about the adolescent shop clerks who blossomed into style setters in London's rock-and-clothes-oriented "noonday underground" of the late 1960s, about the symbiotic relationship between the makers and buyers of "pop art," and much more. His psychedelic style is, of course, characteristic of the New Journalism (itself sometimes regarded as a form of popular culture), which he helped to create.

Arguments rage among academics over the terms "mass" versus "popular" culture. Some writers use the phrases interchangeably. Others more or less define the mass-produced–distributed–consumed product of twentieth-century movies, paperbacks, the press, and TV as constituting mass culture. They reserve the term popular culture for folklore and the kind of phenomenon that country music used to be when Appalachian mountain people made it for themselves, long before it spread across all of America and Europe.

Herbert Gans, in *Popular Culture and High Culture: An Analysis and Evaluation of Taste* (Basic Books, 1975, cloth; 1977, paper), has a term of his own. The Columbia University sociologist lumps the mass, the popular, and the high under what he calls "taste cultures," which he defines as encompassing both "values" and "cultural forms"; everything from music, art, design, literature, news, "and the media in which they are expressed," to consumer goods "that express aesthetic values or functions, such as furnishings, clothes, appliances."

Studies of popular culture are often packaged in glossy picture books of coffee-table size. *The Smithsonian Collection of Newspaper Comics* (Smithsonian Press/Abrams, 1978, cloth and paper), for example, edited by Bill Blackbeard and Martin Williams, is a parade, in black and white and color, of strips from American newspapers, 1896–1976. The characters range from the Katzenjammer Kids (1897) to the Wizard of Id (1964).

A definitive 785-page illustrated reference book is *The World Encyclopedia of Comics* (Chelsea House, 1976, cloth; Avon, 1970, paper) edited by Maurice Horn. It includes a short history of world comics, starting with the publication of William Hogarth's *A Harlot's Progress* in 1734, and a brief analytical summary. Horn concludes that "with the comics' growing cultural acceptance," cartoonists, "no longer dismissed as grubby purveyors of mindless entertainment," and their employers "must expect to be called into account on aesthetic and ethical grounds" like novelists, publishers, playwrights, and film makers.

Leftists often find studies of popular culture a pathway into a critique of American society. The best of this lot is Stuart and Elizabeth Ewen's *Channels of Desire* (McGraw-Hill, 1982) in which the authors emphasize the contradictions inherent in the development of American popular culture over the past hundred years. "On the one hand," they write, "people have experienced industrial hardship and alienation: urban loneliness, dehumanized work, loss of traditional culture and skills, erosion of family and community life. On the other hand, industrialism has broadened horizons, spread literacy, stepped up communications, and promised material abundance beyond the wildest dreams of previous epochs."

Studies in Entertainment: Critical Approaches to Mass Culture (Indiana University Press, 1986), edited by Tania Modleski, assesses the current state of thinking in various Marxist approaches to all forms of American popular culture. This volume is comprehensive and includes an interview with Raymond Williams, possibly the most influential mass culture theorist from the Marxist perspective of the past fifty years.

Some of the greatest rewards in the study of popular culture come from a close examination of the more ephemeral matters. *Mythmakers of the American Dream* (Associated University Press, 1983), by Wiley Lee Umphlett, looks at its thematic subject matter across film, television, books, and comic strips. This is one serious scholarly study of nostalgia that truly covers the media spectrum.

The production of what we know as pop culture began with the print media some 100 years ago when newspapers and magazines began to make serious use of advertising. For an understanding of the role and impact of all forms of advertising in our media-dependent culture see Michael Shudson's *Advertising, the Uneasy Persuasion* (Basic, 1984). An historian, Shudson provides a balanced view of that form of popular culture that most pervades our lives.

But the most significant transformation in reading in the United States has been the coming of the paperback book. We now get instant paperbacks, versions of movies and television shows, and the usual mysteries, romance novels, and non-fiction on all topics. To understand better the coming of the paperback, now about a half-century old, read yet another paperback—Kenneth C. Davis's *Two-Bit Culture* (Houghton-Mifflin, 1984). Here one can learn the details about an industry that grew from Dr. Spock's phenomenal best seller on baby care to a multi-billion dollar enterprise.

One of the most significant selling tools of early paperbacks were the covers. The image of Holden Caulfield and his red hat on the cover of *Catcher in the Rye* inspired a generation and caused author J.D. Salinger never to permit another design on the covers of his books. More about this pop culture phenomena can be traced in *Paperbacks, U.S.A.* (Blue Dolphin, 1981), by Piet Schreuders, who traces cover design from Art Deco inspiration through photo realism.

But pop culture is more than printed works. For example, *Roadside Empires: How Chains Franchised America* (Viking, 1985), by Stan Luxenberg, is a study of economic organization and history of the movement to standardize America's purchase of hamburgers, hair care, mufflers, motels, and assorted other items.

The most successful franchising organization in history is McDonald's, and there is both an authorized version of the rise of this fast-food chain and a behind the scenes story. Ray Kroc, the super-salesman founder of McDonald's, wrote his tale in *Grinding It Out* (Contemporary, 1977). His account is best summed up in his statement, "I have had the satisfaction of seeing McDonald's become an American tradition. Such a dream could only be realized in America." Max Boas and Steve Chain, the authors of *Big Mac* (Dutton, 1976), identify the basis of Kroc's success as cheap labor, mass production, easy access, and uniform sameness, and attempt to convince the reader that he might like the hamburger but not the ideology that goes with it.

Seemingly unrelated is *G-Men: Hoover's FBI in American Popular*

Culture by Richard Gib Powers (Southern Illinois University Press, 1983) in which the author traces how the Hoover image was constructed. In the post–Al Capone era of the Great Depression, the public looked to Washington for a new hero, and Hoover gave it to them. Through newsreels, newspapers, comic strips, pulp magazines, radio series, features, and later television, Hoover made sure the image of the tough, incorruptible G-Man stood tall. Hoover sold himself and the FBI using techniques that Ray Kroc would later use to sell hamburgers.

Popular culture often takes on many forms, and one effective study technique is to examine a dominant genre in all its variations. A once important form, which seems dead at the moment, is the western. Tales of the Old West dominated movies and pulp fiction, and appeared on radio and in newspapers throughout the first half of the twentieth century. John G. Cawelti studies them all in *The Six-Gun Mystique* (Bowling Green University Popular Press, 1971).

Sports have been written about endlessly since the turn of the century. But most books of this genre of nonfiction are part of the mass of pop culture rather than pop culture analysis. One exception is *Ty Cobb* (Oxford, 1984) by Charles C. Alexander, an historian who examines the baseball player who is possibly the greatest hitter the game has ever known. Cobb not only contributed to the ethos of pop culture in the first half of the twentieth century, but also reflected it in his hard-driving perfectionism, ruthless competitive spirit, and shrewd business acumen, which made him the first millionaire athlete.

The United States has long relied on European music to define its high culture music. Other forms are seen as not complex or original enough to rival what has come out of Austria, Germany, and Italy. A contrary view can be found in *Country Music U.S.A.* (University of Texas Press, 1985) by Bill Malone, which examines the nuances and complex variations of an American musical form known only a few decades ago as hillbilly music. Malone argues that the creative talents of Hank Williams, Sr., Bob Wills and his Texas Playboys, and even Ricky Skaggs deserve the acclaim accorded Mozart, Bach, or Stravinsky.

Jazz, yet another form of popular culture, has inspired an enormous literature. The writer always mentioned first among buffs and scholars is Gunther Schuller; his *Early Jazz: Its Roots and Musical Development* (Oxford, 1968) is a basic book. *The Jazz Masters* series, published by Macmillan under the general editorship of Martin Williams, director of the Smithsonian Jazz Program includes one volume by Williams, *Jazz Masters of New Orleans* (Macmillan, 1967), that traces the history and relative importance of the tunes, the bands, and the records. It also evokes a strong sense of what the first jazz capital was like in the years when Jelly Roll Morton, who once asserted that he had invented jazz, was a slim young pianist yet to make his first recording in 1923, and Louis Armstrong was still known only as "Little Louie."

The World's Fair is not a totally American institution but the United States has certainly embraced it. There have been many fairs, but few have had the impact of 1893 Columbia Exposition held in Chicago. This landmark event is described in detail in R. Reid Badger's *The Great American Fair* (Nelson–Hall, 1979).

All in all, the flood of "pop" culture books shows no sign of abating. "Pop" sculpture, twentieth-century musical comedies and country music, nineteenth-century vaudeville, showboat melodramas, penny postcards, and Valentines—all have their interpreters who continue to get into print.

NEWSPAPERS

Chapter 4

NEWSPAPERS IN TRANSITION

by Leo Bogart

When World War II ended, eight daily newspapers in New York City reported the story, as did seven in Boston, four in Philadelphia, five in Chicago, four in San Francisco. Now, not quite four decades later, New York is down to four (if we count the new city edition of *Newsday*, along with the *Times, Post,* and *Daily News*), and Boston, Philadelphia, and Chicago have only two newspapers apiece. The most recent major casualties are the Baltimore *News American, Washington Star,* Philadelphia *Bulletin,* and *Cleveland Press.* In St. Petersburg, St. Paul, Louisville, New Haven, New Orleans, Des Moines, Portland, Tampa, Minneapolis—all one-ownership newspaper towns—publishers have discontinued their less successful papers, usually their afternoon papers. The troubles of other newspapers are still making news. In 1923 there were 503 cities with more than one separately owned daily newspaper; now there are only 49. And in 20 of those cities, competing papers have joint business and printing arrangements.

After the evening *Minneapolis Star* (circulation 170,000) was discontinued in April, 1981, its editor, Stephen Isaacs, responded to a query from *Editor & Publisher:*

> What do I see ahead? I talked to many publishers recently and was startled by the number who have in effect told me that the newspaper business is a dying industry. A dinosaur. Some will survive—the very big and the very small—but the in-betweens are going to face rough going in the electronic era. . . . Frankly, I was stunned by their comments.

SHARES OF NEWSPAPER CIRCULATION, 1986 (by size)

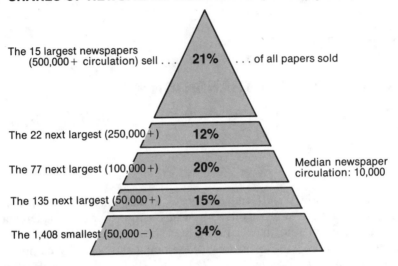

The 15 largest newspapers
(500,000+ circulation) sell . . .   **21%**   . . . of all papers sold

The 22 next largest (250,000+)   **12%**

The 77 next largest (100,000+)   **20%**   Median newspaper
circulation: 10,000

The 135 next largest (50,000+)   **15%**

The 1,408 smallest (50,000−)   **34%**

NEWSPAPER CHAIN OWNERSHIP

10 LARGEST CHAINS September, 1987	Daily Circulation	No. of dailies
Gannett Co.	6,029,745	89
Knight-Ridder	3,840,387	31
Newhouse Newspapers	3,018,247	26
Tribune Co.	2,706,970	9
Times Mirror Co.	2,566,586	8
Dow Jones and Co.	2,536,377	24
New York Times Co.	1,821,089	27
Thomson Newspapers (U.S.)	1,725,799	102
Scripps-Howard	1,598,375	22
Hearst Newspapers	1,441,031	15

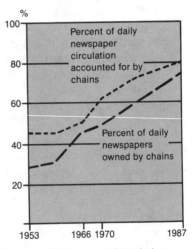

Sources: Morton Research, Lynch, Jones, & Ryan; Audit Bureau of Circulations

Demographic Shifts and the Decline of City Papers

The deaths of great metropolitan dailies are stunning events, and not only to publishers and editors. But do they mean that newspapers, as such, have outlived their function?

The fallen giants in the business have been stricken by the sickness of their home cities. In the twenty largest cities, newspaper circulation dropped by 21 percent between 1970 and 1980, while population fell by 6 percent. This does not tell the whole story, because the big cities have changed character even more than they have lost people. Their white population fell by 20 percent, and the whites now include a higher proportion of Hispanics and the elderly poor.[1] In many blighted inner-city areas, crime, vandalism, and collection problems have wreaked havoc with both home deliveries and street sales.

Changes in the urban economy and social structure have also had disastrous effects on downtown retailers, who have been the mainstay of metropolitan newspaper advertising. Retail chains followed the middle class to the suburbs—and began to put advertising money into suburban papers, give-away "shoppers," and direct mail advertising. Metropolitan evening papers had to print earlier (usually well before noon) just to permit delivery by truck through traffic jams to the sprawling suburbs. Because their circulation was more concentrated in the central cities, they were more vulnerable than their morning rivals to the pressures of urban change. The deaths of metropolitan newspapers help explain why total daily circulation has declined since World War II; the ratio of newspapers sold to U.S. households dropped from 128:100 in 1948 to 71:100 in 1987.

The reasons are many and complex.

The price of a subscription has gone up, and some papers have stopped distribution in outlying areas because of the expense. Young people of the TV generation now read newspapers less often than their parents did. Changes in family life have altered the use of leisure. With more wives at work, both husbands and wives have less time to read when they get home.

Innovations in Form and Content

Still, the worst appears to be over. In spite of the losses in the big cities, overall newspaper circulation and readership have stabilized during the past five years, following eight years of steady decline. The

POPULATION VS. NEWSPAPER CIRCULATION
(25 largest SMSAs)

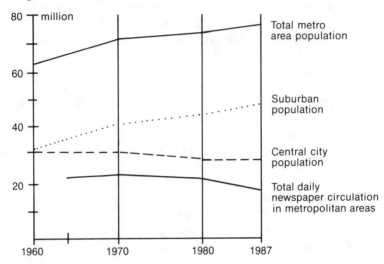

A TYPICAL NEWSPAPER'S EDITORIAL CONTENT

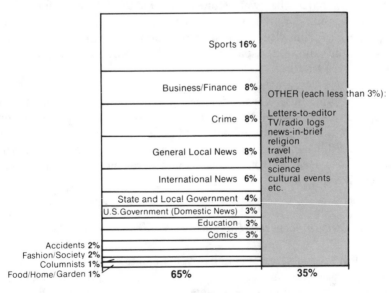

Sources: Morton Research; the Newspaper Advertising Bureau

real question is not whether newspapers will survive into the twenty-first century, but rather *what kind* of newspapers they will be. The answer lies both in the economics of the press and in the perceptions of editors and publishers. Their perceptions have already led to rapid changes in newspaper style and character during the past decade and to an extraordinary amount of editorial innovation.

One theory that quickly gained favor was that TV news was taking away readers—although no evidence directly supported this notion. To the contrary, newspapers have done better (in terms of the ratio of circulation to all households) in metropolitan areas where TV news ratings are high rather than low. Television news viewing went down, not up, in New York City when the *Times, Post,* and *Daily News* were on strike in 1978.

Moreover, many editors appear to have been convinced during the 1970s that more and bigger photographs, and more "features" and "personality journalism" were necessary counters to the visual and entertainment elements of TV in general. Indeed, the *Miami News* billed itself as the newspaper "for people who watch television."

There were other less obvious changes, particularly among dailies with less than 100,000 circulation. One was the emphasis on local, staff-written news—leaving more of the wider world to the TV network news, the *Wall Street Journal,* or *Time* and *Newsweek.* Thirty-five percent of *all* editors who were asked about editorial changes in 1977–9 reported a shift toward "localizing" the news.

"What sells papers is the ability to identify with the news content," said Milton Merz, who in 1976 was circulation director of the Bergen County, New Jersey, *Record* (circulation 150,796). "And people identify with things that affect them directly. Once you get outside their town, their interest drops like a rock."

Among big-city papers, in particular, zoned editions, aimed at specific regions within a metropolitan area, seemed a good response to competition for readers from the mushrooming smaller suburban dailies and weeklies.

Yet the belief that people are mainly interested in "chicken dinner" news runs counter to reality. First, Americans as a whole today are increasingly well educated, cosmopolitan, and mobile, with weak ties to their home communities. Second, as is well known, fewer of any big-city daily's readers now live or work in the city where the newspaper is published and where it deploys most of its reporters (only 32 percent of the *Chicago Tribune*'s circulation, for example, is within the city limits); the suburban dispersion of homes and jobs in

WHAT ADULTS READ AND WATCH

News and information sources and "serious" television programs

	Each Day		*Each Week*
63.0%	Any daily newspaper	24%	*TV Guide*
2.8	*USA Today*	22	*Reader's Digest*
2.4	*Wall Street Journal*	14	*Time*
1.7	*New York Times*	10	*Newsweek*
35.0%	Early Evening Local	19%	*60 Minutes* (CBS)
29.0	Late Local TV News	10	*20/20* (ABC)
27.0	Network Evening News	9	*National Geographic* Specials (PBS)
9.0	Morning TV News	6	*Nature* (PBS)
2.0	*MacNeil/Lehrer Newshour*	6	*This Week with David Brinkley* (ABC)
		6	*CBS Sunday Morning*
		5	*Nova* (PBS)
		4	*Face the Nation* (CBS)
		3	*Masterpiece Theater* (PBS)
		3	*Meet the Press* (NBC)
		3	*Mystery!* (PBS)

Sources: Simmons Study of Media & Markets, 1986. For PBS the percentage is of homes, A. C. Nielsen; PBS figures do not include several repeats of programs outside of prime time each week.

scores of distinct communities over hundreds of square miles means that any particular local event is likely to affect relatively few people. A high proportion of what editors think of as local items that appear in a big-city paper are actually "sublocal"; they deal with events—school board disputes, village politics, accidents—that matter little to most of the paper's readers.

What some editors forget is that TV network news, for all its "show business" flaws, has made national and foreign figures, from Reagan to Begin, vivid and familiar to average Americans, to a degree unimaginable twenty years ago. Of course, as always, people want *both* kinds of news, not just one or the other. Still, national research shows that the average item of local news attracts slightly fewer people who say they are "interested" or "very interested" in it than does the average item of foreign or national news. The same study shows that the "memorability" of local events as "big news," "upsetting news," or "good news" is extremely low relative to the amount of space they occupy in newspapers or relative to more dramatic stories from the wider world.[2]

The *Chicago Tribune*'s publisher Joseph Medill was once asked the secret of his success. "Just publish the news," he said. Today, not every publisher would agree. The most notable change in newspaper content since 1970 has been a new stress on "soft" features, often concentrated in special sections aimed at "upscale" suburban consumers, especially women. Under such umbrellas as "Lifestyle," "Living," or "Style," editors and writers have sought to impart the latest in television, movies, celebrities, "self-help," "women's issues," fashions, food, parties, recreation, and manners. (Less regular coverage has been devoted to the old specialized side dishes of the traditional newspaper menu: stamp-collecting, chess, gardening, and photography.) The new "sectional revolution" was led by the *Washington Post,* the *Los Angeles Times,* and the *Chicago Tribune.*

At the *New York Times,* "Weekend," started in 1976, was followed by "Living," "Home," "Sports Monday," and "Science Times." The strategy worked; *Times* circulation rose by 33,000 during the sixteen months after "Weekend's" birth. In 1977–9, almost half of all newspapers with circulations of over 100,000 added weekday "lifestyle" sections; and many of the remainder already had them.

Said Derek J. Daniels, a former Knight–Ridder executive:

> If [newspapermen] are to meet the new challenges, they must, above all, recognize that reading is work. . . . I believe that newspapers should devote more space to the things that are helpful, enjoyable, exciting, and fun as opposed to undue emphasis on "responsible information."

In some ways newspapers were coming to resemble consumer magazines. Editors had always used feature material as "good news" to lighten the "bad news" that dominates the headlines. But did readers really want newspapers to entertain them rather than to inform them?

Not really. A majority (59 percent) of a national cross-section of people questioned in 1977 indicated they would prefer a newspaper devoted *completely* to news rather than one that just provided a news summary and consisted mostly of entertaining features.

This response should not be dismissed as merely the expression of a socially acceptable attitude. For what it really indicates is that people expect newspapers to do more than cater to their personal tastes. Americans recognize a newspaper's larger responsibility to society; and they want it to cover a multitude of subjects, including ones about which they themselves normally would not care to read.

People perceive that some newspaper articles are "interesting," but others are "important." Thus according to the 1977 study, half of those who found the average sports item "very interesting" also rated it as "not very important." When people's responses to specific newspaper items are surveyed, entertainment features—except for TV and radio program logs, advice columns, and travel articles—all score below average in interest. A typical entertainment feature is rated "very interesting" by only 20 percent of those surveyed, while a typical straight news story is rated "very interesting" by 31 percent.

Editors, then, in remaking their newspapers during the 1970s, may have underestimated their readers. But newspapers in those years were not just changing—they, collectively, were growing. In smaller and middle-sized communities, daily newspapers, most of them without local daily competition, continued to enjoy high levels of readership and prosperity. And the reader got more for his or her money. For a typical (surviving) major metropolitan daily, the number of pages of editorial matter went from 19.8 in 1970 to 32.4 in 1986, keeping pace with an increased volume of advertising.

So, despite the alterations, cosmetic and substantive, newspapers were actually providing more "hard" news and more national and world news. But the proportions were different. There was more icing on the cake, and often the cake itself was a bit fluffier. The *character* of newspapers was changing.

Editorial ingenuity and experimentation did not save the *Chicago Daily News* or the *Cleveland Press*. An article in the *Minneapolis Star,* after announcement of that paper's impending demise, recalled the editors' rescue efforts:

> Suddenly, or so it seemed, the newspaper's most basic ingredients—City Council meetings, news conferences, speeches—were gone. In their place was an unpredictable front-page mixture of blazing illustrations, Hollywood features and all sorts of things that had once been tucked away inside the paper.

The *Star*'s radical changes did not halt its decline in readership.

The Economics of Advertising

Yet the disease that kills off competing newspapers is not lack of readers; it is lack of advertising, which accounts for three-fourths of a newspaper's income. This disease has struck down even highly respected newspapers with considerable numbers of high-income readers, from the *New York Herald Tribune* in 1966 to the *Washington Star* in 1981. From an advertising point of view, "duplication" is considered highly wasteful.

Once a newspaper, good or bad, falls into second place even by a small margin, it becomes a "loser" in the eyes of advertising agencies and big retail chains; more of their advertising goes to the winner, accelerating the decline of the loser.

Why has this winner-take-all doctrine taken hold on Madison Avenue—with all its pernicious side effects on local diversity of information and editorial opinion?

Part of it stems from the desire of advertisers for an exact fit between the kinds of people who buy their products and the characteristics of the media audience. The computer has created an insatiable appetite for marketing data, and the result is that advertising is bought by the numbers, by formula.

This practice has been fostered by the overall trend toward concentration. An increasing percentage of all retail sales goes to chains that operate in a number of different areas, with most of the growth since 1960 in the suburbs. The top hundred national advertisers (for example, Procter & Gamble, General Foods, and Philip Morris) account for 53 percent of all advertising outlays in all media, up from 35 percent in 1960; and the top ten advertising agency groups (led by the British-owned Saatchi and Saatchi) direct the spending of 43 percent of all advertising dollars, up from 17 percent in 1955.

What this means is that the decisions to allocate advertising dollars among newspapers (or among newspapers, magazines, TV, cable, and other media) are increasingly made by fewer people in fewer places. And the decisions are increasingly made on the basis of strictly quantitative data, covering everything from income to life style and personality types ("psychographics").

The established doctrine in marketing on Madison Avenue and elsewhere says this: If 30 percent of the people in a given area buy 60 percent of the product, then you target 100 percent of the advertising dollars at this group. (And for practical purposes you forget the others.) The media attracting the highest percentage of this group get the advertising dollars. What this means is that in Philadelphia, the *Bulletin,* with over 400,000 circulation, strangled on a deficit of $21 million in a market where advertisers spent $1.8 billion on all media in 1981. In that same year, the *Press* had 43 percent of the daily circulation in Cleveland, but only 28 percent of the advertising.

Advertisers try to direct their messages only at the most likely customers, and media have responded by defining their audiences in terms of particular market "segments" in which advertisers might be interested. There are thousands of specialized magazines from *House and Garden* to *The Runner.* Radio audiences have long been broken up into fractions identified with various tastes in music. As cable television spreads, the regular TV networks' share of "prime time" is waning. There are already more than a score of cable networks that advertisers can use to reach specific types of viewers. The newspaper will probably remain the only mass medium in a given community— each day supplying the body of information that provides a shared experience for people who share a geographic space.

To be sure, the death of a metropolitan newspaper is a dramatic story—big news. When a small-town weekly goes daily, that is not such big news. Yet since the end of World War II, newspaper births and deaths have approximately balanced each other out so that the total number of daily newspapers now (1,657) is only somewhat less than what it was on V-J Day (1,763). Twelve daily newspapers stopped publication in 1980 and 1981, but twenty-five new ones were started. Despite the 1981 death of the *Washington Star,* total newspaper circulation in the Washington metropolitan area as of March 31, 1982, was down by only 4 percent from what it had been a year earlier. The reason: Five suburban *Journal* newspapers were successfully converted from weekly to daily publication when the *Star* fell, and a new competitor, the *Washington Times,* emerged.

Despite the funerals of great newspapers, the newspaper industry is, in fact, not faring badly. Daily newspapers are published in 1,525 American towns, more than ever before. Newspapers have 26 percent of all advertising investments (television, local and national, now gets 22 percent; magazines get 5 percent; radio, 7 percent). In 1986 newspapers made capital investments of about $1.2 billion, much of it in new production technology. The latter has transformed newspaper production and greatly cut blue-collar labor costs. Publicly owned newspaper companies have enjoyed considerable prosperity – with a profit rate double the average for all corporations.[3]

Increasing Readership in the 1980s

Nearly nine out of ten Americans still look at a daily newspaper in the course of a week—108 million on an average weekday. Sunday sales are bigger than ever. This decade will see a 42 percent increase in the number of people from age 35 to 44, a prime age group for newspaper reading. With smaller families, the number of households will keep growing faster than the number of people, further improving opportunities for newspaper sales. Despite all the concern about the state of the public schools, the average level of education has been moving upward. Educators are beginning to respond to public concern about students' reading skills. Publishers (and school administrators) have belatedly begun encouraging the use of newspapers in the classroom. And the members of the TV generation are heavy consumers of paperback books and magazines.

What really makes newspapers indispensable is that they give voice and identity to the communities where they are published, and their disappearance somehow diminishes local civic spirit and morale.

It has been suggested recently that newspapers should simply turn themselves into an "upscale" product, aimed at just the top half or third of the social pyramid. This would be folly. There is enough advertising to sustain "elite" newspapers in New York, Los Angeles, and maybe a handful of other places, but certainly not in the average town. Newspapers are inescapably for everybody—and in an era of ever more specialized audiences and markets, that is a significant distinction. Newspapers have a powerful argument to make to the advertisers of mass merchandise, who need to cast their nets as widely as possible so as not to miss any prospective customers.

Still, the trend toward "target" marketing is irresistible, and newspapers are adapting to it. Many of them are able to provide

WHAT PEOPLE WATCH AND READ IN PEORIA

Sources of Daily News for People in Peoria, Illinois

Daily audience for	Home	Percentage
Local Evening News	72,000	33
Network Evening News	82,000	38
Late Night News	85,000	40
Newspaper Circulation	151,000	70
Peoria-Journal Star	91,000	
Bloomington Pantograph	37,000	
Pekin Times	16,000	
Canton Ledger	7,000	

Source: Arbitron, November 1987.

advertisers with ''pinpoint'' coverage in specific areas and to extend their coverage with supplementary distribution of advertising through mail or home delivery to nonsubscribers. But to be able to do this selectively for the largest number and variety of advertisers, newspapers must remain a mass medium.

As it happens, that is also what newspapers must remain if they are to fulfill their principal function, which is not to serve as a vehicle for advertising or entertainment, but to communicate to America's citizens what is happening of importance in their communities, their nation, and the world—and so to sustain informed public opinion in a free society.

NOTES

1. To illustrate this point with an extreme instance, the Bronx lost 19 percent of its total population between 1960 and 1980. The black population rose from 11 percent to 32 percent of the total, and Hispanics now represent 34 percent. The *New York Times* lost 56 percent of its Bronx circulation in those years, the *Daily News* 26 percent.

2. This and other findings cited in this article are from a national survey of 3,048 adults conducted for the Newspaper Readership Project in 1977 by Audits and Survey, Inc. A more comprehensive description of the study will be found in my book, *Press and Public* (Lawrence Erlbaum Associates, 1981).

3. For example, the Knight–Ridder, Gannett, and Washington Post organizations showed net incomes in 1986 of $182.6 million, $540.75 million, and $204.1 million, respectively.

Chapter 5

NEWSPEOPLE

by James Boylan

The press, wrote A.J. Liebling, is "the weak slat under the bed of democracy." Journalists have always liked to think the contrary—that the press keeps the bed from collapsing. They thought so even more after Vietnam and Watergate: Journalism, its champions then argued, deserves the privileges and immunities of a fourth branch of government; and its practitioners should enjoy the status, rewards, and invulnerability that go with being known as professionals.

Unfortunately for the press, its critics took such claims at face value. The press, they said, had become imperial, and journalists an arrogant "elite." Vice-President Spiro T. Agnew put an official stamp on this interpretation back in 1969 when he denounced the power of the "eastern establishment press." Agnew soon left the scene, but he was succeeded by more sophisticated and tenacious critics. Their target was the same as Agnew's—the Big League press and not American journalism as a whole. The latter, in fact, is a potpourri of wire services and syndicates, newspapers ranging in size from big-city tabloids down to mom-and-pop weeklies, and hundreds of magazines and broadcasting outlets.

However, focusing generally on the *New York Times,* the *Washington Post, Time, Newsweek,* and TV networks, such critics as Stanley Rothman, Kevin Phillips, and Michael Novak developed a wide-ranging indictment of journalism's upper crust. These journalists, they charged:

• are better educated and better paid than most Americans, with ideas and values alien to those of "the real majority";

59

• are concentrated in a few national news organizations that exercise disproportionate power over the selection of the news that reaches the American public;

• seek to enhance their own power by taking an aggressive, even destructive, stance toward other major American institutions such as government, the political parties, and business, while making themselves invulnerable to retaliation by wrapping themselves in an absolutist version of the First Amendment;

• have abandoned standards of fairness, accuracy, and neutrality in news to pursue larger audiences and greater power.

Beneath the political animus that fueled such critiques was a residue of harsh truth. But what was not necessarily true was the assumption made by critics that the current state of journalism departed radically from what came before it, that there had been a distinct break with the past.

As British historian Anthony Smith observed in *Goodbye Gutenberg,* "Each decade has left in American newspaper life some of the debris of the continuing intellectual battle over the social and moral role of journalism." For 150 years, journalists have sought success and power and respectability, usually in that order; and society has responded with unease and occasional hostility.

Innovation and Consolidation From the Penny Press to Professionalism

The press, in fact, has gone through at least four cycles of innovation and consolidation. America's first popular newspapers were the penny press of the 1830s and 1840s, typified by James Gordon Bennett's *New York Herald.* The penny press created a first generation of journalists by putting printers in waistcoats and turning young college graduates of literary inclination and poor prospects into reporters. So threatening was Bennett's frank and sensational news coverage that New York's establishment, led by the musty, older commercial papers that Bennett was putting out of business, conducted a "moral war" to stop him. Bennett survived.

A second and far larger journalistic generation appeared during the 1880s and 1890s. By then, the city newspaper had grown into the first mass medium, thanks to the showmanship of such entrepreneurs as William Randolph Hearst and Joseph Pulitzer. In the shrill Hearst–

Pulitzer competition during the Spanish–American War, the sales of an individual newspaper for the first time exceeded one million. Critics again fretted over the power of the press to push the nation into war, to debase society. Like Bennett, Hearst had a "moral war" declared against him, on grounds that his papers had incited McKinley's assassin. Like Bennett, Hearst survived.

Each journalistic generation set its own distinctive "style," but each progressed from rebellion to consolidation, from breaking old rules to laying down new ones. The penny press and its ragtag of "bohemians" angered and shocked the mandarins of the old commercial-political newspapers. Yet it was the old penny journalists who, during the 1870s, declared bohemianism dead and all journalists henceforth gentlemen of clean shirt and college education. Bohemianism reappeared with the "yellow" journalists of the 1890s. When that generation matured, it too set bohemianism aside: Its spokesmen began to claim that journalism was as much a profession as law or medicine, and universities established journalism schools in a flawed effort to prove the point.[1]

Unionizing the Newsroom

For forty years or more, newspapers rode high, but during the middle years of the twentieth century, they were no longer unchallenged. *Time* and other magazines, radio, and TV began to claim a share of the news audience. (Even so, most journalists continued to ply their trade at newspapers; and 75 percent still do.) The character of the popular press, meanwhile, began to turn from yellow to gray, as befitted an aging institution.

The next generation, the third, rebelled not by reverting to impetuous iconoclasm, but by trying to change the harsh economic rules of the game. The Great Depression had sent reporters' salaries plummeting; by 1933 many were out of work. New York columnist Heywood Broun, summoning reporters to set aside snobbery and join together, wrote that he could die happy if, when a general strike began, he saw Walter Lippmann "heave a brick through a *Tribune* window" at a scab trying to turn out a Lippmann column on the gold standard. Broun became president (1933–7) of the first national union for journalists, the American Newspaper Guild, and led it into reluctant affiliation with the U.S. labor movement.

Unionization's immediate effect was to take from management

some of the power it had long enjoyed—the power to fix newsroom wages and to hire and fire as it pleased. In the long run, unionization made newspaper life more orderly and predictable and made it possible for reporters to think of a career. During the years after World War II, as newspaper staffs grew, the newsroom became bureaucratized, even tame. "Somehow," lamented David Boroff, author of a 1965 Ford Foundation study, "the glamor and magic of the craft have leaked out of it." As before, consolidation had followed rebellion.

In fact, the glamor and magic were by then already leaking back in as a fourth generation of newsmen came of age. Like its predecessors, the new generation challenged the rules—not the economic rules, for the 1960s was an era of unprecedented affluence, but the largely unwritten rules concerning the *substance* of a journalist's task: the definition of "news," the authority of the employing institution, and the relation of journalism to the larger society. The groundwork for many of these challenges had already been laid. What the new generation did most successfully was to combine the individualism and flair of *The Front Page* (that is, of yellow journalism) with the ideology and seriousness of "professionalism."

The recipe had several ingredients.

The first was an erosion of "publisher power." By the beginning of the 1960s, most newspapers had lived down their colorful past. Although occasionally caught up in the fevers of, say, a sensational murder trial or sex scandal, most newspapers no longer consistently sensationalized the news. Most major newspapers did not let advertisers regularly control news content. Most publishers had learned to control their hostility to labor and provide balanced coverage of strikes. And most newspapers at least claimed to offer balanced political coverage. The figures most prominently associated with the legendary abuses of the past were fading from the scene. Hearst died in 1951, the *Chicago Tribune*'s Colonel Robert R. McCormick in 1955.

Professionalism was the catchword reporters invoked to insulate themselves from their employers. Aspirants were not required, like doctors or lawyers, to master a certain body of knowledge. But by defining themselves as professionals, journalists could, like doctors or lawyers, claim special rights, notably a degree of individual autonomy in writing and reporting. By the 1960s reporters commonly agreed that attempts, by editors as well as publishers, to shape the news to make it fit predetermined "policy" were wrong. Theoretically, wrote journalist–sociologist Warren Breed in 1955, the only controls should be "the nature of the event and the reporter's effective ability to describe it.'' In the newsroom the actual result was a chronic, usually muted struggle between editors and reporters, between managerial direction and reportorial autonomy.

In addition to the self-image of professional autonomy, the younger journalists inherited from their elders a long-standing antipathy toward officialdom. Publishers during the 1930s had tried unsuccessfully to use the First Amendment to thwart New Deal legislation strengthening labor unions. In the years after World War II, the press's suspicions of government shifted to an editorial, and a more subtle, level. Newspapers during the 1950s mounted a "freedom-of-information" campaign, implicitly suggesting that undisclosed records and closed meetings were a cloak for official misdeeds. Reporters who had submitted to the manipulations of Franklin D. Roosevelt now objected to those of Eisenhower and Kennedy. The term "news management" was coined by James Reston of the *New York Times* during the mid-1950s.

Pulitzer prizes, as always, went to exposers of instances of city hall corruption and Washington chicanery. But steady, continuous muckraking—unless embodied in an institutional "crusade" in the Hearst or Pulitzer tradition—was not yet the fashion. The press had not yet undertaken in its investigations, as Lippmann in his 1922 classic *Public Opinion* had stated it should *not* undertake, "the burden of accomplishing whatever representative government, industrial organization, and diplomacy have failed to accomplish."

News standards were also changing during the late 1950s and early 1960s. Increasingly, the old "objective" format for news was viewed as inadequate to the complexities of contemporary subject matter and to the reporter's desire to demonstrate expertise. The satisfaction of going beyond the facts, once reserved largely for Washington columnists, now came to ordinary reporters, given a new license to "interpret" the news.

One final element helped pave the way for the fourth generation: enhanced pay and popular prestige. Even after the Newspaper Guild helped to stabilize wages and working conditions, newspapers were justly accused of underpaying their employees. Polls taken during the 1950s, moreover, ranked journalism low—near the bottom in fact—in occupational prestige. By 1962 or 1963, however, all of that had begun to change. The combined appeal of gradually rising pay and gradually rising status became attractive enough to draw college graduates from other fields.[2] Journalism school enrollments began to swell.

Newspapering became more secure. In 1965 Walter Lippmann

pondered the overall metamorphosis of the American journalist since World War II: "The crude forms of corruption which belonged to the infancy of journalism tend to give way to the temptations of maturity and power. It is with these temptations that the modern journalist has to wrestle." It was these temptations that confronted reporters as the 1960s unfolded.

The Temptations of Power

Although it was not the first Cold War press–government confrontation over "national security," Vietnam set a decade-long pattern of mutual antagonism that ultimately verged on mutual paranoia during the Nixon years. In reality, the *New York Times*'s David Halberstam and other early birds in Saigon were not, as later painted, antiwar activists in 1963. Rather they heard (from U.S. military field advisers), saw, and wrote, not inaccurately, that U.S. policy in Vietnam was *not working,* even as Washington claimed the opposite.

This conflict between press accounts and official assessments of Vietnam was not all-pervasive, or even constant. But it grew, fed by the inherent ambiguities and rhetorical contradictions of an increasingly costly "no-win, no-sellout" war policy. Under Lyndon Johnson and Richard Nixon, the resulting "credibility gap" began to extend to other matters—to CIA and FBI activities, to diplomacy, and to government generally.

At the same time that he slowly committed America to Vietnam, Lyndon Johnson invited high expectations of government from newsmen and ordinary folk alike with his Great Society programs to "end poverty," to "end inequality," to "end hunger." Few reporters then questioned the need for bigger government (they were, at heart, reformers too). But black riots in Watts in 1965, in Detroit in 1967, and in Washington and a dozen other cities in 1968 seemed to show that government at home as in Vietnam was failing, even as universities seemed unable to cope with campus unrest, and churches and businesses and other institutions seemed unable or unwilling to respond to rising demands for, variously, more equity, more freedom, a cleaner environment, more truth in advertising, more "power." The 1968 Democratic convention, with its attendant Chicago "police riot" against antiwar demonstrators, seemed to show that the political party system could not or would not respond either. Activists on behalf of Hispanics, women, homosexuals, the handicapped, the aged, followed blacks in claiming their due rights, not just in Washington, but in cities all over America.

The younger reporters who tried to keep up with all this were prepared to challenge authority, but they operated within the establishment. Unlike their "underground" contemporaries, they chose to work inside existing and prospering institutions, which alone could offer them the full material, moral, and status rewards of journalism—"status" meaning, above all, status in the eyes of other journalists. The impression given by complaining editors later that they had been overrun by activists hostile to newspaper traditions is largely false.

The claim to professionalism had two striking implications—first, that the press as an institution ought to be a kind of free-floating body in society, encumbered by neither governmental nor social controls; second, that the individual journalist ought to be free of institutional restraint as well. In working terms, this meant that reporters could try to shake free of editors; in social terms, it meant generational conflict even more intense than usual.

For the press as a whole, professionalization meant living more by one's own rules, living, in the words of communications scholar James W. Carey, "in a morally less ambiguous universe than the rest of us." This was the universe inhabited by many young reporters as they covered the civil rights movement, urban decay, campus unrest, the peace movement, and the congressional debates over the Vietnam War. So many things were wrong. The issues seemed so clear. And so dramatic.

The older newspaper generation watched the new breed uneasily. One *Washington Post* veteran later remembered an "often mindless readiness to seek out conflict, to believe the worst of government or of authority in general, and on that basis to divide the actors in any issue into the 'good' and the 'bad.' " This readiness was heightened, perhaps, by the influence of television news and the "thematic" approach that flavored (and often flawed) its documentaries, such as *The Selling of the Pentagon,* broadcast in 1971.

The attitude was replicated in many newsrooms, big and small. The institutional structure of the press was looked on as a barrier to truth. Journalism would be purer and better if it were controlled by the reporters themselves. In the wake of the controversial coverage of the 1968 Chicago riots, young reporters throughout the country established new "journalism reviews"—sometimes in-house newsletters, sometimes magazines meant for a larger circulation. These usually attacked the residual power of publishers, the authority of editors, or the insufficient zeal of reporters in discomfiting politicians, business, and the military. The *Chicago Journalism Review* made its debut in late 1968, *More* magazine in New York in 1971.

These reviews—neither of which is still published—were allied with a reform movement that advocated, at least implicitly, newsroom governance comparable to that of a Swiss canton; or comparable to that of, for example, France's *Le Monde,* where newshands elect their own *redacteur en chef.* "Reporter power" enjoyed a brief heyday, then expired. It never achieved formally in the area of newsroom control what the Newspaper Guild had wrought in terms of security. In part, this was because the battle had been won—newspaper editors had already become more "permissive," and objectivity, as a journalistic standard like the straightedge and compass of classical geometry, was widely accepted as, if not obsolete, then insufficient.

The antagonism between editors and reporters was minor compared with the continuing clash of press and government. Amid the strains of the Vietnam War and civil disorders at home, the Nixon administration in 1969 through Vice-President Agnew and others, had launched a public counterattack on the "elitist" media and their "liberal" bias. Then, in 1971, came the first serious confrontation, over the "Pentagon Papers."

Hawk-turned-dove Daniel Ellsberg had tried for a year to make public the secret Pentagon study of the history of U.S. involvement in Vietnam. He had approached prominent antiwar politicians, among them Senators William Fulbright and George McGovern, but had not achieved his aim. Finally, Ellsberg called *New York Times* correspondent Neil Sheehan, a former Vietnam reporter who had recently begun writing in opposition to the war. Sheehan was interested in the study, and so was his newspaper. ("You have permission to proceed, young man," James Reston has been quoted as telling Sheehan.) In June 1971, the *Times* began publishing the Pentagon Papers.

At first, there was no great stir, except at the rival *Washington Post* where editor Benjamin Bradlee hastened to order a "catch-up." But when the Nixon administration decided to suppress further publication on national security grounds, the confrontation was joined. The *Times*'s and the *Post*'s subsequent victory in the Supreme Court became a landmark in journalistic history. But had the Big League press gone too far in substituting its judgment for Washington's? Had it arrogated to itself a power unsanctioned either by law or by the public it claimed to represent? The debate over such questions continues.

In *Without Fear or Favor* (1980), a history of the *New York Times* centering on the Pentagon Papers case, Harrison Salisbury claims that the *Times* (and, one would think, the rest of the national press) "has quite literally become that Fourth Estate, that fourth coequal branch of government of which men like Thomas Carlyle spoke." The implications of such a claim are immense. "Fourth-branch" rhetoric has been around a long time, of course. (Douglass Cater's *The Fourth Branch of Government* was published in 1959.) But when Salisbury and others take the fourth-branch metaphor as literal truth, they imply that the press, like Congress, for example, enjoys not only independence, but also constitutional privileges and immunities. Time and again, this case, widely accepted among newsmen, has been made before the Supreme Court, but so far, at least, a majority of the justices have refused to concur.

Salisbury puts forth another expansive claim in his book: that Watergate itself and hence the Watergate exposés (in which the *Post* took the lead) would not have happened except for the Pentagon Papers case (in which the *Times* took the lead). Given the security hysteria the Pentagon Papers case touched off in the Nixon White House, the proposition is supportable but unprovable, like much else about Watergate.

Watergate: A Breeder of Myths

Watergate was a breeder of myths. The chief myth is that Hardy boys Joe and Frank (i.e., *Post* reporters Bob Woodward and Carl Bernstein) solved the mystery and toppled a president. Actually, as political writer Edward Jay Epstein noted back in 1973, the government itself cracked the case in its early stages. "What the press did between the break-in in June (1972) and the trial in January," Epstein wrote, "was to leak the case developed by the federal and Florida prosecutors to the public." Congress and Judge John Sirica carried the burden thereafter.

But it was difficult for the mere facts of a complicated story to compete with a glamorized version as compellingly presented in the popular 1974 movie *All the President's Men*. The "Woodstein" model was credited with filling the journalism schools (although, in fact, the influx of students had begun years earlier) and restoring to newspaper work much of its lost glamor.

Watergate also signaled the start of what has been seen as a period in which the press's confrontation with the federal government became excessive and unreasoning. Although some editors noted that the behavior of the government had been far from normal (necessitating, in their view, an abnormal response), others urged journalists to draw back. "The First Amendment is not just a hunting license," warned Associated Press general manager Wes Gallagher in 1975. "We must put before the public ways and means of strengthening the institutions that protect us all—not tear them down," he said.

Under considerable criticism for a variety of sins, the media undertook during the Watergate era to overlay a veneer of public interest on their operations. In 1973 a coalition of foundations and media created the National News Council, a media-dominated, unofficial "ombudsman-at-large" for the national press. At the same time, many publications named their own in-house ombudsmen to handle readers' complaints, explain journalism to the public, and monitor the newspapers' performances. Reporters and editors often greeted these newcomers coolly; their presence seemed not only to promise the embarrassment that accompanies public discussion of newsroom frailties, but to diminish professional autonomy. Newspapers also began running corrections regularly, sometimes in a reserved space, although victims of errors still complained that the corrections lacked substance and prominence.

The temper of journalism after Watergate, as these reforms suggest, was not that of Agamemnon after Troy. To all outward appearances, the press was still acquiring new influence. Investigative, even accusatory, journalism had become more rather than less popular. Yet journalists were uneasy. Chris Argyris, a Harvard management consultant who published in 1975 a thinly disguised study of the inner working of the *New York Times,* observed (perhaps with some malice) that "the innards of the newspaper had many of the dynamics of the White House. I found the same kinds of interpersonal dynamics and internal politics; the same mistrust and win/lose competitiveness."

Although surveys showed that most journalists liked their work, despite its deadline pressures, many reporters seemed fueled by a sense of being under attack or of being in a race; indeed, the Knight–Ridder newspaper chain administered tests to job applicants to gauge just such desirable qualities. Was it surprising then that journalists, especially during the 1970s, tended to see government and politics in the same terms of aggression and competition?

Post–Watergate: Defining New Limits

For a decade the key issue remained "control." "Young reporters have always wanted to change the world," wrote Charles B. Seib, then the *Washington Post*'s ombudsman, in 1978. But, he went on, "in the old days, when a reporter let his opinion show he was quickly brought to heel by an editor" and eventually was turned into "what we called an objective reporter—meaning a reporter who stuck strictly to the raw, unvarnished facts. Nowadays editors are inclined to be more permissive." Seib said he was glad "the days of trying for blind objectivity are over," but he warned: "Too often the new permissiveness is carried too far."

That newspapers indeed at times carried the "new permissiveness" too far became very clear to all in the spring of 1981, when a story by a *Washington Post* reporter was awarded a Pulitzer prize for feature writing. It turned out, however, that reporter Janet Cooke had simply made up "Jimmy's World," her tale of a (nonexistent) eight-year-old heroin addict. Despite certain clues, *Post* editors, including Bob Woodward of Watergate fame, had failed to discern the deception. Cooke resigned, and the *Post* returned her Pulitzer. The next day, the newspaper assured in an apologetic editorial that "more of the skepticism and heat that [we] traditionally bring to bear on the outside world will now be trained on our own interior workings. One of these episodes is one too many."

The uproar over the Cooke affair did not soon abate. Shortly afterward, a *Daily News* columnist in New York was fired when he could not back up some of his reporting from Northern Ireland. Reporters in Minnesota and Oregon were punished for inventing quotations. The Associated Press admitted that an account it had distributed about a California joy ride had been a "composite" story. In February 1982 the *New York Times* admitted on page one that an article written by a freelance writer about his trip to Cambodia, which appeared in December in the *New York Times Magazine,* had been a fabrication. The writer, in fact, had not left Spain.

As a result of the Janet Cooke affair and the ensuing "crime wave" of newly disclosed hoaxes, fakes, and frauds, editors vowed to reassert their authority over reporters. A survey of 312 editors conducted for the American Society of Newspaper Editors Ethics Committee found 30 percent of them had changed their policies because of the Cooke scandal. More than a third said they were keeping a closer eye on reporters and the accuracy of their stories. Fewer than 2 percent of the editors said they would allow reporters to keep identifications of sources from editors; 55 percent said identification had to be provided on request; and 41 percent said it must always be provided.

To outsiders, the press now seemed a little on the defensive. The first "hot" newspaper movie since *All the President's Men* appeared toward the end of 1981; *Absence of Malice*—whose script was written by former *Detroit Free Press* editor Kurt Luedtke—portrayed a venal press cloaking its mischief in the First Amendment.

As the pendulum swung back, journalists began asking tougher questions about their own performances. The *Wall Street Journal* in 1982 attacked other newspapers' coverage of El Salvador as cut from the same cloth as the journalism of John Reed in Russia, Herbert Matthews in Cuba, and David Halberstam in Vietnam. (Halberstam defended himself ably.) When the public appeared to support the Reagan administration's exclusion of the press from the Grenada invasion in 1983, there was a further wave of journalistic soul-searching.

Such intramural debates, however acrimonious, may be a healthy sign that a dilemma, underlined by publication of the classified Pentagon Papers, is at least being brought into the open. Journalists are committed to serving the truth, or at least the "facts." Yet they are unable to avoid wielding influence. Any big story may produce some damaging social or political effect. The public knows this instinctively, but journalists have usually said, "Damn the consequences!" Now, it seems, they are being put on notice that they can be called to account. As Wes Gallagher of the Associated Press warned after Watergate: "The press cannot remain free without the proper functioning of the government, the judicial branch and private institutions in a democracy. The press also is an institution. All rise and fall together."

Journalism's responses so far have been imperfect. One of the most publicized was that of the *New York Daily News*'s Michael J. O'Neill, in a May 1982 farewell address as president of the American Society of Newspaper Editors. He seemed to be accepting, almost point by point, the critique advanced since 1970 by neoconservative intellectuals. Journalists, he said, should "make peace with government," should cure themselves of their "adversarial mindset."

Thus, the most recent generation of journalists, the one that grew up in the Vietnam and Watergate years, received the message that the heyday of autonomy had ended. The nostalgic in that now-aging generation may briefly have glimpsed new dreams of glory in the guerrilla war in Central America and the Iran–Contra scandals of 1986–7. But while the press has pitched in earnestly, neither in Central

America nor in Contragate have its exposures proved better than sporadic or marginal, or both. No new Halberstams or Woodsteins have emerged.

The sobering historical lesson is that journalists, however bright or idealistic, cannot pretend in the long run to live outside society and to live by their own rules. Society wants and needs their services, but at its own price. In the long run American society will determine what kind of journalism it wants; only to a far lesser degree will journalists determine what kind of society America will be.

NOTES

1. Ironically, the romance of bohemianism was even then being forever stamped on the psyche of journalists, most indelibly through *The Front Page* (1928) by Ben Hecht and Charles MacArthur. The playwrights conceded, however, that Hildy Johnson and his feckless colleagues were a vanishing breed—"the lusty, hoodlumesque, half-drunken caballero that was the news-paperman of our youth. Schools of journalism and the advertising business have nearly extirpated the species." Recent films about the news business (*Broadcast News,* 1987, and *Switching Channels,* 1988) are about TV journal-ists—suggesting that the "glamor" side of the media is television, not print.

2. Journalists' salaries vary considerably, even at the 139 Newspaper Guild–organized dailies. As of 1987, a reporter at the *New York Times* with two years' experience earned a minimum of $929.16 a week; at the *Chicago Sun Times,* after five years, $866.03; at the *Sacramento Bee,* after six years, $649; at the *Terre Haute* (Indiana) *Tribune,* after five years' experience, $400.88. The average top reporter minimum for all Guild papers in mid-1987: $590.26. At non-Guild papers (that is, at most papers), the pay is usually lower.

Chapter 6

THE PRESS IN COURT

by A.E. Dick Howard

The First Amendment to the Constitution of the United States consists of a single sentence:

> Congress shall make no law respecting an establishment of religion, or prohibiting the free exercise thereof; or abridging the freedom of speech, or of the press; or the right of the people peaceably to assemble, and to petition the Government for a redress of grievances.

When that sentence became law in 1791, the clause pertaining to the press rendered Congress powerless to enact any law restraining the press in advance from printing whatever it wanted. That, many people thought at the time, did not mean that the press should escape criminal penalty if it published "seditious libels," "licentious opinions," or "malicious falsehoods." Indeed, in 1798, during the presidency of John Adams, Congress enacted the Federalist-sponsored Sedition Act. It prescribed a fine and imprisonment for persons convicted of publishing "any false, scandalous, and malicious writing" bringing into disrepute the U.S. government, Congress, or the president.

Was the act, under which twenty-five persons were eventually prosecuted, constitutional? The Jeffersonian Republicans, at whose publicists it was aimed, thought not. Some of them—including James Madison, the "father" of the Bill of Rights—took an expansive view of freedom of the press. "It would seem a mockery," wrote Madison, "to say that no laws shall be passed preventing publications from being

73

made, but that laws might be passed for punishing them in case they should be made.''

Thomas Jefferson himself harbored a more complex view. On the one hand, he thought the Sedition Act unconstitutional—and, when he became president, he pardoned the ten Republican editors and printers who had been convicted under the law. On the other hand, as he explained in 1804 to Adams's wife, Abigail, the law's unconstitutionality did not mean that ''the overwhelming torrent of slander'' in the country was to go unrestrained. ''While we deny that Congress have a right to control the freedom of the press,'' he wrote, ''we have ever asserted the right of the States, and their exclusive right, to do so.''

A year earlier, New York State had, in fact, indicted a Federalist editor for ''seditious libel'' against President Jefferson. On the editor's behalf, Alexander Hamilton, though a supporter of the Sedition Act, eloquently reasserted the principles enunciated in 1735 in the John Peter Zenger case.[1] Hamilton championed the right of the jury (rather than the court) to determine if there had been libel, argued truth as a defense against libel, and defended the right of the press ''to publish, with impunity, truth, with good motives, for justifiable ends, though reflecting on government, magistracy, or individuals.'' In 1805 New York passed a libel law embodying the Hamiltonian view. Other states soon followed suit. Ultimately, Hamilton's position came to prevail throughout the republic. Because the U.S. Supreme Court under John Marshall and his successors offered no guidance, there matters stood.

Indeed, not until the twentieth century did the Supreme Court begin actively interpreting the First Amendment's press clause. Even then most of its decisions had to await the 1960s when, amid the divisive tensions of war and rapid social change, Americans acquired a taste for litigation, and the press became more assertive in its coverage of local and national governments. The Supreme Court soon had its hands full.

The Court's freedom-of-the-press cases may be arranged into three principal categories:

• Cases in which citizens, of various degrees of renown, seek damages for alleged libels against them by the press
• Cases in which the government seeks to keep the press from publishing what it wants to publish
• Cases in which the press claims special legal privileges, such as the right to refuse to reveal a news source's identity to a grand jury, or the right to be given access to government institutions or proceedings

The Press and Libel: Absence of Malice

A \$9.2 million libel judgment in 1980 against the *Alton Telegraph* forced the 38,000–circulation Illinois daily to file for bankruptcy to avoid having to sell its assets. Although a settlement was reached and the paper remained in business, the case, which involves a never-published memorandum by two reporters, pointed up a lesson that few in the news business have to learn twice: A successful libel action, painful even to a wealthy defendant, can be fatal to a small one. However, thanks to the First Amendment and the Supreme Court, the press has gained certain protective immunities.

The Supreme Court, under Chief Justice Earl Warren, handed down its most important libel decision in 1964 in *New York Times* v. *Sullivan,* a case involving supporters of the Rev. Martin Luther King, Jr. In 1960 they had placed an advertisement in the *Times* criticizing, with some inaccuracies, officials' handling of civil rights demonstrations in Montgomery, Alabama, and elsewhere in the South. L.B. Sullivan, Montgomery's police commissioner, sued the newspaper and the ad's sponsors (though he himself had not been mentioned in the ad). An Alabama jury awarded Sullivan \$500,000. But the Supreme Court, harking back to Alexander Hamilton, ruled that a "public official" seeking damages for a defamatory falsehood relating to his official conduct must prove that the statement had been made with "actual malice"—that is, with knowledge that the statement was false, or with "reckless disregard" of whether it was or not. Otherwise, the Court contended, would-be critics might not speak out, for fear the truth could not be proven in court, at least not without great expense.

Newspaper publishers and reporters were delighted with this decision—which, said *Times* publisher Arthur Ochs Sulzberger, "makes freedom of the press more secure than ever before"—and their satisfaction grew with each subsequent ruling by the Supreme Court. In 1967, the Court (*Curtis Publishing Co.* v. *Butts*) extended the *Sullivan* principle to cover "public figures" (not just *officials*), such as Wally Butts, a former University of Georgia athletic director. Butts had sued Curtis over a *Saturday Evening Post* report that he had given football plays to Alabama rival Bear Bryant. Four years later, in *Rosenbloom* v. *Metromedia,* the Court (by a plurality) extended the *Sullivan* principle still further to include private individuals involved in matters of "public or general interest."

But then the Supreme Court, under Justice Warren Burger, began to change course. Despite its 1971 decision, the Court in 1974 ruled

(*Gertz* v. *Robert Welch, Inc.*) that prominent Chicago attorney Elmer Gertz, who had defended a client in a widely publicized case, was neither a public official nor a public figure—and hence did not need to prove he had been libeled with "malice." Two years later the Court (*Time Inc.* v. *Firestone*) decided that Palm Beach socialite Mary Alice Firestone, who had been a party to a highly publicized divorce proceeding, was also not a public figure. Still more sobering for the press was *Hutchinson* v. *Proxmire* (1979), wherein the Court excluded from the "public-figure" realm a Michigan state mental hospital's research director who had received more than $500,000 in federal grants for research into monkey behavior. U.S. Senator William Proxmire had ridiculed Dr. Ronald Hutchinson's research, and Hutchinson had sued the senator for libel.

Some prominent members of the press were even more upset in 1979 by the Court's ruling in *Herbert* v. *Lando* that the First Amendment did not protect CBS News correspondent Mike Wallace and *60 Minutes* producer Barry Lando from having to answer pretrial discovery questions about their editorial process. The case involved a program questioning the veracity of Anthony Herbert, a former Army lieutenant colonel who had accused the Army of covering up reports of atrocities against civilians in Vietnam. To win his libel case, Herbert, as an acknowledged "public figure," had to prove malice, and hence had to probe CBS's decision-making process. William A. Leonard, then president of CBS News, said the decision denied "constitutional protection to the journalist's most precious possession—his mind, his thoughts, and his editorial judgment." How a public figure was supposed to prove "actual malice" without inquiring into the journalist's state of mind went unexplained. Eventually, most editors seemed to realize that the *Herbert* decision was a natural corollary of *Sullivan*. It had just taken a while in coming.

While the pendulum has swung back toward safeguarding the rights of individuals, nothing the Supreme Court has done of late compares in significance with the 1964 *Sullivan* case. That decision represented an immense shift in favor of the press—one so great that even some newspeople regret it. Kurt Luedtke, former executive editor of the *Detroit Free Press,* argued before the American Newspaper Publishers Association that, prior to *Sullivan,* "the burden on the press was not at all excessive; the 'chilling effect' which the threat of libel action posed chilled exactly what it was supposed to."

Most newspaper publishers, and their lawyers, accountants, and editors, think otherwise. They want not only to feel free to publish critical articles, but also to be assured that newspapers need not pay vast sums to persons deemed by juries victims of libel. Although research by a Stanford law professor, Marc Franklin, has shown that between 1977 and 1980, media defendants won more than 90 percent of libel cases, "winning" is not everything, especially for small papers. Said John K. Zollinger, publisher of the *Gallup Independent,* a 10,795–circulation daily in New Mexico, "We're spending almost 2 percent of our net profit on 'legal.' It's no joke any more. . . . You win and still pay."

Gagging the Press: "Prior Restraint"

If libel is the press's most publicized problem, one even closer to the heart of the First Amendment is "prior restraint"—the chief issue in another cluster of Supreme Court cases.

For centuries authors and journalists have inveighed against censorship or "gagging" of the press by government. "And though all the windes of doctrine were let loose to play upon the earth," advised John Milton in 1644, "so Truth be in the field, we do injuriously by licensing and prohibiting to misdoubt her strength." Yet the principle, and the First Amendment embodying it, underwent a severe test in 1971. In June of that year, the *New York Times* began publishing extracts from the Pentagon Papers (a classified Defense Department history of U.S. Vietnam involvement); and the Nixon Administration went to court to stop further publication. The Supreme Court, however, by a 6-to-3 vote (*New York Times* v. *United States*) ruled in favor of the *Times*—a landmark decision.

In subsequent years journalists savored further gains, even as lawyers and some judges complained of the new "arrogance" of the media. Thus, in 1976 the Supreme Court (*Nebraska Press Association* v. *Stuart*) unanimously ruled invalid a Nebraska judge's gag order preventing the press from reporting salient details of a murder trial. And the Court in 1978 (*Landmark Communications* v. *Virginia*) again unanimously overturned a verdict against Norfolk's *Virginian–Pilot* for publishing, despite a state law, an (accurate) account of proceedings before a state judicial review commission. All in all, the press has largely had its way in specific gag order cases, even though the Supreme Court has not ruled gag orders per se unconstitutional.[2]

Protecting a Source: Journalistic Confidentiality

A third group of cases tackled by the Supreme Court dealing with questions of journalistic privilege has perhaps been the murkiest.

In 1958 Marie Torre, a *New York Herald Tribune* television columnist, refused to divulge the identity of a CBS executive whom she had quoted as saying that singer Judy Garland had "an inferiority complex" and was "terribly fat." As a result, Torre was cited by the judge for contempt of court (Garland, in those pre–*Sullivan* days, had sued CBS) and eventually served a brief jail term. During the tumultuous 1970s, perhaps a dozen newsmen went to jail rather than reveal in court their sources for stories. The newsmen included William T. Farr of the *Los Angeles Times,* Peter J. Bridge of the *Newark Evening News,* and Myron J. Farber of the *New York Times.* Farber, at the murder trial of a New Jersey doctor, refused to turn over his reportorial notes to a judge (although, it emerged, the reporter had signed contracts to write a book on the case). Farber's newspaper articles had been instrumental in the doctor's indictment. The jury found the doctor not guilty.

Journalists have argued that to gather news, they need to be able to preserve the anonymity of their sources. The First Amendment, they assert, puts them in a different category from other citizens. The Supreme Court, however, in a 5-to-4 decision (*Branzburg* v. *Hayes,* 1972) ruled that even a newspaper reporter (in that case, for the Louisville *Courier-Journal*) must respond to a grand jury subpoena and answer questions relevant to a criminal investigation. The *Branzburg* ruling did not prevent state legislatures from enacting so-called shield laws of varying strengths designed to protect reporters from being forced to reveal their sources. After *Branzburg,* eleven states amended existing shield laws or created new ones; fifteen others retained shield laws already on the books.

Privilege of another sort was the issue in 1978 when the Supreme Court, in a 5-to-3 decision, ruled that the First Amendment does not bar police, if they have a warrant, from searching newspaper offices for evidence of crime. (The case, *Zurcher* v. *Stanford Daily,* involved the Stanford University student newspaper, and the evidence sought was photographs of a clash between demonstrators and police.) *Los Angeles Times* editor Bill Thomas said at the time that Justice Byron White's written opinion showed that he "neither cares much nor knows much about the problems of the press." Critics—notably the American Newspaper Publishers Association and the American Society of Newspaper Editors—appeared before Congress, which in 1980 passed a law requiring police, in most situations, to get a subpoena before searching newspaper offices for criminal evidence.

Perhaps the most ambitious First Amendment claim advanced by the press has been that it has a "right" to gather news—a right, that is, to have access to government agencies, documents, and deliberations.

The Supreme Court has approached such arguments cautiously. The Court has ruled that journalists have no constitutional right to interview prison inmates (*Pell* v. *Procunier,* 1974) or to inspect local jails (*Houchins* v. *KQED,* 1978). Most disturbing, from the press's point of view, was the Court's 5-to-4 decision in 1979 to uphold the closing, to both public and press, of a pretrial suppression-of-evidence hearing in a murder case. Justice Potter Stewart's majority opinion in *Gannett Co.* v. *DePasquale* actually revolved around the Sixth Amendment (with its guarantee of a public trial) rather than the First. (The Court said a trial was "public" for the benefit of the accused rather than the public.) But David F. Stolberg, a Scripps–Howard executive, said the decision was "so violative of our whole Anglo–American tradition of open government that the minority position must eventually prevail. In the meantime, it is not just a press fight—it is a freedom fight."

Newspeople are prone to enshrine freedom of the press as an absolute—and to become apoplectic when judges do not display a similarly single-minded zeal in *their* defense of the First Amendment. In fact, however, there are other freedoms, notably those in the other amendments in the Bill of Rights. When various rights conflict, courts must seek a resolution. In any event, the Supreme Court in 1980 (*Richmond Newspapers* v. *Virginia*) assuaged some of the fears inspired by *Gannett* with a decision assuring press and public of access to criminal trials, unless there be an "overriding interest" for closure. Thus, in 1986 the principle of *Richmond Newspapers* was applied to give a California newspaper a right of access to transcripts of a preliminary hearing in the case of a nurse charged with murdering patients by administering drug overdoses.

When it comes to the First Amendment, the men and women of the press are—as is natural and no doubt useful—the first to become alarmed when their prerogatives are even marginally encroached upon. But the modern Supreme Court has hardly been bent on gutting the press clause of the First Amendment.

The Court, to be sure, has manifestly rejected the notion that the press should enjoy any "preferred status" under the First Amendment (and so has insisted that journalists can be called to testify before grand juries). And in balancing a person's stake in his or her good name against the press's right to publish, the Court has unmistakably tended to limit the 1964 *Sullivan* ruling, in favor of individuals and their reputations.

However, when—as in the Pentagon Papers and later cases—government has tried to restrain the press from, or punish it for, publishing information already in its possession, the Court has strongly defended the press and its freedom. As Floyd Abrams, a media attorney and frequent critic of the Supreme Court, concluded in 1980: "The American press has never been more free, never been more uninhibited, and—most important—never been better protected by law."

NOTES

1. Zenger, a New York printer, was accused of seditious libel. His lawyer, Andrew Hamilton, argued that the press should be free to print truthful criticism of a "bad" government (meaning the unpopular Governor William Cosby). Hamilton urged the jury to decide the law as well as the facts. The jury did so—and acquitted Zenger.

2. In a related category of cases, government seeks to force the press to publish what it does not wish to publish. Here, the Supreme Court has sharply distinguished between the electronic and print media. In *Red Lion Broadcasting Co.* v. *FCC* (1969), the Court upheld FCC regulations requiring radio and TV stations to give reply time to individuals criticized on the air. But in *Miami Herald* v. *Tornillo* (1974), the Court ruled that Florida's "right-of-reply" statute requiring newspapers to print a political candidate's reply to editorial criticism violated the First Amendment.

Chapter 7

TAKING COMICS SERIOUSLY

by Arthur Asa Berger

New art forms are often greeted with derision. Attic tragedy was denounced by conservative Greeks, impressionism by highbrow Parisians. Americans, too, have snubbed new, indigenous art forms. The comics, for example, like jazz music, are a home-grown American product; and like jazz, they were long ignored by "serious" critics.

As critic John Canaday recently noted, the pendulum has now swung to the other extreme: The comics have changed from "entertainments to be read while lying on the floor" into "sociological testaments for intellectual evaluation." Perhaps the pendulum has swung too far. Where once Mussolini banned *Popeye* for being antifascist, latter-day commentators point to a perverse relationship between Batman and Robin; an oral fixation in husband Dagwood's eating jags in *Blondie;* and (as the government of Finland helpfully pointed out) an apotheosis of "bourgeois" capitalism in *Donald Duck.*

No longer dismissed as trivial, the comics have other feints to parry. Journalists have great sport with academics who "read meaning" into the comics, and the creators of many comic strips vehemently deny that their work is worth fussing over. We are told, constantly, that comics (or film, or television) should be enjoyed and not analyzed—because there is nothing to analyze.

Comics as Cultural Mirrors

This "know-nothingism" is naive. Like slips of the tongue or dreams, the comics have much to tell us if only we will ask.

One of the first scholarly works to consider the comics was Gilbert Seldes's *The Seven Lively Arts,* published in 1924. Seldes's paean to *Krazy Kat* at once boosted the strip into the comic Olympus and created a cult in its honor back on earth. In *The American Language,* meanwhile, H.L. Mencken began tracing the words and phrases comics have given to English such as "jeep," "wow," and "grr." But until recently, most work in the field was done by non-Americans—Italians in particular—who took the same proprietary attitude toward U.S. comics that Britain's Lord Elgin took toward ancient Greek statuary.

The comics themselves are relatively ancient—by pop culture's standards. They have been with us for more than eighty years, and some have been appearing continuously for fifty or sixty years. *Mutt and Jeff* started in 1907, *The Captain and the Kids* appeared in 1914, *Blondie* in 1930, and *Dick Tracy* in 1931. So rich is the heritage that in 1962, cartoonist Jerry Dumas could introduce *Sam's Strip,* a feature that depended for much of its humor on a kind of camp familiarity with the comics of the past.

Beyond a common affection for the medium, however, cartoonists and scholars approach the comics from different directions. For example, by and large the jokes in the humorous or "bigfoot" funnies are culled from the absurdities of everyday life. To the scholar, this represents a gold mine he or she can sift for clues to the zeitgeist. To the cartoonist, it represents hours of staring at the ceiling. As Mrs. Thurber would say when she caught her husband in a trance at the dinner table, "James, you're writing again!"

The other kind of comic strip—the serial or narrative adventure stories like *Rip Kirby* or *Apartment 3-G*—relies on a different kind of formula and tells us different kinds of things, both about today's world and the worlds we have lost. Here the problem for the cartoonist is sustaining reader interest over a period of months; and it is solved not by rooting the story in everyday life, but by combining fantastic plots with lifelike characters who share the hopes and fears of us all.

Be it through humor or adventure, the comics open a special window onto the past whether they are overtly opinionated (as in *Little Orphan Annie*) or seemingly not opinionated at all (as in *Beetle Bailey*). Indeed, the "value-free" comics may prove the most valuable, for they constitute an implicit record of their audience's attitudes, not an explicit record of their authors'.

It is doubtful, for example, that Richard Outcault intended to leave posterity a record of the tumultuous 1890s when he first penned *The Yellow Kid.* And yet it was inevitable that the waves of immigration and the crowding of laborers into city and factory would leave their mark on his work. And so we find beneath the ostensible humor that the hero of the strip—a strange, bald, jug-eared youth who always wears a yellow nightshirt—inhabits a squalid slum called Hogan's Alley. It is packed with children who are decidedly not childish: they wear derbies, smoke cigars, and may even be bearded. There is something poignant and heroic about the Kid and his friends; they are the first in a long line of spiritual orphans in the comics.

Unlike Outcault, Harold Gray in *Little Orphan Annie* had no qualms about putting his beliefs on the line. But like Outcault's Kid, Gray's Annie is an orphan, not the least because her philosophy is outworn and outdated. Annie spent over forty years (beginning in 1924) railing against the direction American society was taking and championing the old, small-town virtues of yesterday. As James Kehl observed in the *South Atlantic Quarterly,* "She is more than a modern Robin Hood with a heart of gold and a wicked left; she is an outlet for the expression of the political and economic philosophy of her creator and legal guardian, Harold Gray." An extract from a 1945 strip:

> *Annie:* But *why* did some papers and commentators say such terrible things?
>
> *Daddie Warbucks:* Oh, I guess it was fashionable to sneer at "big incomes." They fail to mention that most of those big incomes go to pay everyone's bills and make the load lighter for everyone else. I believe that the more a man makes honestly, the more he helps this country and everybody in it. What I think we need is a lot more million-a-year men! Mighty little *they* can keep anyway.

Consciously or unconsciously, "liberal" or "conservative," the comics *do* speak to the daydreams and ambitions of the many, and they survive only when they do. The comics are a populist institution that depends on a powerful but fickle mass audience. Skeptical newspaper editors are forever "dropping" comics to test their readers' reaction. (When *Prince Valiant* was dropped from the *San Francisco Chronicle* in 1977, the newspaper received over 1,000 phone calls. The strip was restored, and the editors apologized on page one.) These men trace their roots back to editor Arthur Brisbane of the *New York Journal,* who in 1910 refused to let cartoonist Harry Hershfield sign his own strip, *Desperate Desmond,* on the grounds that only "newspapermen" could have bylines.

"But my strip appears in the newspapers," argued Hershfield. "Doesn't that make me a newspaperman?"

"Is a barnacle a ship?" Brisbane retorted.

Comic Themes: From Dick Tracy *to* Doonesbury

The comics survive such occasional hostility because they appeal to a constituency the newspapers will never overrule. To be sure, this may have its drawbacks. *The Gumps,* premier symbol of the "Roaring '20s," declined as the Depression advanced. *Terry and the Pirates* and its unrelievedly cold-warrior outlook sank during Vietnam and detente. Still, dependence on a mass audience can also have its strengths. The same gangster-ridden Depression that weakened *The Gumps* spawned *Dick Tracy;* the tumultuous Vietnam era that toppled *Terry* and angered *Li'l Abner*'s Al Capp helped launch Garry Trudeau's *Doonesbury.*

To what kinds of aspirations do the comics appeal? George Herriman's *Krazy Kat* dealt with two themes that emerge continually in the later strips: the triumph of illusion over reality, and the victory of rebelliousness over authority.

For thirty-five years Herriman's willful, anarchistic mouse (Ignatz) threw bricks at a lovesick Krazy Kat who took the bricks as signs of love. She in turn was pursued by Offissa Pup who tried desperately and to no avail to keep Ignatz behind bars. Herriman's use of shifting, semiabstract backgrounds and his remarkable rhetoric show the possibilities of the comic art form. Listen to one of Herriman's characters rhapsodize about work:

> Indolence—the sin of the century . . . the error of the era—And Labor is so lovely . . . toil so transcendent . . . the witchery of work so wondrous . . . industry looks upon the world with beauty . . . Diligence is a dainty delight . . . Endeavour is an enchanting endowment . . . effort effuses an affluent afflorescent effulgence . . . it is noble to strive, brave to strain, kingly to struggle. . . .

Interestingly, *Krazy Kat,* hailed today as the great comic classic, is more highly regarded now than it was when it was "alive." That it lasted so long was due to the rare intervention of a newspaperman: Publisher William Randolph Hearst so enjoyed the strip that he subsidized its publication for twenty years after it had stopped making money for the Hearst-owned King Features Syndicate.

Some of the other more familiar themes in the comics—the triumph of good over evil, for one—are relative newcomers, arriving with the great adventure strips of the 1930s: *Flash Gordon, Jungle Jim, Secret Agent X-9,* and *Tarzan.* These strips were drawn by master draftsmen like Alex Raymond and Harold Foster and written with skill and imagination (even Dashiell Hammett tried his hand—on *X-9*).

In the adventure strips, the good guys always win. We know that Dick Tracy, who in his forty-seven-year career has been maimed, crippled, and shot countless times, will get his man in the end. But there are many recurrent though less obvious themes: a distrust of rationally ordered societies, of technology, of grand visions. Tarzan prefers the jungle to the encroachments of civilization; X-9 takes aim at totalitarian scheming; and Flash Gordon, who relies on space-age gadgetry, must ever contend with dark forces who put that gadgetry to evil ends. In short, the adventure strips reveal a fear of utopia gone awry.

In most strips these ideas are never spelled out in so many words. In some, however, the political or ideological content, so submerged in *Krazy Kat* or *Flash Gordon,* appears overtly. So it is with *Doonesbury,* our most important new comic strip (though not the most successful commercially; that distinction goes to Dik Browne's *Hagar the Horrible*). Here, the political content is so direct and obvious that the line between comics and political cartoons almost disappears. To the Pulitzer Prize committee that awarded Trudeau a prize for editorial cartooning in 1975 the distinction seems to have already disappeared. Writing social comment under the cover of humor, Trudeau satirizes a number of contemporary figures, ranging from TV correspondents to ex-flower children to Army recruiters. Because his allusions are so immediate, he is a very good guide to the contemporary social scene in America.

Does *Doonesbury* represent the swan song of a dying art form? Some observers think so. They note that many of the adventure strips have been casualties of television, that the syndicates have lagged in developing new talent, and that the edge in innovation has passed from the United States to Latin America, the Philippines, and Japan.

Even if those observers are right, the heritage of eight decades of comic art—and its reflections of our evolving culture—remains. And they may well be wrong: One could as easily interpret the growth of the foreign comic-strip industry as a sign of vigor. The comics are now read by hundreds of millions of people in more than fifty countries. As *Beetle Bailey*'s Mort Walker has noted, that's probably the largest number of countries ever to agree on any one thing. That fact alone deserves some scholarly attention.

Background Books

THE NEWSPAPERS

"News and truth are not the same things, and must be clearly distinguished." So, in 1922, wrote Walter Lippmann in *Public Opinion* (Macmillan, 4th ed., 1965, cloth and paper). "The press is no substitute for [other] institutions. . . . Men cannot do the work of the world by this light alone. They cannot govern society by episodes, incidents, and eruptions."

Such lofty talk was long in coming to American journalism. In *American Journalism—A History: 1690–1960* (Macmillan, 3rd ed., 1962), the University of Missouri's Frank Luther Mott notes that the first continuous U.S. newspaper was the *Boston News-Letter,* founded in 1704 by Boston's postmaster, John Campbell. The weekly did not thrive: fifteen years later, Campbell complained that he could not "vend 300 copies at an impression."

Circulation remained small because Campbell and other early editors catered to a tiny mercantile elite, printing mostly shipping news and advertisements.

That all changed during the 1830s. Jacksonian Democracy, with its egalitarian politics and free-market philosophy, not only encouraged entrepreneurs to start newspapers, but also helped to create an audience for them.

The new papers—the first was the New York *Sun*—cost 1 cent, a sixth of the then-usual cost, and so were labeled "the penny press." They covered "not just commerce or politics but social life . . . the activities of an increasingly varied, urban, and middle-class society" writes Michael Schudson in *Discovering the News: A Social History of American Newspapers* (Basic, 1978). In 1830, Schudson estimates, the combined circulation of all U.S. dailies was 78,000; within ten years, the total shot up to about 300,000.

In the years after the Civil War, a muckraking manic-depressive Hungarian immigrant named Joseph Pulitzer further expanded the newspaper audience. Biographer W.A. Swanberg tells how *Pulitzer* (Scribner's, 1967) wedded reform to sensationalism, and developed the newspaper crusade as a way of hooking America's giant new working-class immigrant population on the daily newspaper habit.

Expelled from Harvard in his junior year, William Randolph Hearst went to work at Pulitzer's *New York World*. That served as an apprenticeship. In 1885 he took over the San Francisco *Examiner,* bought by his father with part of the proceeds from the Comstock Lode. Like Pulitzer, Swanberg writes, *Citizen Hearst* (Bantam, 2nd ed., 1963) was excruciatingly shy in person but explosive in print. Hearst took a lower road to journalistic success, following a "crime and underwear" recipe. He sent his reporters to hunt grizzly bears, or to fall overboard from ferryboats, or to escort Sarah Bernhardt to a San Francisco opium den.

By 1923, two young men fresh out of Yale, Henry R. Luce and Britton Hadden, decided news was so abundant that it needed to be organized, condensed, and (because dry facts did not suffice) inter-preted. Thus was born a new genre of journalism, the news magazine. With *Time* came a new style, notable for its Homeric epithets ("bumper-jawed," "long-whiskered") and odd linguistic shrinkages ("in time's nick"). Former *Time* editor Robert Elson tells the story in the company-sponsored *Time Inc: The Intimate History of a Publishing Enterprise, 1923–1941* (Athenaeum, 1968).

As the mid-twentieth century wore on, technology brought en-tirely new media: radio and television. Broadcast journalists faced a unique problem: people did not buy radios or TV sets primarily to get the news. "You've got to get them into the tent!" CBS evening news producer Don Hewitt used to shout at his crews during the 1950s.

One of the first to get folks "into the tent" was Edward R. Murrow, a man who, in his own words, had not been "contaminated by the conventions of print." Murrow's great feat, notes former CBS writer Gary Paul Gates in his chatty *Air Time: The Inside Story of CBS News* (Harper, 1978, cloth; Berkley, 1979, paper), was to shift radio news from the studio to the scene of the event—in his case, London during World War II. And Murrow succeeded, Gates argued, because he "mastered the art of *playing* himself." Some of Murrow's radio reporting is collected in a book and on a phonograph record. His most recent biography is *Murrow: His Life and Times,* by A.M. Sperber (Freundlich, 1986).

Media critic Edward Jay Epstein's more scholarly *News From Nowhere* (Random, 1974, cloth and paper) concentrates on NBC-TV

News during the late 1960s but finds a similar philosophy of news as entertainment.

New Yorker critic Michael Arlen suggests in *The View From Highway One* (Farrar, 1976, cloth; Ballantine, 1977, paper) that broadcast journalists should not be condemned for failing to provide the facts as well as do their print counterparts. Television news, he contends, seeks to convey not information pertaining to an event but the "feel" of it. Television critic Ron Powers concurs. Looking at local TV news in *The Newscasters* (St. Martin's, 1977), he concludes that during the 1970s it succumbed to the underlying "entertainment bias" of the medium.

Yet the harried gentlemen of the print media are also susceptible to manipulation. So says Edwin R. Bayley, who covered the erratic anti-Red crusades of Senator Joseph McCarthy (R-Wis.) as a reporter for the *Milwaukee Journal*. In *Joe McCarthy and the Press* (University of Wisconsin, 1981), Bayley argues that it was television, not newspapers, that did McCarthy in, when, in 1954, the televised Army–McCarthy hearings brought the ugliness of the senator's attacks into America's living rooms.

The study of the press to most people means the study of great men—the media moguls. Press lords are certainly not a thing of the past. Yet today they often span several continents and several media. The quintessential example is Rupert Murdoch. No biography can be definitive—the saga is far from over—but Thomas Kiernan's *Citizen Murdoch* (Dodd, Mead, 1986) lays out the basic facts of Murdoch's rise in Australian publishing circles, his move to London's Fleet Street, and then to New York and Hollywood.

Richard H. Meeker's *Newspaperman: S.I. Newhouse and the Business of News* (Ticknor & Fields, 1983) is a rare look inside one of the largest U.S. newspaper chains. The founder of this press empire, S.I. Newhouse (1895–1979), and his family have sought to preserve their privacy and to a large extent have succeeded. However, Meeker has applied the tools of the investigative journalist to the Newhouse clan with a fair degree of success. Newhouse cared little for the major issues of the day, but he was a brilliant businessman who saw in newspapers—principally monopoly papers—a passport to wealth. He succeeded by controlling access to newspaper distribution routes and newsstands, and by skillfully playing the takeover game long before it became faddish in the 1980s.

But the story of the news media ranges far beyond vivid tales of ruthless businessmen. There are the newspeople who report and deliver the news. David H. Weaver and G. Cleveland Wilhoit's *The American Journalist: A Portrait of U.S. News People and Their Work* (Indiana University Press, 1986) provides a snapshot of both print and broadcast journalists in the United States, including their educational backgrounds, working conditions, stated values and ethical positions, and their reactions to new technologies. This portrait differs from the prevailing, popular view of journalists as elitist, adversarial, and materialistic. While the educational levels of journalists now put them among the elite of the society, they tend toward middle-of-the-road political views, and their professional values are typified by a sense of altruism and an often-thwarted desire for autonomy. The critics' claim of an adversarial mentality, the authors found, is not reflected in journalists' view of themselves nor in what they identify as their best work.

Newspapers have changed during the past twenty years, principally because of television. One notable victim has been the big-city afternoon daily paper. In *Death in the Afternoon* (Andrews, McNeel & Parker, 1984), Peter Benjaminson describes the sad demise of such PM papers as the *Washington Star,* the *Cleveland Press,* and the *Philadelphia Bulletin,* and concludes that only under special conditions (in a blue-collar town, for example) can an afternoon daily hope to survive.

Because so much important news comes out of the nation's capital, the observations of longtime Washington media watcher Stephen Hess are especially useful. In *The Washington Reporters* (Brookings, 1981), Hess examines the reporters who cover the federal government. In a subsequent work, *The Government/Press Connection* (Brookings, 1984), Hess switches his attention to that small army of government information officers who struggle—usually unsuccessfully—to control the way news is played in the media. His major point: There is little that can be kept secret in Washington once someone determines that it is newsworthy.

One long-ignored aspect of the news business is the important role played by the wire services. These agencies supply most of the out-of-town news heard on radio, read by TV anchorpersons, and published in all but the largest newspapers. In *The International News Services* (Schocken, 1986), a report sponsored by the Twentieth Century Fund, Jonathan Fenby describes the development, operations, and recent troubles of the Associated Press, United Press International, Reuters, and Agence France-Presse.

With attention usually focused on newspapers as purveyors of information, the industry's financial realities are often overlooked. A rare look at the business side can be found in Jon G. Udell's *The Economics of the American Newspaper* (Hastings House, 1978). Udell examines the complexities of advertising, circulation, employee relations, and cost controls in a universe of small enterprises; only 250 U.S. newspapers have circulations of 50,000 or more. It is an industry that offers sizable profits to the owner of a monopoly paper in a medium- or large-size city.

For reasons that are not entirely clear, legal actions against the press have proliferated since the 1964 decision in *New York Times* v. *Sullivan* in which the Supreme Court presumably bolstered First Amendment protection of the press by ruling that public officials suing for libel could win only if defamed through malicious intent. In *Libel Law and the Press: Myth and Reality* (The Free Press, 1987), three media specialists at the University of Iowa, Randall P. Bezanson, Gilbert Cranberg, and John Soloski, suggest some alternatives to the libel litigation that frightens media people into self-censorship yet seldom provides real redress to plaintiffs who feel wronged by the press.

In *Suing The Press: Libel, the Media and Power* (Oxford, 1986), University of Arkansas law professor Rodney A. Smolla reviews many of the more recent lawsuits against the press and offers his own suggestions for reform. These include: requiring the losing side in a libel action to pay the opponent's legal fees, elimination of punitive damages, greater stress on seeking redress through published retractions, and absolute protection for the expression of opinion.

A sure antidote to journalistic smugness can be found in *Reckless Disregard* (Knopf, 1986), an account by the *New Yorker*'s Renata Adler of the much-publicized libel suits brought by General William C. Westmoreland, former commander of U.S. forces in Vietnam, against CBS, and by former Israeli defense minister Ariel Sharon against *Time* magazine. The author's sympathies are clearly with Westmoreland and Sharon, but she argues persuasively that both CBS and *Time* failed to live up to their own professed standards of journalism. After reading Adler's analysis of the two trials, it is difficult not to conclude that, in the public interest, journalists would do well to accompany their rightful claims to First Amendment protection with a far greater willingness to concede error in the practice of their craft.

MOVIES

Chapter 8

HOLLYWOOD'S BUSINESS

by Douglas Gomery

Andy Warhol was lunching poolside, amid the palm trees and exotic bird-of-paradise flowers. CBS News's Mike Wallace had already dashed off for a taping, but director Robert Benton was still sunning himself on one of the 200 chaise lounges. Nearby, a young Paramount Pictures executive was poring over a script. Gossip hounds Susan Mulcahy of the *New York Post* and Barbara Howar of *Entertainment Tonight* were sniffing out stories. In a yellow-and-white striped cabana (rent: $35 per day), executives from Tri-Star Pictures shook hands on a new venture with a group of movie producers.

It was just another day, as the *Wall Street Journal* reported, at the Beverly Hills Hotel pool, long "the watering spot where movie stars and moguls meet to make deals." The hotel management even furnishes poolside secretarial service. In Hollywood legend, the Olympic-size pool (for hotel guests only; their visitors pay $10 for admission) rivals Schwab's Pharmacy as the place to go if you want to be "discovered." Even the pool's manager, Svend Peterson, has appeared on the big screen, in bit parts in *The Prize* (1963) and *Torn Curtain* (1966). He keeps his Screen Actors Guild membership current, just in case. Robert Evans, who became the producer of *Chinatown* (1974) and *The Cotton Club* (1984), was a women's clothing manufacturer until destiny plucked him from his Beverly Hills Hotel lounge chair three decades ago.

A few miles down Sunset Boulevard is the University of California, Los Angeles (UCLA) film school, which emerged during the

93

1970s, along with the University of Southern California (USC) film school across town, as another launchpad for success. Enroll, Hollywood lore says, and before long the film school "mafia," led by George Lucas (B.A., USC, 1966) and Francis Ford Coppola (M.A., UCLA, 1968), will discover you.

Unfortunately, neither the "by-the-pool" nor the "at-school" method has ever produced a very high individual success rate. For anybody who really wants to make it to the top in Hollywood, who wants to be in a position to hire and fire the movie crowd at the Beverly Hills Hotel pool, there is a much clearer path: go to law school, land a job with one of the conglomerates that dominate the movie business, and slowly work your way up.

That is how Ned Tanen of Paramount Pictures and Frank G. Wells of Walt Disney Productions did it.

Hollywood's executives preside over an industry whose public profile far exceeds its economic heft. The annual net *profits* of the International Business Machines Corporation (IBM) are greater than the domestic box-office revenues ($4.2 billion) of the entire U.S. motion picture industry. Including cameramen, actors, secretaries, and film editors (but not theater personnel), it employs only 220,000 people. Why all the glamor? Some of it comes from the high-stakes character of the business and the enormous earnings of the stars. The difference in gross revenues between an expensive flop like *Heaven's Gate* (1980) and a smash hit like *Star Wars* (1977) can amount over a period of years to nearly $1 billion. Big films, such as *Jaws* (1975), *Out of Africa* (1985), and *The Color Purple* (1985), can leave their mark on fashion, fads, behavior, and, sometimes, public debate. But, above all, Hollywood captures the popular imagination because it is still the nation's (and the world's) "dream machine," projecting private hopes and fantasies and fears onto a big screen for all to see and share.

Despite some considerable changes in the way Hollywood does business, an industry "insider" from the 1930s would still recognize today's dominant companies. Gone are the flamboyantly tyrannical movie moguls like Louis B. Mayer and Darryl F. Zanuck, the paternalistic studio system, and Hollywood's old monopoly on stardom, American-style. Many of the vast and glorious backlots, where the likes of Gary Cooper faced *High Noon* (1952) and Gene Kelly went *Singin' in the Rain* (1952) have disappeared or shrunk, now replaced by office buildings and hotels.

Hollywood's "Big Eight"

Yet there is one constant on the Hollywood scene: Eight multinational corporations formed more than fifty years ago still have hegemony over the production and worldwide distribution of feature films. Of the old Hollywood film factory giants, only RKO (producer of the

---

PUTTING TOGETHER *TOOTSIE*

For each of the 350 or more feature films that Hollywood turns out every year, there is a "story" behind the story. But "saga" may be a better word for the making of *Tootsie*.

Tootsie was born during the 1970s as a script called *Would I Lie to You?* by a little-known writer-director named Don McGuire. Purchased by theater owner Henry Plitt and two partners, it made the rounds of Hollywood producers, directors, and agents until 1978, when it landed in the hands of comedian Buddy Hackett. Hackett wanted to play one of the supporting roles, so he took the script to a producer, Charles Evans. Evans bought an "option" on it. (Because of long delays in beginning production, he would be forced to pay to renew the option "one or two" more times.)

Months later, Evans convinced his friend, Dick Richards, director of *Farewell, My Lovely,* to show the "property" to Dustin Hoffman, his partner in a "property development" firm. Hoffman, reports author Susan Dworkin in *Making Tootsie* (1983), liked it immediately. Thus began a commitment that was to last nearly four years.

Hoffman wanted complete creative control, and he insisted that Hal Ashby direct the picture. Evans kicked himself upstairs to executive producer; Dick Richards dropped out entirely (so, eventually, did Buddy Hackett). But with a star like Hoffman on board, Evans had no trouble convincing Columbia Pictures to advance a few hundred thousand dollars in "development" money.

Hoffman set to work rewriting the story with his friend, playwright Murray Schisgal, while interviewing actors and actresses and painstakingly perfecting his makeup.

In the autumn of 1981, Columbia executives, acting as mediators, reported that Ashby was unavailable. Sydney Pollack, however, was free, and they favored him because he was a sound investment: six of his last eight pictures had been money-makers. But Pollack would sign on only if he was guaranteed control over the "final cut"—the final version. Hoffman agreed. Pollack became both producer and director of the picture.

By November 1981, all of the principals were ready to sign on the dotted line. *Tootsie* (Hoffman's title) became a Columbia Pictures presentation of a Sydney Pollack Film, a Mirage/Punch Production. Mirage is Pollack's production company; Punch, Hoffman's. The deal: Columbia agreed to finance production of the movie from its own revolving line of bank credit to the tune of $20 million. (Usually producers must corral outside investors to finance a film; movie investments are a popular tax shelter.) Hoffman was to be paid $4.5 million plus a percentage of the profits; Pollack would get $2 million and a percentage. Among the others entitled to a cut of the profits was Don McGuire, the original writer but long out of the picture.

Money in hand, Pollack (with Hoffman's help) hired his own team—fifty-five actors and actresses and a production crew of sixty-five (including assistant directors, cameramen, and a transportation "captain"). Hoffman's costars—Jessica Lange, Teri Garr, Bill Murray—were signed up. Also on Pollack's staff was a production manager who would file daily budget reports with Columbia.

During nine days of meetings at Pollack's beach house, Hoffman, Pollack, and writer Larry (*M*A*S*H*) Gelbart, who, at Columbia's urging, had replaced Murray Schisgal, worked over the script yet again. By now, the basic plot was clear: An out-of-work actor masquerades as an actress and becomes the star of a TV soap opera. Ultimately, eight writers labored over the script, at a cost of some $1.5 million.

Filming began in New York City on April Fool's Day 1982, lasting, as *New Yorker* film critic Pauline Kael put it, a "rather scandalous" ninety-eight days—twenty-three days over schedule. The production budget was set at $80,000 a day, or $110 per minute, using the usual twelve-hour workday. Having sacrificed his "final cut" privileges, Hoffman knew that he would have to fight his creative battles during the filming; he and Pollack often debated acting technique, dialogue, and lighting as the cast and crew waited. Several times, Hoffman's heavy makeup brought out a rash, delaying shooting.

By late August, when filming (all of it on location in Manhattan and upstate New York) was finished, the picture was way behind schedule for its planned Christmas 1982 release. Pollack had to have a rough cut ready to screen for theater owners by mid-October, and a completed film to show critics by mid-November. He flew back to Hollywood the day the last scene was shot, missing the cast's "wrap" party. Using a cutting room rented from Columbia, he edited the film in five weeks instead of the usual five to six months. Among his concerns: shaping the film to get a PG (Parental Guidance) rating and attract the "family" audience. "For me," says Pollack, "every picture is . . . a hopeless disaster until a certain point in the editing."

Tootsie turned out to be one of the 20 percent of Hollywood films that have a happy ending: it made money, becoming the hit of the 1982 Christmas season. (According to the Motion Picture Association of America, 60 percent of all feature films never recover their costs, 20 percent break even, and the rest make money.) A year later, Home Box Office bought the cable rights to *Tootsie* for a reported $20 million, and Columbia signed a deal to bring out a *Tootsie* videocassette priced at $79.95. In September 1985 the movie had its TV premiere on ABC.

Five years after its release, *Tootsie*'s revenues still roll in from sales of videotapes and rentals to television stations. The "bottom line" will not be known for years, but Columbia's yield from rentals to U.S. and Canadian theaters alone topped $95 million, ranking *Tootsie* number thirteen on *Variety*'s list of all-time hits.

1933 version of *King Kong* and those dazzling Fred Astaire–Ginger Rogers musicals) has gone under, dismantled during the 1950s by its owner, the eccentric billionaire Howard Hughes.

Studio executives still make or break the careers of the Robert Evanses, Jessica Langes, and Richard Geres. They also decide whether to distribute the films of George Lucas, Francis Ford Coppola, and those of every one of Hollywood's legion of aspiring producers and directors. And without a studio distribution contract, few film makers can raise the $15 million required for the average Hollywood production budget, even if they spend a lifetime at the Beverly Hills Hotel pool. (Distribution and advertising expenses add at least another 50 percent to a movie's costs.) Orson Welles, the brilliant director of *Citizen Kane* (1941) who died in 1985, never directed another major release after *Touch of Evil* (1957) because the studios viewed him, as his biographer Joseph McBride put it, as a "wastrel, a rebel, a continuing challenge to the Hollywood system."

"The new Hollywood," as Metro–Goldwyn–Mayer (MGM) executive vice-president David Chasman observed in 1981, "is very much like the old Hollywood."

The Big Eight studios have survived repeated challenges: the breakup of their theater networks, the rise of broadcast television, the advent of cable and "pay" television, and, most recently, the video-cassette revolution. They show no signs of weakening. The studios, despite their age, are among the nation's most adaptable, agile corporations.

Today, old-fashioned entrepreneurs own just three of the eight studios—Twentieth Century Fox, MGM, and United Artists Communications. Yet their economic reach vastly exceeds anything ever dreamed of by the moguls of Hollywood's Golden Age.

The Australian-born press lord Rupert Murdoch, for example, created America's first vertically integrated movie–television company when he bought Twentieth Century Fox for $575 million in 1985 and combined it with the chain of six big-city independent TV stations that he recently acquired from Metromedia Television. This means that a Fox-made film such as *The Jewel of the Nile* (1985) can be shown by the new Fox TV stations after it appears in the nation's theaters, keeping all the film's revenues within the corporate family. Ultimately, Murdoch hopes to expand his television network to challenge ABC, CBS, and NBC.

Ted Turner, of cable television fame, agreed to buy MGM in 1985 for similar reasons: to acquire MGM's film library for his superstation. He made the deal with financial whiz Kirk Kerkorian. In 1986 Turner turned around and sold MGM back, and in 1987 Kirk Kerkorian owned MGM/UA. However, the famed MGM lot is not his. Lorimar–Telepictures, a movie upstart but television power (*Dallas, Knots Landing, Falcon Crest*), took control of the Culver City lot that was once at the heart of America's movie making. MGM/UA has moved across the street into a modern new high-rise.

Paramount Pictures is now part of a large, diversified conglomerate, Gulf + Western. Profits from movies (and television) double each year. Hits roll off the assembly lines: *Top Gun* and *Crocodile Dundee* in 1986, and *Beverly Hills Cop: Part II* in 1987. Nearly one-quarter of the box-office dollars spent on movies in the United States in 1986 went to Paramount. There have been "hot" studios before: Twentieth Century Fox in the late 1970s with the *Star Wars* films, Universal in the early 1980s with *E.T.* All eventually cooled down; pundits expect Paramount to do the same.

Columbia Pictures was part of Coca-Cola from 1982 to 1987. Hollywood prides itself on being a liberal, "creative" community—although Orson Welles once lamented the "gray flannel shadow" over Movieland—and not a few of its celebrities regularly chortled over the tribulations of the button-down corporate types from Coca-Cola, which was not successful in the movie business and sold Columbia.

In recent years top honors at the box office have gone to studios owned by two conglomerates that specialize in entertainment: Warner Bros., owned by Warner Communications, and Universal, a division of MCA. (MCA, following the Murdoch–Turner strategy, recently bought an independent New York television station for $387 million.) The Disney studio, part of the Disney entertainment conglomerate, has not done so well. But with the release of *Down and Out in Beverly Hills* (1986) under its new Touchstone Films banner, it is now pursuing adult audiences, and greater profits.

In Hollywood parlance, the Big Eight corporations are "the majors." Year in, year out, they control almost 80 percent of the movie

Among the matters carefully negotiated in Hollywood contracts are where and how credits will appear in movie advertisements. Here, nobody won billing above the title, a prime spot. But producer-director Paul Mazursky's name appears four times. Although all three star actors are listed in the same size type, Nick Nolte has top billing.

business in the United States and approximately half the market in Sweden, West Germany, and several other nations in Western Europe, not to mention Asia. (Hollywood derives roughly 50 percent of its revenues from overseas film rentals.) Every few years, a couple of bold pretenders (recently, Orion Pictures and New World Pictures) emerge to challenge the Big Eight at home, and as often as not they succeed in creating a modest hit or two. But no challenger has survived over the long haul.[1]

FILM RENTAL CHAMPS: TOP 25

According to *Variety* (January 14, 1987), the twenty-five theatrical motion pictures that generated the most money for their studio distributors in the United States and Canadian markets are:

Title	Year of Release	Total Rentals*
E.T.: The Extra-Terrestrial	1982	$228,379,346
Star Wars	1977	$193,500,000
Return of the Jedi	1983	$168,002,414
The Empire Strikes Back	1980	$141,600,000
Jaws	1975	$129,961,081
Ghostbusters	1984	$128,264,005
Raiders of the Lost Ark	1981	$115,598,000
Indiana Jones and the Temple of Doom	1984	$109,000,000
Beverly Hills Cop	1984	$108,000,000
Back to the Future	1985	$101,955,795
Grease	1978	$ 96,300,000
Tootsie	1982	$ 95,268,806
The Exorcist	1973	$ 89,000,000
The Godfather	1972	$ 86,275,000
Superman	1978	$ 82,800,000
Close Encounters of the Third Kind	1977	$ 82,750,000

(Continued)

Top Gun	1986	$ 82,000,000
Rambo: First Blood Part II	1985	$ 80,000,000
The Sound of Music	1965	$ 79,748,000
Gremlins	1984	$ 79,500,000
The Sting	1973	$ 78,198,608
Gone with the Wind	1939	$ 76,700,000
Rocky IV	1985	$ 75,782,000
Saturday Night Fever	1977	$ 74,100,000
National Lampoon's Animal House	1978	$ 70,778,176

*These figures do not include worldwide grosses or even United States and Canadian box office take because of the inability to collect reliable information. These are raw numbers, not adjusted for inflation.

Film Distribution: The Secret of Their Success

There is no secret to the majors' success. In essence, their power derives, as it always has, from their ability to distribute films. At considerable expense, they maintain offices in about twenty-five cities in America (and up to sixty-five overseas), where their representatives are in constant contact with the heads of regional theater chains. The studios' "hit parade" record at the box office is what impels theater owners (a conservative lot) to rent their products.[2] In the "new" Hollywood, there are dozens of independent producers, but virtually all of them pay the big studios to distribute their films.

In 1945, during the high tide of movie going in America, the majors owned most of the nation's movie theaters. Downtown "picture palaces"—the Paramount in New York, the Oriental in Chicago, the Mastbaum in Philadelphia—were the showcases of the system. "In Hollywood's heyday," notes *Time* magazine, "the films were only celluloid but the cinemas that showed them were marble citadels of fantasy and opulence . . . some of the most exuberantly romantic architecture ever conceived in the U.S." Marcus Loew, the founder of MGM, once said, "We sell tickets to theaters, not movies."

From these Xanadus, with their baroque architectural splendor and acres of seats, came the bulk of any film's revenues, even though smaller neighborhood houses, with about 500 seats, outnumbered the dream palaces by 9 to 1. In the years right after World War II, the theaters sold some 90 million tickets every week.

That all began to change in 1948, when the U.S. Supreme Court declined to hear an appeal of the Paramount antitrust case, forcing the majors to sell their theater holdings. They gradually divested themselves during the next decade—just in the nick of time, as it turned out. As middle-class Americans migrated to the suburbs, many of the downtown movie houses decayed or closed their doors.

From Drive-Ins to Cineplexes

Today, fifty regionally based companies dominate the film exhibition business, led by Cineplex–Odeon, General Cinema, and United Artists Communications, each with more than 1,000 screens. (Total screens in the North American market as of June 1987: 23,000.) Many of these new film exhibition giants got their start as operators of drive-in theaters, the "passion pits" of the 1950s. They prospered not only because they offered a trysting place for older adolescents, but also because they offered a cheap night out for young parents—they could put the kids in the car's backseat, no babysitter needed. (Some families also threw their dirty laundry in the trunk: a few drive-ins offered laundromats for overworked mothers.) Opening a drive-in required only a fence, a macadam parking lot, some speakers for the cars, a projector, and an enormous screen. Best of all, the drive-ins could be built on cheap land at the edge of town.

As the suburbs matured and land became relatively more expensive, "hardtop" cinemas enjoyed a comeback, usually in the form of mini-cinemas with a couple of hundred seats squeezed into a plain box shell in a shopping center. Then, during the 1970s, came the cineplexes, usually with three to twelve screens under one roof.

During the mid-1980s the major Hollywood studios went on a buying spree, acquiring theaters before the deregulation-minded Ronald Reagan left the White House. In 1986 the Department of Justice quietly agreed not to press the longtime restrictions against theater purchase by Hollywood embedded in antitrust decrees signed forty years before.

Paramount kicked things off by buying the Trans Lux circuit and the Los Angeles-based Mann Theaters. But the bombshell hit when, in January 1986, MCA, parent company of giant Universal Pictures, acquired a major interest in the second largest circuit of theaters in North America, Cineplex–Odeon. Quickly Cineplex made use of its new connections and gobbled up Plitt Theaters (the dominant chain in Chicago), the RKO Century Warner chain (a major player in New York City), and Neighborhood Theaters of Virginia (a major player in Washington, D.C.). At the end of one year, MCA had gained unprecedented access to some of the best theaters in three of America's eight largest movie-going markets.

Generally the coming of Cineplex–Odeon has meant good news for potential patrons in those cities. Garth H. Drabinsky, the driven, Canadian-born president of the company, believes in bringing back the luxury, diversity, and technical superiority of the movie theater. Seats in Cineplex–Odeon theaters are wide and comfortable; the butter on the popcorn is "real"; the sound and image achieve a standard many had long forgotten. In Canada, where it began, Cineplex has long had a policy of commissioning original art works for its theater lobbies as well as offering elaborate drink and dessert menus, rather than just the usual popcorn, candy, and soft drinks. Film critics give the company four stars. "Toronto has a film culture because of Garth Drabinsky," says Jay Scott of the Toronto Globe-Mail. "For movies he's been wonderful."

In a way, the exhibition business has come full circle: the new cineplexes essentially are unadorned, chopped-up versions of the glorious Paramounts and Orientals of old. (A few new theaters are even putting on some frills again to lure customers.) The economics, as *Fortune* magazine explained earlier this year, is simple. "A theater with four screens, roughly the national average, is four times more likely than a one-screen house to book a hit picture." A hit movie can be shifted to a big room, a dud to a smaller one.

The cineplexes are far better suited to the film release patterns that developed as the majors sold off their theater holdings. Under the old system, the studios turned out nearly a picture a week to feed their chains: a film would open for a week at downtown picture palaces, return a few months later for a week at the larger neighborhood houses, then appear on successively lower rungs of the distribution ladder. At each set down, the price of admission dropped.

"Once separated from their theater chains," writes film historian Arthur Knight, "the studio heads quickly realized that they no longer had to supply a new movie each week for their own houses. They cut back on their production schedules." The change spelled the end of the already ailing studio system: Why keep stars and directors and screenwriters on costly year-round contracts merely to work on two or three films a year?

Viewing patterns also changed. After 1948 television siphoned off part of the film audience, and moviegoers who once went to the pictures no matter what was showing changed their ways. "Filmgoing used to be part of the social fabric," observes Art Murphy, a USC film professor. "Now it's an impulse purchase."

After dropping from a peak of 4.5 billion during the 1940s, annual admissions leveled off at about one billion during the 1960s and have remained relatively steady at that number. Considering the growth of the population, this represents about a 25 percent decline in the proportion of the U.S. population going to the movies. At the same time, the composition of the movie-going audience has changed. The new schedule targets today's biggest ticket buyers: teen-agers on school vacations. According to the *1986 International Motion Picture Almanac,* young people ages twelve to nineteen make up 40 percent of the typical movie theater audience. They go out to the movies almost three times as often as their parents or grandparents. The over-forty set accounts for a mere 15 percent of ticket sales.

AMERICANS GOING OUT TO THE MOVIES

Age	Percentage of Yearly Admissions	Percentage of Resident Civilian Population
12–15	13	8
16–20	23	10
21–24	18	9
25–29	13	11
30–39	18	18
40–49	8	13
50–59	4	12
60+	3	20

This chart underscores the most important fact about who goes out to the movies in the United States. Simply put, movie going is a social activity of the young. Fully 85 percent of moviegoers in recent years (1984 is typical) are people under forty, with the bulk of these being teenagers, half of whom tell researchers they go to the movies at least once a month. Their parents on average go once a year.

And those young people, by and large, are single. Statistically speaking, married adults patronize movie theaters about half as often as the nonmarried members of their population cohort. It is safe to assume that many young people are at the movies with a date—or wish they were.

Two long-term trends of American movie going continue—American moviegoers tend to be college educated and male, and it was this way even before the advent of television. A moviegoer is three times more likely to be seated next to a college graduate as next to a high school dropout. Skeptics who assert that the average Hollywood movie is aimed at twelve-year-olds must have a bright teenager in mind.

Since the introduction of movies with sound, when reliable statistics were first gathered, it has been the case that males go to the movies in greater numbers than females. Indeed, if we had to sketch an average moviegoer "he" would be a seventeen-year-old male headed off to college. "He" would go to the movies in the summer (July and August are the top months), to a multiplex theater complex not far from his suburban home, to see a recently released feature, chosen on the basis of advice from a friend or because of an advertisement seen on television.

Douglas Gomery

In the cineplex world, summer, beginning before Memorial Day and ending on the Labor Day weekend, is the season when the majors unleash their hoped-for hits. Blockbusters such as *Back to the Future* (1985) hang on for months, sometimes even a year. According to *Variety,* the industry's trade newspaper, the summer movie season accounts for nearly 50 percent of the domestic box-office take. The Christmas and Easter vacation periods are also peak periods.

Where have the older folks gone? Literally, nowhere. Most are staying home, parked in front of their television sets. The "tube" serves up not only cop shows and other standard TV fare, but also a surprising number of Hollywood productions. A quick survey of *TV Guide* reveals that about one-quarter of the average television broadcast day is devoted to movies, most of them aired by independent stations. Add cable television's film-heavy menu, and the movie time vastly increases.

Hollywood Goes Small Screen

During the late 1940s, the majors had tried to deal with the rise of television in a number of ways. Several attempted (unsuccessfully) to establish their own television networks or to ally themselves with existing ones. Others tried to offer more of what the public could not get from television. They came up with "3D" films, wide-screen pictures, and, in two extremely short-lived experiments, AromaRama and Smell-O-Vision. The big shift began in 1955 when Howard Hughes, then in the process of dismantling RKO, agreed to rent pre-1948 RKO feature films to the fledgling TV networks. One by one the major studios followed suit.

Thereafter, Hollywood became indispensable to television. By the late 1950s, all of the major studios had plunged into the production of TV series. Universal's television division now boasts such prime-time hits as *Miami Vice* and *Murder, She Wrote*.[3] During the 1960s Hollywood began to rent recent films (usually three to five years old) to the television networks, which, thus provisioned, mounted a "Night at the Movies" for every night of the week.

Unhappy with the ever-increasing rents that they were paying for Hollywood studio features, the networks moved during the 1960s to create their own movie fare—the made-for-TV movie, then the miniseries and novel-for-television. Some critics dismiss these low-budget productions as the "disease of the week," but in reality today's made-for-TV dramas are successors to Hollywood's "B" movies of yore. In any event these in-house TV products have not eliminated the networks' need to rent Hollywood films.

In 1972 Time Inc. entered the fray with Home Box Office (HBO), which for a modest monthly fee of about $10 offered cable television viewers recent Hollywood motion pictures uncut and uninterrupted by commercials. For the first time in the television age, a way had been found to make viewers pay for what they watched in their living rooms. Thus, the term "pay television." The result was aptly summed up by a headline in *Broadcasting* magazine: "Ten Years That Changed the World of Telecommunications."[4]

Capitalizing on the VCR

Four years after HBO appeared, Sony introduced its revolutionary Betamax half-inch home videocassette recorder (VCR). Originally priced over $1,000 (double that in today's dollars), the cost of Beta machines and their newer rivals, the VHS, dropped to just over $300 by 1986. And the price keeps falling. An enthusiastic American public has snapped up some 50 million machines. Such numbers, notes *Washington Post* critic Tom Shales, give "home video nearly the penetration of cable TV and, thus, virtual 'mass medium' standing." But now the VCR has passed cable. With growth whose speed was like television's, in just about five years home video reached a saturation level that it had taken cable a quarter-century to achieve.

From the beginning Hollywood loathed the new machine. In allowing VCR owners to tape movies from their television sets, and to control when and where they would view pre-recorded films, the device seemed designed to rob Hollywood and the movie theaters of patrons. The VCR, declared Jack Valenti, president of the Motion Picture Association of America, "is a *parasitical* instrument."

But, characteristically, Hollywood has already found a way to make the most of the VCR.

At first the studios tried to sell pre-recorded movies to the public. But the $80 price tag on most popular films kept the public away in droves. Then, in 1980, local entrepreneurs began to buy multiple copies of pre-recorded tapes and offer them for rent. By the mid-1980s stores renting video tapes seemed to be popping up on every street corner. Record stores and even grocery stores jumped into the business, including, most recently, the Southland Corporation, with its 7,250 7–Eleven stores in the United States. These outlets are something like the old neighborhood picture houses—except that today's most popular neighborhood theater is the living room.

The studios have been quick to capitalize on the trend. In 1985 they grossed $1.5 billion at the box office, and between $1.5 billion and $1.8 billion from sales of videocassettes, mostly to the rental clubs. Complaining that there is not enough "product" to satisfy demand, one videocassette manufacturer has announced plans to make its own films.

Videocassettes have created new markets. Some films only become hits when released as videos. For example, director Martin Scorsese's *Scarface* (1984) did reasonably well for Universal at the box office but later commanded the top spot among VCR rentals, thus gaining a fresh new audience.

Citing the 12 percent drop in theater attendance in 1985, the head of one large theater chain remarked recently, "Anyone who doesn't believe videocassettes are devastating competition to theaters is a

Many movie makers use "story-boards" to plan camera angles and action scenes. Here are story-boards from Raiders of the Lost Ark *(1981).*

fool." But Richard Fox, former head of the National Association of Theater Owners, thinks that Hollywood "just didn't make the movies people wanted to see this year." The only certain victims of the VCR revolution are pornographic movie houses: As many as 40 percent of them have closed their doors since viewers gained the ability to watch movies of their choice at home.

For better or worse, the VCR is making an impact on everybody who shows motion pictures. Paradoxically, new movie screens are now going up at the fastest pace since the 1920s, mostly in shopping malls in America's outer suburbs and in affluent city neighborhoods. Why? In order to offer movie-lovers easy access to the latest in first-run Hollywood films. For their part, HBO and other pay television channels are fighting back against the VCR by offering one-time "pay per view" showing of new films after they debut in the theaters but before they appear on videocassettes.

All of this competition guarantees that the TV networks will reduce their reliance on Hollywood's motion pictures. The trend is already well advanced. When CBS aired *Star Wars* in February 1984, that blockbuster looked to be a sure-fire ratings hit. The network doubled its prime-time ad prices. Then *Star Wars* was beaten in the ratings by ABC's *Lace,* a steamy, made-for-TV movie that cost only $3 million to make, less than half what CBS had paid to rent *Star*

THE CART RACES PAST GERMAN AGENT AND TWO ARABS

CROWD PARTS REVEALING MEAN ARAB MARION FREEZES.

—OHORT, — AGENT SIGNALS AND THEY PERSUE —

Wars. Yet, as the networks seek alternatives to Big Eight products, the cable superstations and over-the-air independent TV stations will gladly take up the slack, gradually moving toward round-the-clock showings of the best and worst of Hollywood's past.

All of these changes, from the expansion of cable to the rise of the VCR, add up to one clear trend. More and more people are going to be watching more and more motion pictures. And to filmdom's Big Eight, that is nothing but good news, for they will still be shaping most of what people watch.

In Hollywood the past exists only on film and in memory, and many of the film colony's older folk mourn the Golden Age. The parties were grander, the celebrities more glamorous, the studios more magnificent. But, such memories aside, it is remarkable how little has changed during the last sixty years. The cast of characters is different, but the same studios still direct the action. Old patterns of doing business have survived into the age of television and the VCR. Aiming at new generations of movie-viewers, the studios even turn out the same kinds of pictures—science fiction, Westerns, horror films—in the same predictable cycles. And every picture still represents a big-money gamble on public taste. In more ways than one would have imagined, watching the business of Hollywood today is like watching an old movie that one has seen before.

NOTES

1. The U.S. film industry is unique: In the nations of Western Europe (including Great Britain) and most other areas of the world, directors and producers must secure the backing of a single national government-owned film production authority. The search for more money and wider film distribution occasionally drives noted foreign directors such as Ingmar Bergman and Akira Kurosawa to Hollywood.

2. The studios and the theaters engage in a never-ending tug-of-war. The studios' revenues come from the rental fee and a share of the box-office receipts; both sums are negotiable. To enlarge "profit centers" in which the studios cannot share, some theater owners now deploy ushers hawking popcorn and soft drinks in the aisles as well as in the lobby. One reason: three cents' worth of popcorn can be sold for one dollar. Theaters now ring up some $340 million in popcorn sales annually.

3. The studios are deeply involved in the production of television shows. Even without their old backlots, they retain the sound stages, prop collections, and managerial talent needed to mount elaborate prime-time series, as well as mini-series and dramatic anthologies such as Steven Spielberg's *Amazing Stories*. (Situation comedies, game shows, and soap operas are the province not of major studies but of specialized TV production companies.) In some ways, the studios' TV operations recall the old days: to work on television programs, Universal, for example, keeps over 100 writers and producers on contract.

4. For the film buff, the "superstations" offered by ordinary cable television are even better than HBO. Consider Ted Turner's WTBS in Atlanta. Turner took a typical local independent station, complete with its commercials, sports, series reruns, and old movies, and beamed its output to America's cable systems via satellite. Turner makes his money chiefly by charging advertisers premium rates to reach his large audience. Perhaps half of WTBS's airtime goes to old films, providing a rich repertory cinema in the home.

Chapter 9

BACK TO BASICS

by Noël Carroll

Vampires from outer space, pirate treasure, time machines, cow-
boys defending homesteaders, dinosaurs, a half-naked warrior van-
quishing hordes of enemies, a house that turns into the biggest popcorn
machine in history.

These are the images you would have seen in some of Hollywood's
major productions from a recent year—in *Lifeforce, The Goonies,
Back to the Future, Silverado, My Science Project, Rambo: First
Blood Part II,* and *Real Genius.*

This list may remind some older Americans of the kinds of movie
choices they faced when they were children during the 1930s, 1940s,
or 1950s. Those films could be neatly defined—as science fiction,
horror, Westerns, war pictures, and slapstick comedies. For critics and
movie makers, these labels, along with others, such as musicals,
mysteries, and thrillers, sort out the major film "genres."

Two decades ago the genre film seemed close to becoming an
endangered species. Hollywood had largely turned away from the old
standbys, seemingly forever (although it still produced a fair number
of them), in favor of more experimental films in the vein of *Steelyard
Blues* and *Five Easy Pieces.* "What these films—and others—had in
common," writes Arthur Knight, a film historian, "was their articula-
tion of contemporary attitudes and emotions, in a language that had its
own modern rhythms and nuances."

But Hollywood attentively follows ticket sales at the box office,
and by the mid-1970s, the movie-going public was telling studio executives that it wanted old-fashioned genre films again. This time, instead

111

of churning out simple copies of past hits, Hollywood produced fairly
sophisticated confections, larded with in-jokes and arcane allusions to
motion picture history. Few in the audience understood those references, but crowds flocked to the new movies—science fiction, Westerns, and other variations on old recipes.

Genres, of course, have shaped film production almost since the
beginnings of cinema.[1] The Frenchman George Méliès enthralled turn-
of-the-century audiences with "trick" films that exploited special
effects in frame after frame of miraculous disappearances, apparitions,
and transformations. Later, chase, escape, and rescue films, perfected
during the 1910s by D.W. Griffith and others, introduced suspense as a
staple ingredient of the cinema. The 1920s call to mind the great
slapstick comedies of the Keystone Kops and Charlie Chaplin; the
years of the Great Depression seem inextricably bound up with escapist musicals, swashbucklers, gangster films, and horror shows; the late
1940s recall the *film noir;* the 1950s, Westerns, science fiction, and
thrillers.

During Hollywood's golden era, the general notion of genres
provided film makers with ready-made formulas for large numbers of
films. A genre label, the studios discovered, helped a film find an

*Half-man, half-fish, the creature from the Black Lagoon was one of many
screen monsters that appeared during the 1950s.*

audience. Musical fans could be counted on to turn out for the latest Busby Berkeley creation; werewolf lovers would pay to see many of the movies of that genre. Moreover, the reliance on genre production supplied a sort of common language for the film maker and the audience. Knowing that the audience was aware of the assumptions and conventions of the form—that, for example, in horror films vampires abhor daylight—directors could spare lengthy exposition in favor of continuous action.

In the hands of an especially talented director, the shared genre "vocabulary" was not just a short cut but a means of creative expression. When Orson Welles opened *Citizen Kane* (1941) with a shot of an old, dark house on a hill, for example, he artfully used the imagery of the horror movie to convey the sense that his film (a thinly veiled portrait of ambitious newspaper magnate William Randolph Hearst) would deal with the hidden and unholy. And Alfred Hitchcock often invoked the conventions of the thriller in order to make jokes. In *Strangers on the Train* (1951), the murderer and the hero's wife take a ride in an amusement park's Tunnel of Love. A shadow appears; there is a shriek. But when the pair reappears, the audience discovers that they have simply been flirting.

From the studios' perspective, genres were useful in plotting production strategy. Genre films come in cycles: On the principle that nothing succeeds like success, Hollywood would follow one box-office genre hit with many clones. Each would be refined in its own way. "It is as if with each commercial effort, the studios suggested another variation on cinematic conventions," writes Thomas Schatz, a University of Texas film scholar, "and the audience indicated whether the inventive variations would . . . be conventionalized through their repeated usage." As the audience for one genre was exhausted, the studios could then revive and promote another genre that had lain dormant for several years.

The Horror Film

During the late 1930s and early 1940s, for example, Hollywood tried, without much success, to repeat the popular horror cycle of the early Great Depression years. Makeup men busied themselves with *Son, Ghost,* and *House of Frankenstein,* as well as *Son* and *House of Dracula.* During the same era, comedians Abbott and Costello met monsters W, X, Y, and Z.

More than one film critic has seen the constant repetition and recycling in the history of popular movies as a sign that celluloid is a significant repository of contemporary myth. "When a film achieves a certain success," the French director François Truffaut observed in 1972, "it becomes a sociological event, and the question of its quality becomes secondary." Laconic cowpokes, bug-eyed monsters, singing sailors, and sinister, domineering gangsters rehearse on the screen the audience's hopes and fears, its notions of loyalty and authority, and of masculinity and femininity.

The chief preoccupations of each genre tend to change very little over time, but the inflections shift from one cycle to the next. Take the horror film. Its essential ingredient is Otherness, epitomized by a monster. Frankenstein, Dracula, and the Mummy made their screen debuts during the early 1930s, when distraction from the day-to-day difficulties of the Depression was good box office. Often, the movie monsters of the 1930s were themselves creatures of some pathos: Not a few tears were shed in movie houses over the demise of King Kong. But when Hollywood recycled the horror genre during the 1950s, the early Cold War years, things had changed. There was nothing sympathetic about the giant insects and repulsive aliens who ravaged the cinematic Earth during those years. In *The Invasion of the Body Snatchers* (1956), for example, aliens from outer space slowly infiltrate a California town, taking over the bodies of its human inhabitants. Only one telltale sign gives the aliens away: they lack emotion. The Other had become a completely repulsive force bent on dehumanizing us, a stand-in for the Soviet menace.

By the late 1960s, however, it appeared that the curtain was coming down on genre movies. Amid growing domestic disarray over the war in South Vietnam and black riots in the nation's big cities, none of the old formulas seemed to work, on the silver screen or in real life. Most clearly, there was bad news at the box office.

The 1960s: Epics and Musicals

In their perpetual quest to offer something TV could not, the studios had hit on two new high-budget genres during the early 1960s. Epic spectacles such as *Ben Hur, Lawrence of Arabia,* and *Spartacus* often seemed to use Pax Romana and Pax Britannica as metaphors for Pax Americana to illustrate the trials and tribulations of imperium. (Other epics, such as *The Longest Day* and *Fifty-Five Days at Peking,* meditated more directly on American military history.) The runaway success of *The Sound of Music*, starring Julie Andrews, in 1965 marked the apogee of a series of lavish musicals celebrating the bright optimism of the times with uplift and gaiety: *Music Man, Mary Poppins*, and *Hello Dolly*.

When the big-budget genre balloon finally burst, notably with the flop of Twentieth Century Fox's $15 million *Star!* in 1968, it blew up with a bang. In 1969 five of the Big Eight studios were deeply in the red; and Wall Street was bearish on their future.

The 1970s: "The-Small-and-Weird-Is-Beautiful" Revolution

In that same year, the year of Richard Nixon's inauguration, Hollywood witnessed the monumental success of *Easy Rider*, a low-budget motorcycle tour of America's emerging counterculture starring Peter Fonda and the then-unknown Jack Nicholson. The studios were quick to climb aboard the new bandwagon, ushering in a period of cinematic experimentation unprecedented in a half century of American film making.

Traditional genre films were thrust into the background by a slew of original offerings that included *Alice's Restaurant, Zabriskie Point, Drive, He Said, Brewster McCloud, Harold and Maude, Mean Streets, Five Easy Pieces, M*A*S*H,* and *Carnal Knowledge.*

These films reflected the nation's (or at least Hollywood's) Vietnam-afflicted, antitraditional mood. *Carnal Knowledge* was sexually explicit; *M*A*S*H*, a black satire on war; and *Harold and Maude* recounted the love affair of a teen-age boy and an eighty-year-old woman.

The films were experimental in form and composition as well as content. The plots were loosely constructed and the editing disjunctive, reflecting the influence of Jean-Luc Godard and other directors of the French New Wave.

J. Hoberman, film critic of the *Village Voice*, recently described it all as the "small-and-weird-can-be-beautiful revolution."

The most remarkable genre pictures of this period—such as *Bonnie and Clyde, McCabe and Mrs. Miller,* and *The Long Goodbye*—were not straightforward genre exercises, but self-conscious and reflective. The directors were well aware of the old formulas and turned them upside-down in order to thumb their noses at the established order. In *McCabe and Mrs. Miller* (1971), for example, Robert Altman set up McCabe as a typical Western hero, rugged individualist and founding father of a pioneer town, then exposed him as a weakling and a loser. The unrelenting hail of bullets in many of these movies echoed the domestic and international strife of the day, so the critics said; while the astounding stupidity and seediness of the new "antiheroes"

THE CRITICS

Anybody who knows anything much about current movies knows these chaps. One is tall and thin, described by his partner as "cold and detached" on camera; the other is short, a bit on the rotund side, voluble.

They are not actors. They do not even live in Hollywood. They are Gene Siskel and Roger Ebert, the odd-couple hosts of "At the Movies," a weekly half-hour syndicated TV show, based in Chicago, in which they applaud and/ or deplore Hollywood's latest offerings. And Hollywood listens. "We pore over every word," one Metro–Goldwyn–Mayer executive said a few years ago.

Few of the duo's counterparts at newspaper and magazines can claim as much influence. Movie reviews have been around since the earliest days of motion pictures, when short notices of new films began appearing in newspapers. James Agee, Vachel Lindsey, and Carl Sandburg are among the noted American writers who scratched out a living as movie reviewers at one time or another during their careers. But even during the movie-happy 1920s, the limited influence of reviewers was obvious. The general public, Sandburg flatly declared, "doesn't care about [reviewers'] recommendations."

On rare occasions, a magazine critic can alter a movie's fate at the box office—as the *New Yorker*'s Pauline Kael did when she broke with other reviewers and praised *Bonnie and Clyde* to the skies in 1967. Today, *Bonnie and Clyde* is considered a classic American hit. Eleven years later, Kael was right on target again when she dismissed *Grease* as "a bogus, clumsily jointed pastiche of late '50s high school musicals." This time, many other reviewers echoed her opinion. But millions of young Americans were eager to see John Travolta dance and romance with Olivia Newton-John, no matter what the critics said. They made *Grease* one of Hollywood's all-time money-makers.

Every week, *Variety,* in its inimitable style, mocks the judgments of the critics with reports on which movies audiences paid to see. In 1978, it reported that *Jaws II,* shrugged off by many critics, was "biting big" at the box office. The next year, the critically despised *Rocky II* was "Socky" in New York; *Heaven Can Wait* was "celestial."

The most that writers usually can hope for is to alter subtly the way Americans talk about the movies. Consider the case of Andrew Sarris, long-time film critic for Manhattan's *Village Voice*. Most moviegoers have never heard of him. But, during the 1960s, by popularizing the French auteur theory—the notion that directors are the real "authors" of movies—Sarris revolutionized the way many Americans think about films. Before Sarris, most filmgoers regarded the great Western *Rio Bravo* (1959) as a John Wayne–Dean Martin picture. Thanks to Sarris and his influence on other critics, many would now say that *Rio Bravo* is a Howard Hawks film.

If he were starting out today, however, Sarris and his opinions would not go very far. Critics' theories do not play well on television. And, since Siskel and Ebert made their first appearance in 1976, a host of local and network TV imitators have taken to the airwaves, diminishing further the influence of newspaper and magazine commentators. The Chicago partners, with more than 10 million viewers, remain the undisputed kings of the aisle. They have also become stars in their own right, with each probably earning upwards of $500,000.

The opinions of print reviewers are still (selectively) quoted in movie ads. But the scribes cannot hope to match the audiences and influence of their TV counterparts. And the studios know that. They cater to the TV folk by delivering conveniently packaged film clips of their latest releases, hoping for a few precious seconds of airtime, even if the critics turn thumbs down on the picture. What matters most to Hollywood is public attention of almost any kind—*then* favorable word-of-mouth. As the old Hollywood saying goes, "All publicity is good publicity."

Douglas Gomery

---

made it hard to tell who wore the white hats and who wore the black ones.

This is not to say that "experimental" and revisionist genre features monopolized the nation's movies screens. Hollywood still churned out standardized Westerns (*The Stalking Moon*) and cops-and-robbers pictures (notably, *Bullitt* and *The French Connection*). These films too, indirectly reflected popular anxieties about the war against evil, foreign and domestic. In Clint Eastwood's *Dirty Harry,* a San Francisco cop deals with a psychotic terrorist named Scorpio the old-fashioned way: He kills him. And a spate of disaster films—*The Poseidon Adventure, Airport, Skyjacked, Earthquake,* and *The Towering Inferno*—exploited the theme of entrapment, whose political and social correlates were easy to identify.

But these efforts were the exception. For a time experimentation thrived, commanding much greater critical and public attention than the more pedestrian genre offerings.

The 1980s: Return to the Genre

It was an unexpected string of blockbuster hits—William Friedkin's *The Exorcist* in 1973, Steven Spielberg's *Jaws* in 1975, and then George Lucas's *Star Wars* two years later—that sent Hollywood producers rushing back to genre films. Or, as one film title later put it, back to the future.

One by one, the blockbusters slowly rose to high rank on *Variety*'s list of all-time hits. Indeed, today all of *Variety*'s Top Ten are movies made since 1975.

The success of these genre features underscored the fact that movie audiences had changed. No longer was Hollywood mainly in the business of offering entertainment for all ages: More than half of the people lining up at the theaters were under twenty-five, many of them teen-agers. The older folks were staying home with TV. "If Hollywood keeps gearing movie after movie to teen-agers," quipped comedian–director Mel Brooks, "next year's Oscar will develop acne."

Youth was also making its mark in Hollywood. Spielberg (who was twenty-four when he agreed to make *Jaws*) and Lucas were among the first "movie brats," a new cadre of young film makers who were beginning to make their way up the Hollywood ladder when *Jaws* swam onto the scene.[2] Raised in the age of television, the newcomers had watched endless late-night reruns of Hollywood's trash and treasures. Many were also trained in university film schools when the reigning form of criticism, *auteurism,* accorded special emphasis to such Hollywood classics as Hitchcock's *Psycho* and John Ford's *The Searchers.* In the view of the auteur critics, Hollywood's previously unrecognized contract directors were maestros of film who made sharp personal statements in their works. The new directors were more than ready to follow in their footsteps.

Whatever else might be said of these film makers—that, as some critics contend, their works are clever but often empty—they know their craft. Spielberg, Lucas, and company can put the old genres through their paces with awesome precision, invent new plot twists, graft old tricks into contemporary subject matter, and combine genres into new alloys.

But that is not all that they do. Often, the works of these new directors contain sly and not-so-sly allusions to film history—a camera movement here, the re-creation of a famous scene there. *Time* said of *Star Wars* that it was "a subliminal history of the movies wrapped in a riveting tale of suspense and adventure." The new genre films often appear to have been designed with two audiences in mind: the connoisseurs on the lookout for "scholarly" references, and a mass of younger viewers in search of thrills.

One of the first genres to reappear was horror. Revived by the success of *The Exorcist,* which generated a half-dozen spinoffs, the trend did not appear long for this world. However, *Jaws* and *The Omen,* with its Grand Guignol stagings of stylized murders, gave the cycle a second push. Every kind of monster that audiences had ever seen rose up from its Hollywood grave: werewolves (*The Howling, American Werewolf in London*), vampires (*Dracula, Lifeforce, The Hunger, Fright Night*), psychics (*Firestarter*), and zombies (*Dawn of the Dead, The Fog*). With *The Car* and *Christine,* the studios added a new family of monsters to the Hollywood immortals: old cars.

Many of these movies share the same basic plot structure. First the monster appears, committing ghastly atrocities (the shark's mauling of a young girl in *Jaws*). Next, someone (the boy next door in *Fright Night*) discovers the agent of death (a vampire, in this case). Then, he or she must convince unbelievers that there really are vampires, big sharks, or whatever. And together the good guys go off to confront the monster in a final showdown.

This kind of plot seems to appeal to young audiences because it is a kind of parable about growing up. It highlights the discovery of hidden knowledge, while also dramatizing a moment when adults are finally forced to listen seriously to the young. And many horror films stress biological deformity and Otherness, thus broaching adolescent anxieties about the body.

Sometimes just the act of viewing a film can be a kind of rite of passage for teen-age boys: Are you man enough to sit through a gruesome "slasher" film, such as *Halloween, Friday the 13th* and its sequels, or *Prom Night,* or an even gorier "splatter" film like *Scanners* or *The Evil Dead?*[3]

Space Operas and Rites of Passage

A sizable share of the current menu of science fiction offerings—such as *Alien, The Thing,* and *The Dark*—are really horror films, films about monsters. They are classified as sci-fi only because their monsters hail from outer space. A new twist in this old genre is the beatific, in contrast to horrific, sci-fi movie: *Close Encounters of the Third Kind, E.T.,* and *Cocoon.* These films, with their friendly extraterrestrials, confirm the adolescent wish for a universe filled with warm and compassionate beings.

Even more appealing to teen-age audiences is that these pictures involve quests or rites of passage. *The Last Starfighter,* for example, not only enacts the notion of a trial in cosmic proportions but exploits the desire of every girl and boy to escape the humdrum world of school and family. Because of his prowess in video games, Alex, otherwise an ordinary earthling boy-next-door, is drafted by the Star League of Planets to defeat the forces of the traitorous Xur.

The projection of adolescent fantasies onto big screens does not happen by accident. When Lucas was working on the script of *Star Wars,* he recalls, "I researched kids' movies and how they work and how myths work." "Do not call this film 'science fiction,'" he told the marketing men at Twentieth Century Fox. "It's a space fantasy."

The commercial success of the space operas spawned several variants built around the quest and rite-of-passage themes. In the sword-and-sorcery genre—*Excalibur,* the *Conan* series, and, in twentieth-century garb, *Time Bandits* and *Raiders of the Lost Ark*—swords and whips replace ray guns, and magic, science. The *Mad Max* series depicts a postapocalyptic world cloaked in imagery of the Dark Ages. Castles and chargers are made out of old cars, the barbarians are at the gates, and the spark of civilized life hinges on the outcome of stock car races between knights in punk regalia.

Today's comedies are not much closer to reality. With the exception of such sex farces as *10* and *Unfaithfully Yours,* both starring Dudley Moore, most of them are keyed to younger sensibilities. This is apparent in the flurry of films about high school romance, often in a light comic mood (*Sixteen Candles, Risky Business*). It is even more obvious in the aggressive irreverence of the gross-out/fraternity-house humor of *Animal House* (and its numerous progeny) and the Burt Reynolds redneck car films. When they decide to sabotage their college homecoming parade with "a really futile, stupid gesture," Bluto and his *Animal House* brothers sum up the new comedy's attitude toward adult values.

Physical humor—slapstick, sight gags, and comic chases—has also gained a new lease on life. But the same sense of unreality prevails. Slapstick shares several traits with science fiction and supernatural films. All three genres demand the suspension of the laws of physical probability: the world becomes a kind of playground. In Woody Allen's *Zelig,* for example, a man metamorphoses into whomever he is with; in *The Purple Rose of Cairo,* a character steps off a movie screen that the characters are watching. This assault on the reality principle is so extreme that it verges on vulgar surrealism in films such as *The Blues Brothers,* the *Cheech and Chong* series, and *Pee Wee's Big Adventure.*

Fantasy prevails even when the settings seem real. In 1976 Sylvester Stallone restored the power of positive thinking to the screen with *Rocky,* a story about a "ham 'n egg" prize fighter who nearly wins the heavyweight boxing crown from the glamorous Apollo Creed. *Rocky* paved the way for a slew of uplifting sports films, of which Britain's *Chariots of Fire* is aesthetically the most noteworthy, as well as success stories about all sorts of down-and-outers, such as *The Verdict.*

There have been three *Rocky* sequels so far, all of them exercises in improbability. In *Rocky IV,* a boxing match becomes the solution to East–West tensions. Some of the most effective wish-fulfillment films, such as *Breaking Away* and *The Karate Kid,* have adolescents in the leading role. And, of course, the resurgence of the teen musical, spearheaded by *Saturday Night Fever, Fame,* and *Flashdance,* owes much to the success-story motif.

The darker side of adolescent fantasy is evident in Stallone's two *Rambo* pictures. The Rambo movies have several ingredients that make them especially compelling to young audiences: the figure of the misunderstood loner, and the themes of betrayal and revenge. In *Rambo: First Blood, Part II,* the Pentagon dispatches Rambo back to Vietnam to rescue American soldiers who have been declared "missing in action" (MIA). But then officialdom deserts him, claiming that there are no MIAs. So he uses his perfect, high-school-weightlifter's body to execute unstoppable rampages, leading his MIAs back to the United States over the dead bodies of scores of his foes. On the screen, Rambo transforms teen-agers' feelings of alienation and frustration into cinematic delusions of grandeur.

Of course, Hollywood has always emphasized escapism. Yet, it is astounding what a high percentage of its products today are literally fantasy films—horror, sci-fi, and absurdist comedies—or, in the case of *Rocky* and its kin, psychological fantasies. Even during the Great Depression, the heyday of Hollywood escapism, the studios released a fair number of gritty "realistic" pictures. But *The Grapes of Wrath* has no real counterpart today. *The Color Purple,* Steven Spielberg's effort to explore the unhappy history of the black family in America, was filmed like a fairy tale. *Country* and *The River,* two recent films that dramatized the plight of the nation's farmers, were thoroughly drenched in sentimentality. And there were many empty seats in the theaters where they were shown.

In Hollywood, there is never too much of a good thing. Each of Sylvester Stallone's Rocky *movies has earned more than $40 million at the box office.*

Lucas and the other new university-trained directors, with only a few notable exceptions, are no more interested in the "real world" than are their audiences. During the 1970s they set out to rescue their heroes—not only Alfred Hitchcock and Howard Hawks, but also Superman and Flash Gordon—from critical contempt and oblivion. In their eyes, the Hollywood genre movie was one of America's great art forms: How could so many people fail to see that?

In a sense, the movie brats have accomplished their revivalist mission in grand style. Indeed, they have managed to achieve a level of financial success and celebrity beyond the imaginings of their predecessors. But now they have nothing left to do. Movies have become the subject of movies, as though the most vital elements in our contemporary environment are representations and images rather than the "real world."

If today's directors are paid handsomely to indulge themselves, it is because their audiences make it profitable for the studios to sign the checks. And the youthful ticket-buying public seems to find more comfort and authenticity in honey-spun fantasy films than in those that confront political and social themes or simply dramatize the often painful realities of everyday life. Until the nation's movie audiences change their minds, Hollywood is sure to travel ever deeper into its past in search of its future.

NOTES

1. The word *genre* comes from the Latin *genus,* a kind or a sort, a category based on regularly recurring patterns. Westerns, for example, repeat certain settings (the American West in the nineteenth century), action (gun-fights), and certain hero–villain plot structures. But there is no one set of criteria for identifying genres. A Western must be set in the West, but a musical can be set in any time or place, as long as there is singing and dancing. A *film noir,* on the other hand, has more specific demands: a downbeat mood, signaled by dark lighting and rain-slick streets, a contemporary setting, and a pessimistic plot line. Horror films, to cite a final example, are named after the emotion they provoke.

2. The directors and their credits include: Joe Dante (*Gremlins*); Brian De Palma (*Body Double*); Tobe Hooper (*Poltergeist* and *Lifeforce*); Lawrence Kasdan (*Body Heat* and *Silverado*); John Landis (*National Lampoon's Animal House* and *The Blues Brothers*); Nicholas Meyer (*Star Trek II: The Wrath of Khan*); Irving Reitman (*Ghostbusters*) and Robert Zemeckis (*Romancing the Stone* and *Back to the Future.*)

3. "Slasher" films, in the tradition of *Psycho,* are those in which victims are done in by knives and axes. "Splatter" movies take advantage of sophisticated new special effects: victims either explode on-screen or deteriorate in gruesome ways.

Chapter 10

THE AVANT-GARDE

by David Bordwell

If Louis B. Mayer, the Hollywood mogul, had lived until the late 1960s, he would have been startled by some of the changes in the tastes of movie-going Americans.

True, the lines would have been longest at theaters offering such easily recognizable Hollywood fare as *Dr. Dolittle* or *Paint Your Wagon.* But in the larger cities and college towns, a good many movie fans would have been elsewhere. Some would have been thronging local "art" theaters to see Ingmar Bergman's *The Hour of the Wolf* or Luis Buñuel's *Viridiana.* Others would have been at the museum watching experimental works by Stan Brakhage or Andy Warhol. And the local campus film society might have been packing them in with Jean-Luc Godard's *Weekend,* a savage denunciation of bourgeois lifestyles.

Most Americans were (and are) still going to the movies to be entertained. But the emergence after World War II of a big new generation of college graduates—some of them with film appreciation courses under their belts, many with some exposure to modernism in the arts—created a sizable audience in the United States for experimental films.

The Illusion–Reality Theme

Such films were nothing new. Almost as soon as it was born, cinema encountered modernism. The meeting occurred not in the

125

Hollywood studios but, during the 1920s, in the cafes of Paris and Berlin and the chilly meeting rooms of Moscow. Painters were attracted to cinema by its capacity to become what one artist called "drawings brought to life." Composers found its dynamic movement and montage a counterpart of musical rhythm. For artists in many fields, the new medium represented modernity itself. "Most forms of representation have had their day," declared Antonin Artaud, the French poet and founder of the "theater of cruelty," in 1930. "Life, what we call life, becomes ever more inseparable from the mind. The cinema is capable of interpreting this domain more than any other art, because idiotic order and customary clarity are its enemies."

It was thus not simply the technical side of cinema that appealed to modernist artists. Cinema was an ideal vehicle for the modernist urge to question the solidity of reality, to probe the way the world seems to the beholder.

Among the first film makers to take this approach was Germany's Robert Wiene, in *The Cabinet of Dr. Caligari* (1920). With remarkable sets painted in the expressionist style, the film conveyed the hallucinatory vision of a madman named Francis. Only in the end is it revealed that Dr. Caligari is the warden of the insane asylum where Francis is an inmate. Yet the audience is led to wonder whether there is some larger metaphorical truth about society in the hallucinations of the madman. This theme is well-worn today, but it was novel in its time. Not until after World War II did the probing of psychic ambiguity become a common theme for movie makers.

And there were other ambiguities. A samurai has been killed and his wife raped; a bandit has confessed. So much is fact. Yet, through flashbacks, the wife, the bandit, and a witness each present a different version of events. Was the rape resisted? Did the samurai fight bravely, or did he try to flee? That is the substance of Akira Kurosawa's *Rashomon* (1951), which inaugurated the illusion–reality theme in post–World War II cinema. Although considered "too Western" in Japan, the film had an enormous impact in the West—not least for its refusal to answer the riddles it posed. The audience never learns the truth; Kurosawa suggests that each version *is* the truth, at least to each character.

The inquiry into the relativity of perception preoccupied a whole generation of European film makers during the 1950s and 1960s. In *Wild Strawberries* (1957), Sweden's Ingmar Bergman used flashbacks to detail an old man's nostalgic revision of his past. Later, in *Persona* (1966), Bergman merged almost seamlessly the chaotic dreams of a

In a scene from Robert Wiene's hallucinatory The Cabinet of Dr. Caligari *(1920), Caligari's hypnotized servant, Cesare, looms over one of his victims. Many film critics argue that Cesare represented the "enslaved" German working class.*

nurse on the edge of a nervous breakdown with his portrayal of her reality. Bergman suggests that film making itself is as mysterious and impenetrable as the lives he portrays:

> The illuminated face, the hand raised as if for an incantation, the old ladies at the square, the few banal words, all of these images come and attach themselves like silvery fish to my net; or, more precisely, I myself am trapped in a net, the texture of which I am not aware.

Federico Fellini's lively *8½* (1963) advanced the theme further with its hero, a harried movie director whose memories and fantasies are filtered through film conventions and cliches. Fellini thus introduced a reflection upon cinema itself, the machine for producing realistic-seeming illusions. Just as Pablo Picasso's work questioned realistic conceptions of painting, so such films as *Rashomon* and *8½* challenged the "customary clarities" of the Hollywood film. As Alain Resnais, codirector of *Hiroshima Mon Amour* (1959), put it,

> My aim is to put the spectator in such a state that a week, six months, or a year afterwards, placed before a problem, he would be prevented from cheating and be obliged to react freely.

Cinematic Visions of Light and Form

But Resnais and his colleagues clung to the belief that a film should tell a story. Other modernists, not only in film, were going a step further, deemphasizing story telling, or even eliminating it altogether. They aimed to draw the audience's attention to the medium itself, to the tangible patterns of words, gestures, and scenes. The idea originated in modern painting. Some painters, such as the Soviet constructivist Vladimir Tatlin (1885–1953), held that doing away with "stories" would return the spectator to a state of innocent perception, allowing him to see the elements of art clearly. Artists of a more mystical turn believed that the purist approach could provide a glimpse of the ineffable—what Kazimir Malevich (1878–1935), inventor of the school of abstract geometric painting known as suprematism, called "the semaphore of light across an infinite abyss."

Malevich's ideas were echoed after World War II in the work of young directors influenced by abstract expressionist painting. In the films of Missouri-born Stan Brakhage, perhaps the most important

American avant-gardist of his generation, the "story" is no more than an episode from his personal life or a sketchy mythic formula, transformed into a purely cinematic vision of flickering hues, flowing shapes, and endlessly changing views of mundane objects. In *Scenes from under Childhood* (1967), Brakhage produced the most poetic of home movies. He interspersed photos from a family album with images of domestic activity, as well as with superimpositions, reflections, and other distortions, to suggest the lyrical deformations of memory. In *The Text of Light* (1974), he put an ordinary ashtray close to his camera lens to create a startling play of color and shape.

The classic example of the "purist" avant-garde is probably Michael Snow's *Wavelength* (1967). *Wavelength* tells a "story," but it is completely fragmented. The scene is a New York loft: People come and go, play a radio, answer a phone call. Perhaps a murder is committed. But the film is organized around a camera technique. The camera is in a fixed position. Snow's zoom lens begins with a long shot inside the loft and jerkily enlarges the room little by little until the distant wall fills the frame to reveal a photograph of ocean waves. The film's forty-five-minute duration is thus revealed as a "wavelength."

As the frame enlarges, the audience is invited to play a perception guessing game. How will the shot's composition change? Will the fragments of story ever coalesce? Snow's explanation of *Wavelength* shows that his intentions were purely abstract:

> The image of the yellow chair has as much "value" in its own world as the girl closing the window. The film events are . . . chosen from a kind of scale of mobility that runs from pure light events, the various perceptions of the room, to the images of moving human beings.

Issues and Innovation

To which playwright Bertolt Brecht (1898–1956), another father figure of modernism, would have replied that art is about society, not just light and figures. The political and rhetorical uses of film technique had been pioneered during the 1920s by a group of young Soviet film makers, notably Sergei Eisenstein in *Strike* (1925) and *Potemkin* (1925). Four decades later, it was to Brecht and the Soviets that young leftist film makers turned to merge experimentation with social criticism.

From the Soviets they adopted the notion that film should not passively copy reality but challenge it through disjunctive editing, explicit commentary, and by allowing audiences to see that scenes have been staged. From Brecht came the "estrangement effect," the notion that by calling attention to the mechanics of presentation instead of concealing them Hollywood-style, actors and directors could make audiences think critically about what they were seeing.

This trend shows clearly in the work of the West German film-making team of Jean-Marie Straub and Danile Huillet. In *Not Reconciled* (1965), they depicted a fascist specter haunting Germany by interrupting scenes from the daily life of a contemporary family with an elliptical series of flashbacks to Germany during the two world wars. The characters are barely identified; the chronology of events is unclear. The camera dwells ominously on empty spaces, as if waiting for the hidden meaning of history to emerge. *History Lessons* (1972), adapted from a Brecht novel, uses anachronism to make viewers think about the links between economic and political power. Set amid the ruins of imperial Rome, it is a portrait of Julius Caesar, busily juggling state business with the pursuit of private profit, drawn largely through fake TV interviews with his toga-clad colleagues.

From Soho to Paris, today's film makers are still experimenting with these three modernist "traditions": the illusion–reality theme, the purely cinematic statement, and the political critique built on innovative film techniques. Raul Ruiz traces the convolutions of memory and misunderstanding in such elusive films as *Three Crowns of the Sailor* (1983). The American film maker Jim Jarmusch, in *Stranger Than Paradise* (1984), dramatizes his portrait of three wandering down-and-outers with a rigorous, almost mathematical use of framing and editing. Hans-Jurgen Syberberg's *Our Hitler: A Film from Germany* (1977) uses Brechtian techniques to trace the links between Germany's Wagnerian romanticism and the rise of Hitler.

In recent years, many avant-garde film makers have trimmed their sails a bit. During the late 1970s, younger directors like Wim Wenders and Rainer Werner Fassbinder (1946–82), raised on a steady diet of Hollywood classics, created a more popular "art cinema." With his parodies of the early Frankenstein and Dracula movies, Andy Warhol moved into straightforward feature film making, and several experimentalists have followed. Even Bruce Connor, master of the surreal compilation film, now makes commercial music videos for Devo and other rock groups. And many directors with a political message have set off in search of larger audiences, a trend best seen in such films as the popular *Night of the Shooting Stars* (1982), about Italy's internal wrestling with fascism during World War II, by the brothers Vittorio and Paolo Taviani.

The relationship between avant-garde and popular cinema is, as always, complex. The Hollywood classics of the 1930s and 1940s, for example, inspired the experiments of the French New Wave directors of the 1950s, which influenced the young directors who began arriving in Hollywood during the late 1960s. The makers of popular horror and science fiction movies, always in search of new cinematic shocks, are quick to exploit new avant-garde techniques.

At the moment, the avant-garde is in a bit of a lull. But there remains a large and growing audience, ready to welcome all manner of films that would have been unthinkable during the heyday of the Hollywood studio system. The experimentalists are sure to thrive.

The work of Jean-Luc Godard perfectly exemplifies the fluctuations and adjustments within the alternative cinema. From New Wave cinephilia during the early 1960s, he shifted to strident and forbidding Marxist works later in the decade, and then to serene, voluptuous studies like *Passion* (1982). In 1987 he released *Hail Mary,* a mystical retelling of the Virgin Birth in contemporary times. It is anything but conventional.

To many film connoisseurs, Godard is the symbol of cinematic modernism's vitality. The twisting path of his career suggests that there is always a new avenue for experimentation, that many possibilities remain open to avant-garde film makers imaginative enough to seek them out. An exasperated inquisitor once demanded of Godard: "But surely you will admit that a film must have a beginning, a middle, and an end?"

"Certainly," he replied. "But not necessarily in that order."

Chapter 11

WE ARE NOT ALONE

by Frank D. McConnell

At one point in Graham Greene's *The Confidential Agent,* the hero—a hunted spy—hides out in a movie theater. A nondescript Hollywood romance is on the screen, but the hero discovers in it a significance deeper than any intended by its makers: "It was as if some code of faith or morality had been lost for centuries, and the world was trying to reconstruct it from the unreliable evidence of folk memories and subconscious desires."

A splendid film critic in his own right, Greene realized that the movie comes closer than any other product of our culture to the happy status of the novel in Victorian England. It is at once attuned to individual human concerns and sensitive to the daydreams of the masses. And, a rarity in this century of lugubriously self-conscious art, the movies are genuinely fun.

That is why they have taken so long to be accepted as a legitimate object of study in the university. American academics, good Calvinists all, have operated for years on the assumption that Kulchur (as poet Ezra Pound contemptuously called it) should hurt, at least a little; that there must be a gulf between esthetics and entertainment. This attitude was concisely captured by the turn-of-the-century wit who said of Wagnerian music, "It's better than it sounds." By contrast, our best "serious" novelists and poets have understood that we live in a creative and often profoundly humanizing popular culture—and that much of this culture is stored on celluloid.

The Mythology of Film

American literature of the twentieth century is filled with writers who built their vision of America upon a vision of Hollywood: F. Scott Fitzgerald in *The Last Tycoon,* Norman Mailer in *The Deer Park,* and Saul Bellow in *Humboldt's Gift.* Others, like Brock Brower in *The Late Great Creature,* and especially Thomas Pynchon in his towering novel *Gravity's Rainbow,* have begun using not simply the fact but also the basic themes and myths of popular film genres in their work. To understand *Gravity's Rainbow,* for example, it is not sufficient to have a background in modern fiction and physics. One must also understand that this awesome tale, which seeks refuge in fantasy from the terrors of the modern city, swings unfailingly and recognizably between the extremes of *King Kong* and *The Wizard of Oz.*

The popular film, of course, is not of value simply because it prepares us to read Brower, Pynchon, and the rest. The serious celluloid fairy-tale genres—science fiction, melodrama, the Western— are much like officially sanctioned myths; their formulas are predictable. At the same time, these formulas undergo subtle shifts with time. To understand these shifts is, in its way, to excavate that mental city we all inhabit privately—and in common.

As Norman Mailer wrote in his 1961 open letter to President Kennedy on the Bay of Pigs invasion: "I can't believe the enormity of your mistake: You invade a country without understanding its music." Substitute "movies" for "music" and one comes close to stating the necessity of understanding film. In movies that catch the popular imagination, we see ourselves as in a funhouse mirror: distorted, yes, but distorted in a way that reveals more than photographic accuracy ever could. For it reveals who—and where—we really are, what we want and want to believe.

Rocky: *A Western for the Eighties*

It is widely believed, for example, that our post-Vietnam, post-Watergate mood is one of moderate self-congratulation. But what is the real shape of this mood? How do we, in our film daydreams, project the new confidence in ourselves we think we have earned? Sylvester Stallone's *Rocky* is a film of obsessively unbounded optimism. It insists so strenuously that everything will be all right that we are forced to ask: What is it that we were afraid would go wrong?

The continually implied and finally averted possibility of disaster in *Rocky* is the failure of community. Rocky Balboa is a never-was, a club fighter in the Italian neighborhood of Philadelphia who supplements his scanty fight earnings by breaking bones for the local loan shark, a nobody whose great romance is with the clerk in the neighborhood pet store, a drab girl named Adrian.

In a bizarre public relations gimmick, Rocky is selected to fight heavyweight champion Apollo Creed on the Fourth of July. The whole community falls in behind him, helps him train, gives him money, lets him pound away on beef carcasses. The night before the fight, Rocky tells Adrian he wants, if not to win, at least to go the full fifteen rounds. "If I can do that, I'll know I wasn't just another bum from the neighborhood." He lasts the fifteen rounds, losing to Creed only by a split decision. At that moment, bruised, bloodied, exhausted, he is able to tell Adrian, for the first time, "I love you."

Sentimental, of course, but intelligently so. We can trust it because it is so aware of its own sentimentality. Rocky begins as a lonely man trying to be a lonely hero. He discovers that he becomes a hero when he stops being alone. The film is a celebration of the single man who redeems the honor of his town.

It is, in other words, a Western. For in the Western—despite the bitter inversion of such films as *High Noon* (where the town abandons the hero) or *The Magnificent Seven* (in which the Seven are driven from the town they save)—our hopes for the tiny communities of the film West are always, implicitly, our hopes for the larger community in which we all live. Main Street is always Main Street, and *Rocky*, complete with final showdown, simply translates the myths into elementary terms. It tells us that little people can survive, but only if they are faithful to each other.

Star Wars: *The Possibility of Heroism*

George Lucas's *Star Wars* makes the assertion in a different key. Far from simply a science-fiction adventure, this highly self-conscious film is a virtual history of past motifs, situations, and even characteristic bits of dialogue from old Westerns, swashbucklers, war movies, and of course, science-fiction movies. Ontogeny recapitulates phylogeny, at least on the celluloid level.

This does not mean that *Star Wars* is "camp"—to use that shibboleth of critics who are excited by popular works they don't understand. Like *Rocky, Star Wars* is an experiment to see if the myths of popular culture have any life left in them. That these myths are still alive is reflected by nothing so much as the movie's phenomenal success—in cold cash ($500 million), the most successful film in history. And for all its self-consciousness and formula predictability, it is a serious film about the possibility of heroism, not within a community but within our own imagination: Can we still believe in ourselves as heroes?

A hero, after all, is a corny thing to be; a century of psychoanalysis, sociology, and political science has taught us that. But *Star Wars,* great popular myth that it is, reminds us that the corniness of heroism, like that of love or honor, does not render it less important. The real "force" behind the famous *Star Wars* blessing—"May the Force be with you"—is that of fairy tales and their power to humanize even after we no longer believe in their literal reality.

Close Encounters: *Everyman and a Vision of Transcendence*

If *Star Wars* attempts to revivify some of the oldest conventions in the movies, Steven Spielberg's *Close Encounters of the Third Kind* does something more subtle, risky, and important. A resolutely popular myth, it is also an uncanny critique of the relationship between popular mythology and our nostalgia for the sublime—for a desire to believe, as the film's advertising copy says, that We Are Not Alone. Roy Neary, the Indiana electrical worker who sees a UFO and is thereafter compelled to visit the site where the alien visitors will show themselves, is a modern Everyman who in his boredom and confusion has become obsessed by a vision of transcendence—a terrible thing to experience, as St. Paul told us long before director Spielberg got around to it.

But Neary is an Everyman whose vision is itself shaped by the pop mythologies of transcendence that surround us. When we first see him, he is watching television: watching Cecil B. De Mille's *The Ten Commandments,* that earlier translation of miracle into special effects, of transcendence into kitsch. Later, his daughter watches a Bugs Bunny cartoon about invaders from Mars. And in the climactic sequence, when the UFOs land and speak to us, they speak through a lovely, funny jazz fugue, transforming the giant mother ship into a cosmic synthesizer playing the Muzak of the spheres.

The point is not that *Close Encounters* is a pop gospel of transfiguration. It is something better, an examination of our lives as already transcending their own limitations, if only we can understand our own daydreams. We are not alone because we speak to one another—and nowhere at a deeper level than through the mythology of film.

To say this much implies that the hieroglyphics of popular myths are at once naive and highly sophisticated about their own naivete. For they rediscover the dignity of cliches and tell us again and again what we can never hear too often: We are most human not in despair or self-loathing but in shared laughter and delight—when, indeed, we are having fun.

Chapter 12

A FOOTNOTE TO HISTORY:
MGM MEETS THE ATOMIC BOMB

by Nathan Reingold

In February 1947, barely eighteen months after an American-made atomic bomb known as Little Boy leveled the Japanese city of Hiroshima, Metro-Goldwyn-Mayer released to the world what would today be called a "docudrama" about the making and deployment of that bomb. It was the first such movie of the atomic age, the first full-length feature film describing what *Life* magazine called the "biggest event since the birth of Christ."

In theaters across the United States, before millions of moviegoers, the MGM lion growled his customary two growls. Below his mane appeared the company's celebrated motto: *Ars Gratia Artis,* "Art For Art's Sake." Then came what purported to be a newsreel, showing canisters of film—supposedly, copies of the film that the audience was about to see—being buried in a grove of California redwoods.

"A message to future generations!" the voice-over proclaimed. "Come what may, our civilization will have left an enduring record behind it. Ours will be no lost race."

Thus began *The Beginning or the End,* Hollywood's ambitious and ultimately ill-starred portrayal of the World War II Manhattan Project and the people behind it.

No one man or woman was responsible for the way this motion picture turned out (badly). Then as now, docudrama film making in Hollywood involved a triad of conflicting interests: the commercial

139

hopes of the producers, the perceived demands of a mass audience for entertainment, and the personal qualms of the participants in the events described in the film. Taken together, these proved to be a recipe for a fiasco, in terms of both historical veracity and box-office receipts.

Happily, we can reconstruct what happened, thanks to a legal requirement that no longer exists. In order to depict living, well-known public figures, MGM had to secure their permission in writing. These individuals, in turn, often demanded the right to review the script. The result is a vast harvest of correspondence scattered among MGM files, the National Archives, the Library of Congress, and various universities. The letters, along with the film, supply a bizarre footnote to the dawn of the atomic age.[1]

The idea for *The Beginning or the End* grew out of contacts between MGM producer Sam Marx and members of the so-called atomic scientists' movement, a group of young, liberal, rather antimilitary Manhattan Project alumni who hoped to educate the lay public about the nature of atomic weapons and their disturbing implications for both domestic and foreign policy. (The movement soon developed into the Federation of American Scientists.) Edward R. Tompkins of the Clinton Laboratories, now the Oak Ridge National Laboratory, in Tennessee, seems to have been the first to suggest the idea of a movie—in a letter to a former high school student of his, actress Donna Reed, who brought the concept to MGM's attention. MGM eventually paid Tompkins a modest honorarium of $100.

Sam Marx was as much in awe of the new atomic weapons technology as the scientists were of Hollywood; initially, at least, Marx approached the subject of the bomb with unusual care. During the autumn of 1945, in preparation for his film, the producer visited the Clinton Laboratories and on the same swing east visited Harry S Truman in Washington. MGM officials later assured the president that "a great service to civilization" might be done if "the right kind of film could be made."

Mixing Fact with Fiction

High-minded though its intentions were, MGM faced a forbidding challenge: how to present complex, often cerebral, feats of science and engineering in a way that American audiences would sit through, without fidgeting, for 120 minutes. Then as now, the solution, inevita-

"They held in their hands the fate of millions!" The stars of MGM's **The Beginning** or the End; *from left, Robert Walker, Audrey Totter, Tom Drake, and Beverly Tyler, pose for a publicity photo.*

bly, was to veer, often sharply, from factual accuracy in the interest of entertainment.

Screenwriters Robert Considine and Frank Wead, abetted by Marx and by director Norman Taurog, added several fictional characters and the mandatory "love interest" to the story. To build tension, they depicted the Manhattan Project as a race pitting America against both the Germans and the Japanese, who were said to be nearing completion of their own atomic bombs. (In reality, there had been little concern about Japan.) The film makers invented numerous other aspects of both nuclear technology and the development of the Manhattan Project.

The members of the atomic scientists' movement, active in shaping the script during its early stages—they naively hoped to determine its point of view and, through a substantial contribution from MGM, to swell their organization's meager coffers—withdrew their cooperation when they saw what Hollywood was doing to the story. In the opinion of Sam Marx, who did not want his film to be "a big, long speech for world government," this was just as well.

The scientist-activists withdrew with the expectation that the senior scientists and military men in the Manhattan Project, people such as J. Robert Oppenheimer, General Leslie R. Groves, Vannevar Bush, and James B. Conant, would likewise withhold their endorsements. In this they proved to be, for the most part, wrong.

Why? One reason was that some of the key military participants in the Manhattan Project had already accepted fees from MGM—$10,000 in the case of General Groves—in return for their permission to be depicted on film. For their part, many of the important scientists (none of whom accepted money) seem to have assumed that helping the film makers was a professional obligation. Moreover, only by cooperating could the Manhattan Project's "big shots" exercise any control over the film's content. MGM's need to get waivers gave all of them a certain leverage that the younger, unknown scientists did not possess.

To be sure, the senior Manhattan Project personnel protested the direction in which the movie appeared to be heading when, in the spring of 1946, the first screenplay was sent to most of them for approval. MGM, in response, agreed to make some small changes. Some of the scientists protested once more after viewing the first completed film version in autumn of the same year. Once again MGM made some changes. But when it came to what the studio insisted was a matter of both artistic principle and commercial necessity, MGM stood its ground.

In the words of an MGM memo passed on to Albert Einstein by studio head Louis B. Mayer in 1946, "It must be realized that dramatic truth is just as compelling a requirement on us as veritable truth is on a scientist." The studio reminded General Groves, who headed the Manhattan Project in its later stages, that MGM was not an endowed institution "like Harvard" but a commercial enterprise. The requirements of "dramatic truth" helped shape the film into a familiar narrative form with stock characters and stock situations.

In the original screenplay, the movie begins with J. Robert Oppenheimer (who would be played by Hume Cronyn) recounting the flight of physicist Lise Meitner from Berlin when Nazis overrun her laboratory in 1938. She takes refuge with Nobel laureate Niels Bohr in Denmark. Soon, word of the pair's work in nuclear fission reaches America; Albert Einstein, at the behest of a fictional physicist named Matt Cochran (played by Tom Drake), writes his historic 1939 letter to Franklin D. Roosevelt suggesting the theoretical possibility of constructing an atomic bomb. An Office of Scientific Research and Development (OSRD) is set up, leading to physicist Enrico Fermi's first controlled chain reaction at the University of Chicago's Stagg Field in 1941. ("Dr. Fermi, scientifically detached from the world, enters," reads the screenplay.)

Among the scientists at Stagg Field, the fictional Cochran is the most vocal in airing doubts about going forward with the atomic bomb. His concerns are typically dismissed out of hand. ("Get it done before the Germans and the Japs, then worry about the bomb," he is told.) After the successful experiment at Chicago's Metallurgical Laboratory, a small group of scientists is shown resigning from the bomb project; both correspondence and the script make it clear that these men were intended to be perceived as Quakers. The walkout, which never occurred, gives the Enrico Fermi character an opportunity to say: "Sometimes, it takes greater principles to stay than to go." In general, *The Beginning or the End* slides over issues of morality that some atomic scientists at Stagg Field, hardly pacifists, debated intensely among themselves.

Skipping over much important scientific work of the period, the screenplay shifts to the domain of the Manhattan Engineer District, which superseded the OSRD. General Groves (played by Brian Donlevy) is shown exhorting industry to support the weapons effort. We see the DuPont representative grandly waive all potential patent rights, an easy position for DuPont to take fictionally since the real Leslie Groves and Vannevar Bush would never have let atomic weapons technology fall into private hands. The movie screen bustles with a panorama of factories, railway yards, and busy assembly lines.

The action moves to Los Alamos, where rather little is shown, given the requirements of military security. (Until 1958, the town of Los Alamos was off limits to the general public.) Then comes the first test explosion. For the movie, the A-bomb blast at Alamogordo, New Mexico, would be impressively recreated in the MGM studios in Culver City, California. Right after the test, a turtle is seen walking across Ground Zero, a symbolic affirmation that, yes, life can survive a nuclear blast.

Declaring in the original script that "I think more of our American boys than I do of all our enemies," President Truman decides to drop the bomb on Hiroshima. Matt Cochran and his equally fictional friend Jeff Nixon (played by Robert Walker), an Army colonel on General Groves's staff, travel to Tinian, a small Pacific island, to prepare the first of two atomic bombs for use against Japan. In an impossible accident, Matt suffers a fatal radiation injury while setting up the bomb one evening all by himself.

Then, the *Enola Gay* takes off on its historic mission, braving heavy flak over Hiroshima. (In reality, the B-29 encountered no hostile fire.) Little Boy devastates the city in a spectacular film sequence that demonstrates Hollywood's skill at special effects. (The special effects won the movie an Oscar.)

Matt dies, though not before writing the obligatory final letter, resolving his own doubts about the bomb. The screenplay (like the movie) ends with Matt's pregnant widow, along with Jeff Nixon and Jeff's girlfriend, standing before the Lincoln Memorial in Washington and talking inspirationally about how the world will be better for the young scientist's sacrifice.

This, in outline, was the screenplay that those Manhattan Project alumni depicted in *The Beginning or the End* were asked to review and approve during the spring of 1946.

Eliminating "Unreasonable Distortion"

The senior participants in the Manhattan Project did not like what they read and said so in no uncertain terms. The first hurdle for MGM was physicist J. Robert Oppenheimer, who had served as director of the atomic laboratory at Los Alamos. Oppenheimer's chief complaint was artistic; the characters appeared "stilted, lifeless, and without purpose or insight." Producer Sam Marx wrote back, agreeing to fix certain minor factual details and to spruce up the personalities. In

---

THE RUSSIAN THREAT—1980s STYLE

If MGM met the atomic bomb as a feature film in movie houses of the 1940s, forty years later this type of film would have appeared on television as a movie-of-the-week, or better yet a mini-series. Indeed, early in 1987 ABC invaded the United States with unprecedented hype to sell its vaunted fourteen and one-half hour mini-series *Amerika*. The third-ranked network spent $35 million for a story depicting a future Soviet occupation of the United States, an idea that ABC entertainment president Brandon Stoddard called "provocative, interesting, different and fresh."

ABC spent millions publicizing the series. It could have saved the money. Critic Todd Gitlin spoke for many when he called it "simply right-wing propaganda." The United Nations objected to its name being used in connection with troops occupying the United States. Political critics (including star Kris Kristofferson) felt the show would undermine U.S.-Soviet relations. The Chrysler Corporation withdrew planned advertising dollars. (Nonetheless the show "sold out" its ads at $150,000 per thirty-second spot.)

And all for naught. The mini-series started out big on Sunday, February 15, 1987, smack in the middle of a crucial sweeps rating period as the curious (about a quarter of the nation) tuned in; then the bottom dropped out. Fewer and fewer stayed tuned. ABC would have done better with a regular series such as *Moonlighting*. Pundits estimate the fiasco cost the network about $20 million. Later that month, American TV viewers voted on what they really wanted to watch that spring; CBS's *I'll Take Manhattan,* an eight-hour adaptation of Judith Krantz's frothy best-seller, scored a rating triumph.

The notion that a dramatized Soviet attack on the United States could be a network money-maker began three years earlier with the November 20, 1983, presentation of *The Day After*. That two-hour-and-twenty-minute made-for-television movie depicting a nuclear doomsday in Kansas drew a record (for a TV movie) 47 percent of all American households. Indeed, in the capital of news junkies, Washington, D.C., trendy restaurants reported business off 25 percent to 50 percent as potential viewers stayed home.

Initially, ABC had trouble selling advertisers on a film depicting the horror of a nuclear attack. But advertisers who stuck it out reaped an enormous bargain. At a discounted price of only $100,000 per thirty-second advertisement, they were able to reach audiences most advertising executives only conjured up in their dreams. Those companies that benefited: Commodore computers, Dollar Rent-A-Car, Certs breath mints, Orville Redenbacher's popcorn, and English Leather cologne. ABC did make one concession. The twenty-five network commercials appeared during the first hour in order to avoid having advertisers hawk their wares between scenes of carnage.

The high viewing levels carried over for the forty minutes ABC used to fill out the third hour. To explore reaction to *The Day After,* Ted Koppel interviewed Secretary of State George Shultz who called the movie "a vivid and dramatic portrayal of the fact that nuclear war is simply not acceptable," and then discussed its implications with Henry Kissinger, William F. Buckley, Jr., Robert S. McNamara, Carl Sagan, and Elie Wiesel. This public affairs program was watched by a third of all households in the United States, a record that still stands for public affairs programming.

Douglas Gomery

---

particular, Marx said, "the character of J. Robert Oppenheimer must be an extremely pleasant one with a love of mankind, humility, and a fair knack of cooking." Marx added that the film would make it plain that Oppenheimer, not Groves, was in command at the Alamogordo test.

Somewhat mollified, Oppenheimer signed a release in May 1946. He would be depicted in the movie as an earnest scoutmaster who accidentally had a doctorate in theoretical physics from Gottingen. Queried later by an incredulous member of the atomic scientists' movement, physicist James J. Nickson, Oppenheimer replied that while the screenplay was not "beautiful, wise, or deep . . . it did not lie in my power to make it so."

While Oppenheimer withdrew from further involvement in *The Beginning or the End* after May 1946, both General Groves and Vannevar Bush corresponded with MGM throughout the year. Groves was determined that the movie not violate national security (a sensitive issue in the immediate postwar era) or discredit anyone involved in the Manhattan Project. He sought assiduously, though with limited success, to correct inaccuracies.

Among other things, Groves was disturbed by the way he was shown barking orders at industrialists; relations with business, he insisted, had always been polite and respectful. The general was outraged by his fictional subordinate, Jeff Nixon, the long-haired (for an officer) womanizer and wise guy. Such a man, Groves argued, would not have been tolerated in the Corps of Engineers and would never have been asked to join his personal staff. As to his own film image, the rumpled, pudgy Groves raised no objection to being portrayed by the handsome Brian Donlevy.

In the end, the general won some small concessions, notably the elimination of a highly imaginative scene in which Groves tells Roosevelt and Secretary of War Henry L. Stimson that if the United States did not use the atomic bomb at once against Japan, Japan would greet a U.S. invasion of the home islands with nuclear weapons of its own. Essentially, though, Groves went along with MGM's plans. He was no doubt relieved by the report of an aide who attended a sneak preview of the final film version in 1947. The aide concluded that the public impact of the movie would be minimal because the film would be a box-office flop.

Vannevar Bush, formerly director of the Office of Scientific Research and Development, had better luck than Groves with the creative folk at Culver City. Bush had held the crucial discussion with FDR about launching the Manhattan Project, but in the screenplay, MGM gave the credit to another man, the National Bureau of Standards' Lyman J. Briggs. Bush objected and the movie makers rewrote the script accordingly.

Bush did not like the rewrite either. In the new version, Bush was shown with Roosevelt (and with FDR's Scotch terrier, Fala, who leaves the room when Bush announces that he has a top-secret matter to discuss); he was portrayed as uncertain over whether an atomic bomb could be built "in time" or would even be small enough to fit inside an airplane. On the contrary, Bush insisted, he had had no doubts on either score.

Sam Marx agreed to soften but not eliminate this angle. It was Hollywood fiction that had been deliberately introduced to heighten dramatic tension—to suggest the possibility that the Axis powers might get the bomb first.

Bush also disliked being shown leaving the White House disgruntled at not getting an immediate go-ahead from the president. The scene implied, he believed, that American scientists were "arrogant enough to feel [they] should either make the decision [themselves] or force the Commander-in-Chief into making it then and there." Again, MGM gave way. The released film shows a rather prosaic parting of Bush and Roosevelt, followed by the president placing a transatlantic call to Winston Churchill to give him the details.

On the eve of the film's release in 1947, Bush could write to financier Bernard Baruch that, insofar as his own role was concerned, "history was not unreasonably distorted" by *The Beginning or the End.*

Harvard president James B. Conant, a key administrator in the A-bomb effort, proved even more persnickety than Bush. Conant was hardly publicity shy. Indeed, he and Bush willingly played themselves in a 1946 March of Time documentary, *Atomic Power,* which showed the pair stretched out on the desert (actually, a sand-strewn garage floor in Boston) awaiting the first nuclear blast at Alamogordo. *The Beginning or the End* was another matter. Conant agreed to being shown at Alamogordo but not to having any words put in his mouth.

The foreign-born scientists depicted in the movie gave Sam Marx his biggest headaches. Having been told by members of the atomic scientists' movement that *The Beginning or the End* would reflect the Pentagon's viewpoint, Albert Einstein twice refused his consent to be portrayed, reluctantly giving in only at the urging of colleague Leo Szilard. Appalled by inaccuracies and outright fabrications, Lise Meitner and Niels Bohr spurned all of MGM's entreaties and had to be written out of the movie altogether.

From MGM's standpoint, the most serious refusal was that of Bohr. The early scenes of the screenplay featured him in Europe. To highlight the race against the Nazis, much was made of smuggling the physicist out of Copenhagen and then bringing him to the United States. That Bohr was essential to the A-bomb project was more than strongly implied—though in fact he was not a member of the Manhattan Project. For dramatic effect he was placed at the Alamogordo test site; but in fact he had not been there.

To make up for the absence of Bohr and Meitner, MGM in December 1946 hastily began cutting the movie and reshooting scenes, a process that continued into January.

The intransigence of Bohr, Meitner, and others cost *The Beginning or the End* one of its more vivid fictional interludes. In the original script, Niels Bohr shocks Oppenheimer when he brings the news that the Germans are sending atomic experts and know-how to Japan. Later, the screenplay has a U-boat leaving Hitler's doomed Reich with a fictional German physicist aboard named Schmidt—identified as a former worker in Lise Meitner's Berlin laboratory. The submarine surfaces in Tokyo Bay, and the Japanese promptly rush Schmidt off to a modern laboratory they have built for him—in the city of Hiroshima.

Columnist Walter Lippmann was responsible for another excision. After previewing the original version of the movie in the fall of 1946, Lippmann complained that Truman's order to drop the bomb was depicted as a snap decision. This, he wrote, was an "outright fabrication and reduces the role of the President to extreme triviality in a great matter." Lippmann also objected to the movie Truman's seeming unconcern for the loss of Japanese lives. The entire scene was reshot.[2]

Neither Herr Doktor Schmidt nor a shoot-from-the-hip Truman appeared in the final film version, but many of MGM's other revisions of the record made it through. Before a first atomic bomb is tested at Alamogordo, for example, Oppenheimer and General Groves's deputy, Brigadier General Thomas F. Farrell, discuss the frightening possibility that the nuclear chain reaction would go around the world, converting the planet into one big fireball. In the movie, Oppenheimer rates the possibility at less than one in a million. Asked after the test if he really had been worried, the Oppenheimer character says: "In my head, no, in my heart, yes."

In fact, the Manhattan Project physicists had no such worries; the possibility was raised only *after* the bombings of Hiroshima and Nagasaki, by people with little expertise in nuclear fission.

A Box Office "Bomb"

Until the world premiere of *The Beginning or the End* in Washington, at least some MGM officials were certain they had a hit on their hands. Carter T. Barron, MGM's man in Washington, cabled to Culver City on January 7, 1947:

> Seldom have we experienced more enthusiasm for the dramatic entertainment of a film than that demonstrated by small preview groups comprised of immediate friends, staff members, and associates of persons impersonated or otherwise associated with the project. It appears to be a daringly strong audience picture.

Then came the reviews. *Time*'s critic wrote that "the picture seldom rises above cheery imbecility" and scolded Hollywood for "treating cinemagoers as if they were spoiled or not-quite-bright children." (Few reviewers, however, questioned the factual accuracy of the movie.) At least seventy-five films in 1947 grossed more at the box office than what MGM billed as "the story of the most HUSH-HUSH secret of all time."

The reaction of groups of scientists invited to special screenings was typically one of disappointed silence punctuated by outbursts of raucous laughter. Sam Marx had once allowed that he was interested "not in how a scientist would talk but how the public thought he would talk." Hollywood's notion of how science was done—amid batteries of blinking lights and a cacophony of electronic noises—proved irresistibly comic to real scientists.

Ironically, had the reactions of Bohr and others not forced so much cutting and reshooting of scenes, MGM might have produced a box-office hit. At a sneak preview in October 1946, the first, uncut version of the film won an overwhelmingly enthusiastic response from the audience. Imagine the impact on popular memories of World War II if tens of millions of American moviegoers had watched the fictional Herr Doktor Schmidt disembarking from his U-boat in Tokyo Bay, with a blueprint for an A-bomb in his briefcase!

Did *The Beginning or the End* really matter? Not in any way that is easy to describe. Although its distortions went largely unremarked, they also went largely unseen. The making of *The Beginning or the End* is chiefly of value as a parable of sorts. And it may serve as a timely reminder that, as the years go by, Hollywood fictions sometimes take on lives of their own. "Engrossing account of atomic bomb development, depicting both human and spectacular aspects"—that is how *The Beginning or the End* is described in Leonard Maltin's *TV Movies* (1983–4 edition). The film gets three stars, no less.

NOTES

1. For related reading, see also Alice K. Smith's *A Peril and a Hope* (1965) and Michael J. Yavenditti's "Atomic Scientists and Hollywood: The Beginning or the End?" in *Film and History* (December 1978, vol. 8, no. 4).

2. Because Truman's visage did not actually appear—the camera shot over an actor's shoulder—MGM did not need a signed waiver from the president. Truman read the screenplay of the first film version and, judging from private letters, disliked the same sequence that Lippmann criticized, and for the very same reasons. However, wishing to avoid charges of censorship, he refused to intervene.

Background Books

THE MOVIES

"The coming of the motion picture," newspaper publisher William Randolph Hearst once said, "was as important as that of the printing press."

Hearst, as was his wont, exaggerated a bit. But during its humble beginnings in a Menlo Park, New Jersey, laboratory, nobody could have guessed what an enormous impact on Americans' fantasies, mores, and morals the motion picture would have—least of all its inventor, the redoubtable Thomas Alva Edison.

Edison and his assistant, William Dickson, at first saw the moving picture as something to accompany music from Edison's phonograph, notes Emory University's David A. Cook in *A History of Narrative Film* (Norton, 1981). So they experimented with ways of putting pictures on rotating cylinders like Edison's early audio records. In the process, they created the world's first motion picture "star," a burly Menlo Park mechanic named Frederick Ott, who shamelessly hammed it up in front of the camera dressed in a white sheet belted around his middle.

In 1889 Dickson came up with the idea of putting pictures on a single film strip with sprocket holes on each side, and the Kinetograph was born. (Edison and Dickson stuck with their star; their first picture was called *Fred Ott's Sneeze.*) In most of its essentials, it was the predecessor of the modern movie, with one crucial exception. The Kinetograph did not project pictures on a screen; it was a peepshow. And Edison did not think enough of the machine's potential to pay the $150 needed for an international copyright. Seizing the opportunity, Auguste and Louis Lumière, of Lyon, France, adapted Edison's technology and invented a projection system, the Cinématographe. Other projectors followed, including Edison's Kinetoscope.

So quickly did American film makers churn out new movies that by 1926, Terry Ramsaye, a journalist turned newsreel producer, could offer up a serious 868-page study of the American cinema, *A Million and One Nights: A History of the Motion Picture* (Simon & Schuster, 1926). "For the first time in the history of the world," Ramsaye observed, "an art has sprouted, grown up, and blossomed in so brief a time that one person might stand by and see it happen."

Arthur Knight's *The Liveliest Art: A Panoramic History of the Movies* (Macmillan, 1957; rev. ed., 1978), living up to its title, is the best popular survey of film history through the late 1970s.

After attracting curious throngs during their first years, Knight recalls, movies were relegated to the clean-up spot in vaudeville revues. Most were novelty items, running no longer than a minute. Then, in 1903, Edwin S. Porter filmed one of the first coherent cinematic narratives, *The Great Train Robbery,* and before long, movies were everywhere.

American film makers soon began to head West, to the sunshine of Burbank and Hollywood, where year-round outdoor filming was possible. In the beginning the locals were not happy to see them. Los Angeles boarding houses hung signs that read, "Rooms to Rent—No Dogs or Actors."

The rest, as they say, is history.

Most of the insider chronicles of Hollywood's Golden Age have been lost among the countless exposés and kiss-and-tell memoirs that bring in profits for booksellers. For a distillation, consult *Hollywood on Hollywood: Tinsel Town Talks* (Faber & Faber, 1985, paper), an entertaining compendium of words wise and otherwise by Hollywood's notables, collected by freelance writer Doug McClelland.

"I am paid not to think," said a straight-faced Clark Gable, commenting on the studio system's control over his acting career. The first words Fay Wray heard about her role in *King Kong:* "You will have the tallest, darkest leading man in Hollywood." On the semiserious side, studio boss Louis B. Mayer suggested in 1937 that Hollywood's celluloid creations were "important to world peace."

In recent years film scholars have moved away from the "great man" view of Hollywood, the notion that a handful of top studio executives and directors dictated the way movies would be made.

By 1920, for example, Hollywood had unconsciously defined a "proper" style of film making and ruled out most alternatives. The results are still with us: the emphasis is on telling stories with seamless narratives, usually set in more or less realistic surroundings, with at least a few characters sure to engage the sympathies of the average moviegoer. Avant-garde directors may make statements by shooting entire films composed of one-second scenes or populated by pathetic characters; in Hollywood, such things simply are not done.

Such is the thesis of *The Classical Hollywood Cinema* (Columbia University Press, 1985) by David Bordwell, Janet Staiger, and Kristin Thompson, all at the University of Wisconsin–Madison.

A more obvious influence on movies—at least until the 1960s— was Hollywood's self-censorship at the hands of the Production Code Board (1930–68), better known as the Hays Office. Jack Vizzard's account of his years on the board, *See No Evil: Life inside a Hollywood Censor* (Simon & Schuster, 1970) is an engaging, sympathetic look at the censor's work.

The Hays Office worried not only about nudity, blasphemy, and profanity (among the taboo words were "cripes" and "fanny"), but also about plots that seemed to let sinners and malefactors off too lightly. The war between the censors and the studios was unrelenting. One story has it that a screenwriter once tweaked the censors by penning the stage direction: "From offstage, we hear the scream of a naked woman."

Vizzard admits the excesses and absurdities of the old censorship, but he laments that under the industry's current rating system (G, PG, PG-13, R, X), just about anything goes, if it sells tickets.

Of all the many writers who have journeyed to Hollywood in search of fat scriptwriting fees, only F. Scott Fitzgerald, in his unfinished portrait of *The Last Tycoon* (Scribner's, 1941), has written a lasting novel about movieland.

The problem for novelists may be that it is very difficult to wrap an illusion around an illusion. As David Lees and Stan Berkowitz note in *The Movie Business* (Random House, 1981, cloth and paper), even Hollywood's palm trees, its brick and concrete, are deceptive. "The uninformed," they write, "show up at Hollywood and Vine and see nothing but tacky tourist traps and hookers of both sexes breathing in a lot of brown smog. Visitors find it hard to imagine that at that very corner, and nearby as well, movies are happening."

A loyal book-buying public never seems to tire of true confessions or lurid exposés of movie stars, however obscure. David Thompson's *A Biographical Dictionary of Film* (Morrow, 1981) skillfully summarizes the lives of the most important and influential of Hollywood's past luminaries, as well as a number of significant directors and producers in a manner that is meant to inform rather than titillate.

Since the 1960s, more serious students of the cinema, following a more rigorous biographical form of analysis, have begun to create career studies, particularly of directors. A model can be found in Richard Schickel's *D.W. Griffith: An American Life* (Simon & Schuster, 1984). In this mammoth work the author asserts that we can best understand the early history of the American cinema through analysis of this one major figure.

Many would disagree. Hollywood has always been more than great stars and powerful directors. Behind the shiny veneer lies a highly profitable machine that has long been turning stories into dollars for the owners of the major movie companies, some of which they grudgingly share with actors and directors. The Golden Age of Hollywood began in 1930, and the following year former film company executive Benjamin B. Hampton skillfully surveyed the peaks and valleys of the industry he was about to leave. His influential book

History of the Film Industry (Dover, 1970) should be read by all students of the cinema.

During the 1930s and 1940s Hollywood movie making was a big business on the scale of a major manufacturing industry. As Douglas Gomery has detailed in *The Hollywood Studio System* (St. Martin's, 1986), eight companies—including the still familiar Paramount and Universal—completely defined the conditions for the production of movies, their distribution to theaters throughout the world, and even the ownership of theaters.

The focus of this game has always been Hollywood, but insiders have long kept a close eye on the nation's 20,000 movie screens to understand how the money was entering the system. From 1920 through 1940, movie theaters defined the centers of American communities. Baroque picture palaces underscored the elegance of movie going. Ben M. Hall, in his breathtaking homage to the grand movie theaters of the past, *The Best Remaining Seats* (Bramhall House, 1961), skillfully tells the story of the glories of the picture palace. The lure of these fabled cathedrals of pleasure can best be conveyed through a simple *New Yorker* cartoon in which a mother is seen dragging a gaping child through the rotunda of the Roxy Theater in New York City. The child gasps: "Mama—does God live here?"

Americans have long feared the power of the movies. Garth Jowett in his book, *Film: The Democratic Art* (Focal Press, 1976) notes that the first official court case involving movie censorship was *People* v. *Doris* in 1897. From that moment on, defenders of public morality have sought to protect blasé moviegoers from the evils of the cinema. Both Jowett and Robert Sklar, author of *Movie-Made America* (Random House, 1975), examine in exhaustive detail how religious and moral leaders from Jane Adams to Billy Graham have tried unsuccessfully to restrict the movies Americans could see.

A brush with television during the 1950s seemed to cripple Hollywood, but the invalid has come back healthier than ever. And the public has never tired of reading about the film business and its perennial scandals. A major mess at Columbia Pictures during the late 1970s was dissected in great detail in David McClintick's *Indecent Exposure: A True Story of Hollywood & Wall Street* (Morrow, 1982). Steven Bach examines a single great movie failure in *Final Cut: Dreams and Disaster in the Making of "Heaven's Gate"* (Morrow, 1985).

But what has captured the fancy of film fans and students alike has been a new set of Hollywood stars—Steven Spielberg, George

Lucas, and Francis Ford Coppola. The rise of these auteur producer/ directors is artfully chronicled in Michael Pye and Lynda Myles's *The Movie Brats* (Holt, Rinehart & Winston, 1979).

It took the French with their *auteur* theory of film criticism to convince Hollywood that one person—the movie director—could and indeed should be treated as an artist who could create a vision of the world as moving as any created by a composer, novelist, or poet. Andrew Sarris, in his widely read *The American Cinema* (Dutton, 1968) has codified the *auteur* theory in the United States.

Before Hollywood decided in the 1970s to place the film director's name above the title of the film, it emphasized the genre of the film. Year after year came Westerns, gangster films, and science fiction fare. The most interesting writing on Hollywood film genres focuses on the musical. Jane Feuer's *The Hollywood Musical* (Indiana, 1982) and Rick Altman's *Genre: The Musical* (Routledge & Kegan Paul, 1981) dissect what seem to be the simplest of works and find complexity in the way the best musicals copy each other. But before tackling the history and theory of the musical, one would be wise to read a very useful anthology edited by Elisabeth Weis and John Belton, *Film Sound: Theory and Practice* (Columbia University Press, 1985).

At their best, film scholars have now developed methods by which to analyze cinema in general, any film in particular, and the history of the medium itself. These units of film study are artfully summarized in J. Dudley Andrew's *The Major Film Theories* (Oxford, 1976), David Bordwell and Kristin Thompson's *Film Art: An Introduction* (Knopf, 1986), and Robert C. Allen and Douglas Gomery's *Film History: Theory and Practice* (Knopf, 1986).

TELEVISION

Chapter 13

TELEVISION IN AMERICA: SUCCESS STORY

by Lawrence W. Lichty

In many households in the United States during the early 1950s, Father came home one night, often just before Christmas, and placed a television set in the living room where the radio had stood. It came sooner to families in big cities and suburbs, sooner to people with higher incomes, and sooner to those living in the Northeast where most of the new TV stations were. Because postwar America was the most affluent place on earth, television, like the automobile, eventually came to everybody.

In one sense, television seems to be the world's first dispensable major technology. Theoretically, the complex industrial societies of the United States, Western Europe, and Japan could function quite well without it. This is not true of the printing press, the telephone, the radio, or the digital computer. Were any of these to disappear, our economy, our public administration, and our defense system would be thrown into chaos.

Television, too, would become essential. We have adjusted to it, allowed it to alter our perceptions and choreograph the rhythms of daily life. Television, if only by default, is one of the tools modern societies now must use to sustain themselves. In many countries, as in our own, television and the central government are the only *national* institutions. Television is a baby-sitter, an initiator of conversations, a transmitter of culture, and a custodian of traditions. It is the creator—and showcase—of heroes. Psychologically, TV performs other, ineffa-

159

ble functions. If it were suddenly to disappear, what would happen to the 20 percent of Americans who watch twelve hours of television a day? On average, half of all American's leisure time is spent watching television, though much of that time we might also be talking, eating, even reading. Television *is* our nightlight. One need not concede that TV is "good" to recognize that getting rid of it, like keeping it, entails a certain cost.

Television's roots go deep. It is the inheritor of functions once performed by serialized novels, by newspapers and photographs, by movies and the phonograph. But its content, like a froth, exists on the surface of things. The "substance" of TV is a derivative amalgam flavored by Madison Avenue and Hollywood, endlessly percolating the grounds of popular culture: the fiction of women's magazines, the cliches of newspaper headlines, the plotlines of best sellers, the fleeting tyrannies of political fads, the shifting banalities of the conventional wisdom. All of this television ingests, then throws back, reshaped and reinforced and trivialized. It happens over and over again, day after day. In relation to American society, television is always in the same place. It possesses a peculiar, implacable kind of stability.

For forty years television has been a flickering constant in American life. The TV industry and its structure, the nature and quality of television programs, the ratings system, the raised eyebrow of federal regulation—remarkably, none of these has changed, in its essential lineaments, since commercial TV emerged after World War II. Television thrives within a constellation of forces on which it depends but over which it has only limited influence. Its character, in effect, has been locked into place. Television might be a different medium if broadcasters did not have to rely for their revenues on advertising, but they do. Television would certainly be different if the audience were different (imagine the result if only people with mortgages or Ph.D.s in physics owned TV sets) or if it had been the offspring of the federal government, or even the Ford Foundation, instead of network radio.

Television: Radio's Child

Nothing was so important to the development of television as radio. Radio-as-progenitor gave television a voice, a code of conduct, and a way to make a living, just as radio itself had drawn its form and content from vaudeville, the concert hall, and the newspaper.

In 1923, when émigré engineer Vladimir Zworykin, late of the

TV VIEWING BY AGE, SEX, TIME
(December 1987)

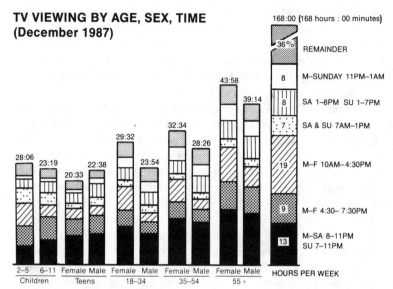

Source: A. C. Nielsen Company

RADIO LISTENERS VS. TV WATCHERS

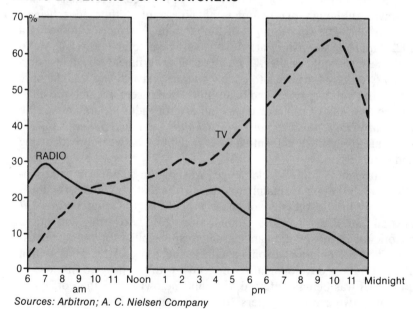

Sources: Arbitron; A. C. Nielsen Company

Russian Army Signal Corps, sought his patent for the first electronic TV tube (the iconoscope), the radio broadcasting business was growing rapidly. In 1922 the number of U.S. radio stations rose from fewer than 30 to 570.[1] The Radio Corporation of America (RCA), founded in 1919 as a U.S. government-promoted holding company for radio patents, grossed $50 million in 1924 from sales of radios.

By the time of the Great Crash, a network structure was in place. Building on several years of experiments, RCA through its subsidiary, the National Broadcasting Company, inaugurated a "Red" Network in 1926 by providing music and various talk shows to twenty-one affiliate stations. A second NBC "Blue" network was started a few months later. (NBC was ordered to divest itself of one network in 1943, and the Blue network became what is now ABC.) In 1929, cigar-fortune heir William S. Paley, then 28, took control of a floundering network, the Columbia Phonograph Broadcasting System—now CBS and still directed by Paley. Together, the networks provided about 130 hours of programming a week in 1931. For a quarter-century, the networks would dominate radio programming. Interestingly, in the late 1980s, NBC, now owned by General Electric, was the first to sell its radio network and all of its radio stations.

As the radio audience grew, advertisers turned increasingly to the airwaves, although many found the notion of "ether advertising" distasteful. "The very thought of such a thing," wrote the author of a 1922 *Radio Broadcasting* article, "is sufficient to give any true radio enthusiast the cold shakes." Yet, barring government subsidies, or a rush of Andrew Carnegies to endow stations, advertising was the only long-term way to pay for radio. In time, advertisers became the chief source not only of radio revenues but also of radio programming (the *Eveready Hour,* the *Cliquot Club Eskimos,* and the *General Motors Party* are examples), cementing forever the link between broadcasting and commerce.

Throughout radio's golden age, Washington stepped in occasionally from the sidelines, mainly to prune a tree that was otherwise doing nicely. With the blessing of most broadcasters, Congress in 1927 created the Federal Radio Commission (FRC) to straighten out a chaotic technical situation and assume responsibility for station licensing. The FRC eliminated some channels and consolidated others, then allowed radio's development to proceed—with the proviso that use of a channel was being conferred "but not the ownership thereof." The regulators were not reformers. In any event, the FRC found, as its successor, the Federal Communications Commission (FCC) would find, that life and death power over individual stations did not bring much leverage over the system as a whole.

By the time of the Depression, as radio became a vehicle of popular entertainment, the broadcasting industry had acquired the shape it now generally maintains. Stations were organized into networks, AT&T "longlines" linked them up, and advertisers paid for programming. Broadcasters were experimenting with program formats that have since become familiar: news, drama, comedy, music, and variety shows. Politicians began using radio to publicize their conventions, FDR to broadcast his "fireside chats." Radio, with its capacity for virtually instantaneous nationwide communication, had become America's first *universal* mass medium.

Slowly, working from the inside out, television displaced radio. It took radio's programming, its networks, its audience, its advertisers, its talent, its executives, its benign relationship with the FCC, and its way of doing business. Over time, the TV moguls made some changes; but the basic formula remained.

Television was radio's child. Although the idea was not new— *Scientific American* had used the word *television* in 1907—it was not until the early 1920s that such pioneers as Charles F. Jenkins and Philo T. Farnsworth in the United States and John L. Baird in Britain reported the first successful video transmissions. The radio networks built on this foundation. NBC televised images as early as 1927, and in 1931 began broadcasting from an experimental station, W2XB5, on the fifty-third floor of the Empire State Building. Atop the Chrysler Building, CBS soon had its own experimental TV station.

After World War II, the electronics industry finally got television out of the infant stage. Television sets reappeared on the market in 1946, costing an average of $280. Within two years, four networks— ABC, CBS, NBC, and the short-lived DuMont network—were in operation. By 1952, 108 stations were on the air.[2] Of these, more than half were owned by a company that operated an AM radio station before 1925, half were owned by a company that owned another TV station, and four out of five were owned by a company that owned a radio station in the same market as its TV station. Ninety percent of the stations were showing a profit. Television's advance was abetted by skillful promotion. "How can a little girl describe a bruise deep inside?" asked one television manufacturer's advertisement. "No, your daughter won't ever tell you the humiliation she's felt in begging those precious hours of television from a neighbor."

Radio was the obvious source of much television programming.

TV HOUSEHOLDS

	TV households (millions)	Households with TV (percentage)	Households with color TV (percentage)	Households with two or more sets (percentage)
1950	4.6	9	—	—
1960	45	87	—	—
1970	60	95	41	12
1980	78	98	85	35
1985	86	98	93	51
1986	86	98	95	59

Source: *Television 1987 Nielsen Report*, A. C. Nielsen Company.

NUMBER OF CHANNELS AVAILABLE

Number of Channels Available	Percentage of U.S. households in:		
	1964	*1972*	*1985*
1–4	41	17	3
5–10	51	52	22
11–29	8	31	56
30 or more	—	—	19

Source: *Television 1987 Nielsen Report*, A. C. Nielsen Company.

In sum, in the early 1960s about half could get no more than four channels; by the mid-1980s three-fourths could get more than ten, and one in five got more than thirty channels.

U.S. TV HOUSEHOLDS IN 1987
(percentage)

28	TV only
23	TV + VCR
12	TV + Basic Cable
10	TV + VCR + Basic Cable
9	TV + Basic Cable + Pay Cable
18	TV + VCR + Basic Cable + Pay Cable

Sources: Cable and pay cable (November 1987) from *Channels*, January 1988, *VCR*, May 1987, Nielsen press release; A. C. Nielsen Company.

**PRIME-TIME AUDIENCE CHOICES
(percentages)**

	1983	1985	1987	
Networks	80	77	72	21 ABC
				23 CBS
				27 NBC
Independents and PBS	17	20	23	18 Independent stations
				5 Public stations
Basic cable	4	6	8	
Pay cable	6	6	5	

Source: A. C. Nielsen; totals more than 100 percent because of homes with multiple sets.

Most of the radio stars of 1950—Martin and Lewis, Lucille Ball, Bob Hope, Groucho Marx, and scores of others—became TV stars a few years later. To this ready-made menu, the networks added movies and a bigger dollop of sports than radio, lacking pictures, had ever been able to sustain. Puppet shows and, later, cartoons drew young children into the broadcast audience, just as action/adventure serials had done for radio. Television news combined the traditions, good and bad, of radio and newsreel reporting, but it made journalism a more prominent feature of broadcasting than it had ever been.

TV Programming: Raising Parthenogenesis to a Science

Television programming, like that of radio, consists of a finite number of trends mutating within a closed system. Most of them have radio precedents: the courtroom dramas (beginning with *They Stand Accused* in 1949), the "adult" westerns (*Gunsmoke* and *Wyatt Earp* in 1956), the medical dramas (*Ben Casey* and *Dr. Kildare* in 1962), and so on.[3] "Spinoffs" were not unknown on network radio—the Green Hornet, for instance, was the Lone Ranger's nephew—but television raised parthenogenesis to a science.

If something works, imitate it; if one show soars in popularity, put on others like it; if the ratings fall, take them off. One can study an electrocardiogram of this phenomenon, reflecting the variable vitality of "action" shows, in the incidence of TV violence, which rises and falls but oscillates from a nearly constant level. Few trends, or programs, last very long.

Typically, only about one-fourth of the programs in any season have been on for five years or more. Many radio and television programs of the 1950s usually survived at least one season, but life on

---

THE ULTIMATE TELEVISION SPORT

A crowd of 93,173 fans jammed the Pontiac Silverdome outside Detroit, surpassing a record set by an earlier Superbowl. Closed-circuit television carried the three-hour event to 163 U.S. sites and 26 foreign countries. More than one million cable subscribers paid $20 each to watch. A dream heavyweight boxing match? A long awaited World Series appearance by the Detroit Tigers? No, Wrestlemania 3, a twelve-card professional wrestling extravaganza on March 29, 1987.

Television had come full circle. Professional wrestling, as we know it today with all its rousing zaniness, was invented during the 1930s to draw crowds to legitimate heavyweight title matches that provided too little crowd-pleasing action. Fans flocked to see Ed "Strangler" Lewis and Lou Thesz, and television discovered wrestling. Gorgeous George—and a host of friends and enemies—filled time on the now defunct DuMont network and the then struggling ABC. In the 1940s and 1950s, television broadcasters did not care whether the grunters and groaners were respectable or not.

Later, more middle class "sports" pushed wrestling off the networks; but the rise of independent stations in the 1970s brought it back—with a vengeance. By the mid-1980s wrestling extravaganzas still filled the needs of marginal independent television stations and also provided NBC its highest Saturday late night ratings as a once-a-month replacement for "Saturday Night Live." Moreover, wrestling served as a staple for the fourth largest cable network and helped convince a skeptical cable television industry that pay-per-event programming was a potential gold mine.

One wrestling television show from the World Wrestling Federation was the third most popular syndicated program in 1986 and 1987, trailing only the record setting *Wheel of Fortune* and its companion game show *Jeopardy*. Local sportscasters soon discovered that they could enliven a dull listing of the latest sports scores with highlights from a recent wrestling match.

Professional wrestling reached a peak of television popularity in 1985. In May of that year, NBC aired its first *Saturday Night Main Event* in the former *Saturday Night Live* time slot, a new children's program premiered *Hulk Hogan's Rock 'n' Wrestling,* and even the TV soap operas became involved. In June NBC's *Search for Tomorrow* featured a plot line with Hulk Hogan, the Magnificent Muraco, and the manager, Mr. Fuji.

Television has always loved professional wrestling. The matches are all orchestrated so that there are none of the aggravations that afflict other sporting events, such as games that run over their alloted time or visually devastating injuries. Boxers may be seriously injured or even killed. Professional wrestlers are seldom hurt except by freak accident.

Professional wrestling is also cheap programming to produce. In most instances the wrestling promoters give the show away for nothing or even pay stations to take it. Why? Because they want to advertise future local matches.

Wrestling's popularity is universal. Through the modern miracles of videotape and communication satellites, wrestling matches are taped in the United States and sent throughout the world. Statistical evidence of this pirating is sketchy; but the best markets appear to be in the Middle East, especially Oman, Kuwait, and Egypt.

Professional wrestling has now infiltrated other realms of entertainment. Popular music stars such as Cyndi Lauper double as managers. Ray Charles, Alice Cooper, and Aretha Franklin have helped referee matches. Television personalities Joan Rivers, Susan Saint James, Cathy Lee Crosby, and Dick Clark serve as guest referees or time keepers. Wrestlers regularly move to Hollywood and star in movies, beginning with Hulk Hogan in *Rocky III*.

Is wrestling sport or theater? Any fan knows the answer. It is both . . . and more. The complexities of foreign policy may baffle even the most knowledgeable citizens. But when the "Russian" Nikolai Volkoff and the Iron Sheik from "Iran" appear together as a tag team, fans of all ages and educational backgrounds know it is time to hiss the villains.

Professional wrestling has always been a form of low comedy, usually aimed at lower class, blue collar audiences. Then cable television, home video, and the cynicism of the 1980s were skillfully manipulated to give the grunt and groaners a middle class respectability. For a time in 1985 the "sport" even became chic. Professional wrestling was made for television and will always be with us unless television changes into some unrecognizable form.

Douglas Gomery

---

prime time TV today is usually very short. Of 104 regular program series of the 1987 television season, 29 survived for less than five episodes.

To maintain the flow of new programming, the three networks require a total of about eighty "pilots." Only one-third of these will be added to network schedules; and of those, only one in five will survive for a second season. But the few that do last five seasons—or about 100 individual episodes—may play on and on as syndicated programming for local stations and cable networks.

NETWORK PRIME TIME PROGRAM TRENDS (hours per week)

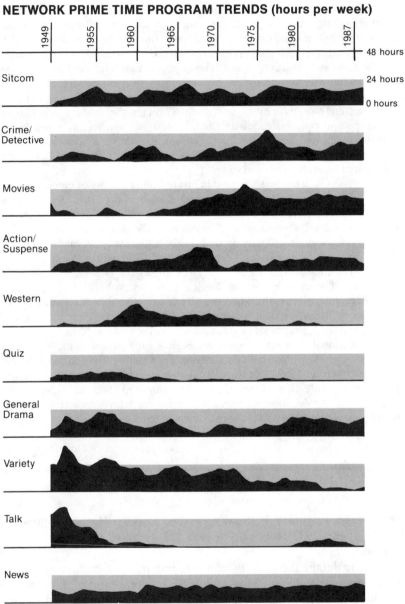

Source: Compiled by Lawrence W. Lichty, Christopher Sterling, Susan Leakey, and Mary-Teresa Cozzola.

The Ratings Game

Contrary to the claims of the high-minded, television is not free to break this cycle. Broadcasters are in business not to produce bold, innovative programs but to attract audiences to view commercials. Audience taste—what the largest possible audience will stand for—sets television's immutable boundaries. Fred Smith, then director of radio station WLW, identified the fundamental principle in 1923. "The nature of radio programs," he wrote, "eventually will follow demands of economic conditions, which in other words, is but the demand of the public."

Most early radio stations kept track of audience response, usually by monitoring the mail and phone. But as advertising increased, so did the accuracy and importance of polling. In 1930 Archibald Crossley and his Cooperative Analysis of Broadcasting Company began publishing once-a-year ratings based on telephone surveys. By 1935, the C. E. Hooper Company was providing "Hooperatings" on a monthly basis. Seven years later, the A. C. Nielsen Company introduced a mechanical "black box" that could be affixed to radio sets in selected homes to record listening habits. A more sophisticated version was then developed to measure TV ratings. For the 1987 season, Nielsen and a competitor introduced "people meters" that remind viewers to feed additional information, such as who is in the room with the television set, into the "box." A more sophisticated version comes with a "wand" that will read universal product codes so that sample households can provide information on products they buy and answer other questions. Sponsors and advertising agencies rely heavily on this and other information to cancel programs or develop new ones. Networks and stations charge prices-per-minute based on the size of the audience. "Nothing in American life," author Martin Mayer has written, "certainly not politics, is so democratic, so permeated with egalitarianism, as the use of television ratings to influence program decisions."

Television programming is tethered to the audience. Like a kite, it has a bit of latitude; but it always responds to a tug from the viewers. As is the case with TV violence, public opinion rises and falls, though never straying very far, or for very long, from a glacial mainstream. When audience tastes and preferences change in a superficial way, television reflects them in a superficial way. If the audience itself changes profoundly, so does television. There are many reasons for the end, in the mid-1950s, of the "Golden Age" of live, often inspired,

THE TOP-RATED SHOWS IN HISTORY

Rank	Program	Telecast Date	Rating	Share
1	*M*A*S*H Special*	February 1983	60.2	77
2	*Dallas*	November 1980	53.3	76
3	*Roots* (Part 8)	January 1977	51.1	71
4	*Super Bowl XVI*	January 1982	49.1	73
7	*Gone with the Wind* (Part 1)	November 1976	47.7	65
8	*Gone with the Wind* (Part 2)	November 1976	47.4	64
11	*Bob Hope Christmas Show*	January 1970	46.6	64
15	ABC Theatre, *The Day After*	November 1983	46.0	62
16	*Roots* (Part 6)	January 1977	45.9	66
17	*The Fugitive*	August 1967	45.9	72
19	*Roots* (Part 5)	January 1977	45.7	71
20	*The Ed Sullivan Show* (Beatles appearance)	February 1964	45.3	60
21	*Bob Hope Christmas Show*	January 1971	45.0	61
22	*Roots* (Part 3)	January 1977	44.8	68
26	*Roots* (Part 2)	January 1977	44.1	62
27	*Beverly Hillbillies*	January 1964	44.0	65
28	*Roots* (Part 4)	January 1977	43.8	66
29	*The Ed Sullivan Show*	February 1964	43.8	60
30	*Academy Awards*	April 1970	43.4	78

Source: A. C. Nielsen Company, 1987.

Rating is percentage of households viewing; share is percentage of households using television tuned to that program. Ranks 5, 6, 9, 10, 12, 13, 14, 18, 23, 24, and 25 are other *Super Bowl* games.

TV drama. Not the least of these is that television's early core of affluent, urban viewers by then constituted a minority of TV households.

Television did induce, though it did not initiate, one major change in the relationship of advertiser to broadcaster. Throughout most of the radio era, advertisers paid for *and produced* their own programs. Then, in 1946 CBS radio regularly began producing shows of its own—notably *My Friend Irma* and *Arthur Godfrey's Talent Scouts*—and selling the time to advertisers. The notion was transplanted to television. By 1959 only one-quarter of all prime-time TV shows were produced by advertisers. (Today, the practice survives mainly in soap operas.)

The chief catalyst here was the rising cost of production. A typical hour-long variety show cost only about $6,000 in 1949, but more than $100,000 a decade later. By 1988 the cost of a typical one-hour drama

**LARGEST ADVERTISERS ON TV
(in $ millions)**

Procter & Gamble	779
Philip Morris	478
McDonald's	303
Pepsi Co	266
R. J. Reynolds	263
General Motors	259
General Mills	239
Pillsbury	232
Ford	229
Anheuser–Busch	227

Source: Television Bureau of Advertising, *Broadcasting Yearbook,* 1987, p. xv.

**ADVERTISING REVENUES
($ millions)**

	TV Networks	*National Spots*	*Local TV*	*Syndicated TV*	*Cable*
1980	5,130	3,269	2,967	50	58
1985	8,285	6,004	5,714	540	767
1987	8,915	6,964	6,905	760	1,147

(National spots are national and regional time buys on local stations)

Sources: TV Advertising Bureau and Cable Advertising Bureau, 1987; 1987 estimates are from *Channels,* January 1988.

was about $1,200,000. Bearing production costs plus network fees represented a big commitment—and an act of faith—by even the wealthiest sponsors. At first advertisers reacted by sharing the costs of a program with one or more other companies. Eventually, they moved out of the business altogether, content to spread their bets and buy time on programs created by the big Hollywood production companies: Paramount, Universal, Twentieth Century Fox, Warner Bros., and Columbia.

The decline for advertiser-produced TV coincided with the quiz show scandals, an episode that constitutes a parable of government attempts to regulate the TV industry.

Introduced in 1955, within six months Revlon's *$64,000 Question* was being seen in almost half of all TV households. True to the cycle of imitation described above, prime time was suddenly blinking with sponsor-produced quiz shows, all of them hungrily competing for viewers. By 1957 reports of "rigging" were being investigated. The climax came during congressional hearings in November 1959 when Charles Van Doren, a teacher at Columbia University and an NBC *Today* show celebrity, confessed that he had been briefed on questions and answers while competing on the quiz show *Twenty-One*. "I would give almost anything I have," Van Doren testified, "to reverse the course of my life during the past three years."

The FCC and Public Affairs Programming

Amid a brief public uproar, the FCC in 1960 raised an eyebrow and enjoined the networks to clean house. Then—as atonement, it was implied—FCC Chairman John C. Doerfer proposed that each of the three networks begin providing an hour of public affairs programming each week. The networks agreed. During the 1962 season, there were more hours of documentary programming on television than any season before or since—253 hours. Yet, as the memory of the quiz show scandals receded, so, quickly, did the number of documentaries.

The FCC's "prime-time access rule," which went into effect in 1971, has suffered a similar fate. In essence, the rule requires TV stations in the fifty largest markets to carry no more than three hours of network-supplied programming during the prime-time hours of 7:00 to 11:00 PM. The goal was to promote *local* programming, especially news and public affairs. To a certain extent, the rule was effective: some stations now broadcast informational programs such as *PM Magazine*. Yet its primary—and unanticipated—effect has been to stimulate the growth of first-run, nationally syndicated quiz shows, created by independent producers. After 1975 two-thirds of the programs on all TV stations in the 7:30–8:00 PM time slot consisted of quiz shows. The first success as a syndicated, first-run program in that time period was *Family Feud*. Later, *Wheel of Fortune* was often seen every week night in about one-fifth of American homes. Costing only about $12 million a year to produce, it returned nearly ten times that amount to its producers. Broadcasters have neatly finessed the intent of the access rule while following it to the letter.

The Network Shuffle

Perhaps the greatest change for television came in 1986. At the beginning of the year, Capital Cities, a relatively small station owner, surprised the industry by taking over the ABC television and radio networks and stations. In May, General Electric bought RCA and thereby acquired the NBC network and stations. And before the year was out, Laurence Tisch and his Loews Corporation became the major force in the operation of CBS. For the first time in thirty years NBC "won" the battle for prime-time supremacy in large part because of

FORTUNES FROM THE WHEEL

In the mid-1980s it was a force so powerful that it rendered news anchorman Dan Rather almost invisible in Cleveland and placed aspiring actress Vanna White on the cover of *Newsweek*. *Wheel of Fortune* is a simple game show featuring an eight-and-a-half foot wheel, a former weatherman as host, and Vanna White as a letter turner. In 1986 *Wheel of Fortune* became by far the most popular nonnetwork (syndicated) program in the history of American television, watched by some 40 million people a day.

"Wheel," as it is known in the trade, became such an attraction that station managers built their daily schedules around it. Nightly news shows were overwhelmed by it. A station owning the rights to the "Wheel," won the time slot and with that victory nearly all the millions in local advertising dollars. Over on competing channels the news shows languished as audiences steadily drifted away.

In Cleveland Dan Rather and the "CBS Evening News" were doing fine in the ratings until the rival ABC affiliate bought rights to the "Wheel." Pitted head-to-head against *CBS Evening News,* the game show was devastating competition. For a time, the CBS station had trouble selling all its news show advertising time.

But in New York City the "Wheel" was a gold mine for CBS. There, the network-owned CBS station bought the rights to the popular syndicated show and placed it *after* the "CBS Evening News." The audience for the news shot up. Why? Because audiences tuned in while waiting for the "Wheel" to begin.

One frustrated station manager summed it up this way: "It really shows the ultimate zaniness of this business. You try to do everything right journalistically and then the most successful game show in history comes along and cuts your head off. It's unbelievable."

What explains the game show phenomenon? It can't be its novelty. *Wheel of Fortune* has been on NBC in the morning as a game show since the mid-1970s. Prizes, a car being generally the most valuable item, are modest compared to other shows. The game itself is hardly a challenge. One wins by determining a simple phrase or name. Some credit the droll wit of host Pat Sujak, or the attractiveness of Vanna White, the woman of the eighties. The show began its extraordinary popularity when Sajak and White came aboard in 1982.

Roger King, the multimillionaire head of the company that sells the program to TV stations, ascribes the appeal of the "Wheel" to its simplicity. "It can be played by a rocket scientist and by an eight-year-old."

Douglas Gomery

---

the phenomenal success of the *Bill Cosby Show,* previously rejected by ABC.

The impact of the *Cosby Show* was incredible. There had been many highly rated, often short-lived programs in the early days of television. But just as many predicted the era of sitcoms was over, *Cosby* was first in its time period every week from its premiere through most of the first year. It moved NBC from third to first place and helped NBC's affiliates as well. In 1983 only 31 NBC stations were first in their markets; in 1985 more than 100 were. *Cosby* also increased the audiences for other shows around it: *Cheers* went from fifty-fourth to third, *Family Ties* was up 48 percent in 1985 and another 34 percent in 1986. This was sweet music for stations that could charge advertisers much more based on these increased audiences.

A "fourth network" was born in 1987 when Rupert Murdoch's Fox Broadcasting began offering a daily late-night comedy-talk program and a Saturday and Sunday prime-time schedule of situation comedies and crime shows. But it was still not clear that there was audience enough to support another national television network. Barry Diller, who at the age of twenty-five changed television programming by developing the made-for-TV movie series at ABC, entitled *Movie of the Week,* was put in charge of the Fox network. As chairman of Twentieth Century Fox Film Corporation, Diller understands the structural advantages that flow from control of a production company and ownership of stations in half of the nation's ten largest markets. ABC, CBS, and NBC generate about as much revenue from the television stations they own—reaching nearly a quarter of all TV homes—as they do from all other broadcasting operations, including radio, and from supplying TV programming to more than 200 affiliate stations.

With the number of independent TV stations increasing during the 1980s from about 100 to more than 300, the networks' share of audience has dropped from 90 percent to about 67 percent. Pay cable and other television services gained prime-time viewers. But although the networks are forced to survive on leaner budgets, they still greatly

ENTERTAINMENT VS. INFORMATION

Average rating and share for the top ten programs, and three information programs during the 1986–87 and 1987–88 seasons.

	1987					*1988*	
Rank		*Rating*	*Share*	*Share*	*Rating*	*Rank*	
1	*Cosby Show*	34.9	53	44	27.8	1	*Cosby Show*
2	*Family Ties*	33.4	50	39	25.0	2	*Different World*
3	*Cheers*	27.5	41	37	23.4	3	*Cheers*
4	*Murder She Wrote*	25.4	37	37	21.8	4	*Golden Girls*
5	*Golden Girls*	24.5	41	32	21.3	5	*Growing Pains*
6	*60 Minutes*	23.3	37	33	21.2	6	*Who's The Boss*
7	*Night Court*	23.2	35	33	20.8	7	*Night Court*
8	*Growing Pains*	22.7	33	34	20.6	8	*60 Minutes*
9	*Moonlighting*	22.4	34	30	20.2	9	*Murder She Wrote*
10	*Who's The Boss*	22.0	33	30	18.8	10	*Wonder Years*
50	*20/20*	14.2	24	23	12.6	57	*20/20*
82	*West 57th*	10.9	18	15	9.5	87	*48 Hours*
104	*Our World*	6.5	10	15	7.8	96	*West 57th*

Source: Nielsen season's series ratings, September 1986 to April 1987, *Variety,* 20 May 1987, p. 42. Nielsen ratings are regularly published in *USA Today, Broadcasting* magazine, and *Variety.*

Rating is percentage of households viewing; share is percentage of homes using television tuned to that program. Note the decline in ratings from 1987 to 1988, in part because of increased competition from other programming on independent stations and cable and available for rent on videocassette.

overshadow all their competitors in providing home video entertainment.

There has been great growth in the number of channels available to viewers, but there is considerable duplication in programming. About 300 movies are shown on the five largest pay movie channels every month. However, more than half of these, including the vast majority of recent releases, appear on two or more channels, sometimes virtually simultaneously.

One still reads, from time to time, laments in the press or in academic journals about what television "could have been," as if it could have been any different than what it actually became. Its future, as a mass marketing tool, was determined well before its birth, in a very Darwinian sense. A fish cannot fly; it swims.

Some dreamers now hail cable TV and videodiscs as technologies that may finally pull television into an era of "quality" and "innovation." They won't. They may supplant commercial TV just as TV in some ways brushed radio aside. But radio adjusted by becoming more "specialized," and so will network television. The new video media, for their part, will be subject to the same market forces that shaped radio and television broadcasting. Even though the audience may have more choices, the proportion of "quality" programming appearing on the home screen will not be much different than it is now. The prospect is not a noble one, but it has, at least, the virtue of familiarity.

NOTES

1. Much of radio remained "amateur" throughout the 1920s, with programming sometimes patched together minutes before broadcast time. Most stations with any real "staff" were owned by department stores and other retail outfits that sold radios, or by radio manufacturers themselves, for example, Westinghouse and General Electric.

2. From 1948 to 1952, the FCC imposed a "freeze" on new TV station applications while it corrected certain technical problems—allocation of stations to various market areas, use of the ultra-high frequency (UHF) band, color television, and other matters. Following the precedent set by the Federal Radio Commission twenty-five years earlier, the FCC then allowed the development of television to proceed. Within one year after the end of the freeze, the FCC authorized creation of more than 400 new TV stations.

3. Throughout this essay, the date given for programs is that of the TV "season." Thus, *Dr. Kildare* appeared during the 1962 season, which began in the autumn of 1961.

Chapter 14

HISTORY AS SOAP OPERA?

by Steven Lagerfeld

In 1492 Christopher Columbus was welcomed to the New World by scantily clad dancing girls. General George Custer was court-martialed for his performance at the Little Big Horn. Wayne Williams did not commit the Atlanta Child Murders.

That is not, to paraphrase Walter Cronkite's old sign-off, the way it was. It is the world according to television's "docudramas."

In Hollywood, or at network headquarters in New York, somebody thought that Columbus's actual landfall in the Indies was a bit dull. General Custer's death alongside his men at the Little Big Horn was a historical inconvenience. The producer of *The Atlanta Child Murders* (1985) disagreed with both the jury that convicted Wayne Williams and the appellate court that upheld the verdict.

For the past dozen years or so, ever since the commercial success of *The Missiles of October* in 1974, about the 1962 Cuban Missile Crisis, the Big Three television networks have been airing dozens of "fact-based dramas" annually. During the 1986–7 television season (from September to April), the networks broadcast thirty-three. What accounts for the popularity of docudramas? "When a [character] is known, the audience gets involved more easily," one NBC executive explained a few years ago. "If [a program] is just fictional, it would be less attractive."

For that very reason, relatively few docudramas deal with subjects of great historical moment. *Elvis and Me* (1988) is more typical of the form than is *The Missiles of October*. Yet, the historical docudrama is common enough to merit some concern.

177

Traditional "pure" documentaries score low in the Nielsen audience ratings and, like television histories, suffer from the fact that their creators cannot get all aspects of the story on film. As Hollywood producer Alan Landsberg explained at an Academy of Television Arts and Sciences (ATAS) symposium on docudramas in 1979:

> As one who has struggled . . . long in the vineyard of the pure documentary, and finally found it a frustrating form, I was delighted to find that docudrama is an avenue that can communicate more than the existing or shootable film allowed. After all, I could film the bloody White House for just so long, and I couldn't get into the damned Oval Office where the action was, so I was forced to conclude that the action going on inside the White House was my guess as to what happened. Now in the docudrama, at least, I can mount that guess so you can properly see it.

What is a "guess," and what is not? Where does the "docu" end and the "drama" begin? The audience is never told.

Of course, as nearly everyone in the TV business quickly points out, Shakespeare mixed fact and fiction in *Richard III* and his other historical plays. But the Bard called it theater, and his histories were performed on the same stage as his comedies and tragedies. Docudramas, on the other hand, appear side-by-side with TV news and documentaries; and they make claims to historical truth. Moreover, if anyone in Shakespeare's audiences somehow mistook the stage for reality, the confusion was limited; the Globe Theater held only about 2,000 people. A popular docudrama may be seen by 80 million Americans or more.

Of necessity, docudrama enters the realm of fiction as soon as a scriptwriter picks up his pen to write a line of dialogue. How does he know what President Dwight D. Eisenhower said to Mamie over dinner? Or what Marilyn Monroe said between the sheets?

The makers of docudramas maintain that such invention is inconsequential if done "in the spirit" of the truth. As *Roots* producer David Wolper put it: "I do not think we are dealing in fiction because we are inventing words between people. . . . Whether a man said exactly 'I love you, my dear' or 'My dear you are beautiful and I love you' is not relevant."

The courts apparently agree. In 1976 NBC broadcast *Judge Horton and the Scottsboro Boys,* a docudrama in which the chief witness against the nine black "Scottsboro Boys" in the racially charged 1931 Alabama rape case was called a "whore," a "bum," and a "perjurer."

The real-life witness filed a $6 million libel suit against NBC. As scriptwriter John McGreevy testified in federal court, those lines of dialogue were pure invention. Yet, deciding that they were not written with reckless disregard for the truth, the judge in the case dismissed the suit.

The spirit of the truth often dwells in strange places. ABC's *Young Joe, the Forgotten Kennedy* (1978) shows the eldest Kennedy son volunteering for the dangerous World War II mission that cost him his life. "I'm glad I'm not going with you, Joe," says a fellow flyer named Mike Krasna. "Like us," remarked novelist Mark Harris in *TV Guide*, "Krasna is at first suspicious of Joe Kennedy's wealth and aristocratic bearing." His acceptance of Kennedy encourages viewers to accept him too. The problem: Not only was the Krasna–Kennedy dialogue made up, so was Mike Krasna. He never existed.

Docudramas and the Presidency

The less trivial cases include ABC's *Collision Course: Truman and MacArthur*, a 1974 docudrama about the conflict that ultimately led President Harry S. Truman to relieve General Douglas MacArthur of his command of U.S. forces in the Far East during the Korean War. As *Collision Course* relates, Truman and MacArthur met for the first time at Wake Island in 1951. On TV, an arrogant MacArthur circles Wake in his plane, trying to get Truman to land first. After finally being ordered to land, MacArthur keeps the Commander in Chief waiting for forty-five minutes before joining the welcoming committee on the airstrip and later gets a severe tongue-lashing from Truman.

In reality, MacArthur reached Wake Island the night before Truman did and greeted him promptly. MacArthur was not dressed down. Truman "radiated nothing but courtesy and good humor during our meeting," the general later recalled. "He had an engaging personality, a quick and witty tongue, and I liked him from the start." *Collision Course*'s creators apparently relied almost exclusively on the aging ex-president's hazy recollections ten years after the fact, which appeared in Merle Miller's *Plain Speaking*. Unfortunately, TV offers few opportunities to insert "footnotes" indicating that other versions or interpretations of events exist, and docudramatists rarely take advantage of them.

Docudramatists have taken a special interest in the private lives of the presidents. There was *Eleanor and Franklin* (1976), *Ike* (1979), which focused on Eisenhower's alleged romance with his wartime aide, Kay Summersby, and *Backstairs at the White House* (1979), a grand tour of White House domestic life during much of the twentieth century. History as soap opera. In 1976 Christopher Lasch, a University of Rochester historian, wrote that docudrama "reduces great lives to ordinary lives, heroes to ordinary citizens indistinguishable in their perceptions and feelings from everyone else, at the same time it invests them with the spurious glamour of stardom."

Docudramas as Social Commentary

Sometimes docudrama writers and producers have an ax to grind. NBC's *Unnatural Causes* (1986) entered the debate over the effects of Agent Orange on veterans exposed to the chemical in Vietnam, suggesting that Washington was trying to cover up the facts. *The Trial of Lee Harvey Oswald* (1977), on ABC, in effect argued that President John F. Kennedy's assassination was the work of a conspiracy that may have included the Federal Bureau of Investigation (FBI), the Central Intelligence Agency (CIA), the Mafia, and anti-Castro Cubans. The scriptwriters created scenes in which President Lyndon B. Johnson tried to squelch a federal investigation, and Oswald hinted that "they" would never let him live to tell the truth. The conspiracy theory got a second airing in 1986, in Showtime's *On Trial: Lee Harvey Oswald*.

Capital punishment was the villain in *Kill Me If You Can,* which was broadcast twice by NBC during the late 1970s and once by CBS in 1983. The producers played down the crimes of California sex offender Caryl Chessman (played by Alan Alda) and lingered over his extended, gruesome execution in the gas chamber. The last scene showed a telephone ringing, with a moments-too-late reprieve for Chessman—pure fiction.

A more amusing case was noted by *Wall Street Journal* critic Martha Bayles, who observed that CBS's *Christopher Columbus* (1985) portrayed the Italian-born "Admiral of the Ocean Sea" as tormented over the enslavement of New World Indians and relatively indifferent to their gold. (His Spanish second-in-command, by contrast, was depicted as a stereotypical conquistador.) Actually it was slavery that left the great explorer unmoved; he had a keen interest in precious metals. The fact that the production of the show was handled mostly by Italians, Bayles speculated, may have had something to do with the way reality was rearranged.

WHAT IF LEE HARVEY OSWALD HAD LIVED TO STAND TRIAL?

The controversy that has haunted America for fourteen years. The bizarre story behind the man accused of assassinating John F. Kennedy. Was he part of a conspiracy? Recruited by Anti-Castro Cubans...the FBI? A patsy for the CIA and the Mafia?

Guilty or Innocent? Watch the conclusion of...

THE TRIAL OF LEE HARVEY OSWALD

And voice your opinion.

STARRING:

BEN GAZZARA · LORNE GREENE MO MALONE · JOHN PLESHETTE
AS MARINA   AS OSWALD

To participate in this National Opinion Poll, fill in the ballot and mail to:

Lee Harvey Oswald Survey
P.O. Box 2200, Westbury, New York 11591

Results of this National Opinion Poll will be reported on **Good Morning America, ABC Television, Friday, October 14.**

I think Lee Harvey Oswald was...
☐ Innocent   ☐ Guilty

If guilty...
☐ He acted   ☐ He was part of a
on his own.   conspiracy.

A WORLD TELEVISION PREMIERE
ABC SUNDAY NIGHT MOVIE 9:00PM ⑦⑧

"Guilty or Innocent?" ABC asked viewers of its 1977 docudrama The Trial of Lee Harvey Oswald. *A ballot in* TV Guide *allowed them to vote. Seventy-nine percent of the "jurors" who voted "guilty" felt that Oswald was part of a conspiracy. In December 1986 cable TV's* Showtime *broadcast a fictional Oswald trial, this one more than five and a half hours long. In a telephone poll of viewers only 15 percent said Oswald was guilty "beyond a reasonable doubt."*

Few of the regular TV critics who write for the nation's newspapers and magazines have strained to keep the docudramatists honest. In reviewing CBS's *Robert Kennedy and His Times* (1985), for example, Tom Shales of the *Washington Post* declared the show a success "not because its portrayal of Robert Kennedy is so authentic and complete but because it successfully reconstructs the sensibilities of a decade." Among the presumably minor inauthenticities were scenes showing Kennedy enthusiastically backing the 1963 March on Washington led by the Reverend Martin Luther King, Jr., although Kennedy and his brother, John, were ambivalent at best about the march. The show also neglected to mention that when he was the U.S. Attorney General, Kennedy authorized FBI wiretaps on King's telephones.

However, CBS's *The Atlanta Child Murders* (1985) went too far, even for the TV critics. Abby Mann, the show's producer, forthrightly declared that he was engaged in a "crusade" to demonstrate that

---

TOP 25 MADE-FOR-TV MOVIES 1961–1984

According to *Variety* magazine, six docudramas, appearing here in bold-face type, can be counted among the twenty-five most popular made-for-TV movies since 1961. In order of their ratings, the twenty-five are:

Film	*Network*	*Year*	*Rating**
The Day After	ABC	1983	46.0
Helter Skelter, pt. 2	CBS	1976	37.5
(A dramatization of the Charles Manson murders.)			
Little Ladies of the Night	ABC	1977	36.9
Helter Skelter, pt. 1	CBS	1976	35.2
The Waltons' Thanksgiving Story	CBS	1973	33.5
Night Stalker	ABC	1972	33.2
A Case of Rape	NBC	1974	33.1
Dallas Cowboys Cheerleaders	ABC	1979	33.0
Brian's Song	ABC	1971	32.9
(The story of Chicago Bears running back Brian Piccolo and his losing battle against cancer.)			
Women in Chains	ABC	1972	32.3
Jesus of Nazareth, pt. 1	NBC	1977	32.3
Something About Amelia	ABC	1984	31.9
Heidi	NBC	1968	31.8
Guyana Tragedy: The Story of Jim Jones, pt. 2	CBS	1980	31.7
My Sweet Charlie	NBC	1970	31.7

The Feminist and the Fuzz	ABC	1971	31.6
Something for Joey	CBS	1977	31.5
(Dramatization of the relationship between Heisman-trophy winning football star John Cappeletti and Joey, his leukemia-stricken brother.)			
Dawn: Portrait of a Teenage Runaway	NBC	1976	31.5
Kenny Rogers as the Gambler	CBS	1980	31.3
Coward of the County	CBS	1981	31.1
The Amazing Howard Hughes, pt. 2	CBS	1977	31.0
Sarah T.—Portrait of a Teenage Alcoholic	NBC	1975	31.0
Call Her Mom	ABC	1972	30.9
A Death of Innocence	CBS	1971	30.8
The Autobiography of Miss Jane Pittman	CBS	1974	30.8

*Represents the percentage of all households with television sets (85 million in 1985) watching.

Atlanta's black mayor was at first indifferent to the murders, which eventually claimed the lives of nearly two dozen ghetto children between 1979 and 1981, and that the city's police department botched the investigation. Mann's docudrama strongly implied that Wayne Williams, the man convicted in 1982 of two of the murders and assumed to have committed the rest, was railroaded by authorities eager to get the story off the front pages.

Mann uncovered no new facts that might have justified an exposé. Indeed, he left out a number of crucial details, notably the fact that the killings stopped after Williams's arrest. *The Atlanta Child Murders* was ostensibly based on the official records and trial transcripts. But, as John Corry of the *New York Times* noted, evidence on television is different: "A smile is meaningful; a leer says something else. Truth shall be known by a character's persona. Jason Robards, the defense attorney, could not possibly be on the wrong side; he's far too decent for that. . . . Rip Torn, the prosecutor, is only another politician."

The CBS verdict: not guilty.

The "Roots" of Docudrama: From Dreyfus to Huey Long

Television did not invent the docudrama.[1] Ironically, the probable progenitor, Georges Mlis's silent film *L'Affaire Dreyfus* (1899), concerned another trial, the court-martial in which French Army officer Alfred Dreyfus was convicted of treason. Mlis re-created the trial days after the event itself; it was so effective that some of the trial's participants thought that they saw themselves on the screen.

D. W. Griffith's fictional silent film on life in the post–Civil War South, *Birth of a Nation* (1915), which cast the Ku Klux Klan in a favorable light, was another landmark. Griffith was one of the first directors to use a soundtrack (preplanned sheet music for theater orchestras) purposely to shape audience perceptions. In 1922 came the successful U.S. documentary, *Nanook of the North*. By the 1930s the Hollywood studios were churning out film biographies of famous Americans: Abraham Lincoln, for example, was the subject of three films between 1930 and 1940 (and also appeared as a minor character in eight other movies). Orson Welles's thinly veiled portrait of newspaper magnate William Randolph Hearst, *Citizen Kane* (1941), created a whirlwind controversy. On radio, Welles had discovered the power of simulated newscasts and studio sound effects in his famous 1938 *War of the Worlds* broadcast, describing an invasion of New Jersey by Martians. Harry Truman and the scientists who worked on the Manhattan Project were the stars of a 1947 film that traced the development of the atomic bomb in *The Beginning or the End*. (Chapter 12, "A Footnote to History: MGM Meets the Atomic Bomb," gives a full account of this unsuccessful effort to blend historical truth with artistic principle and commercial necessity.)

Radio gave birth in 1931 to the famous *March of Time* series, which featured actors speaking lines attributed to the powerful and famous. In 1935 a film version of the *March of Time* premiered in the nation's movie houses. As the stentorian "Voice of Time" narrated, a blend of stock footage, reenactments, and news film dealing with such subjects as Hitler's rise to power, the strange career of Pierre Deibler, France's chief executioner, and the life of Father Divine, the popular black religious leader, appeared on the screen.

The *March of Time*'s imaginative interpretations were often criticized. Sen. Huey ("Kingfish") Long of Louisiana was enraged when, after helping the film makers reenact scenes from his career, he found himself lampooned on the screen. The *New York Times* politely called the series "an interesting, well-made supplement to the newsreel, standing in about the same relationship to it as the weekly interpretative news magazine bears to the daily newspaper."

A few *March of Time* episodes were made for television, but they contained no dramatizations. The quick death of the series in 1951 was an object lesson for network executives in the fate of the TV documentary. But the networks did not seize upon the docudrama as a replacement during the 1950s and 1960s. One reason was that the Federal Communications Commission's (FCC) "fairness doctrine" required networks airing controversial programs to give free time to opposing points of view. All in all, it was easier and more profitable for the networks to stick to Westerns and variety shows.

By the early 1970s several things had changed. The fairness doctrine had been relaxed. Rising production costs prompted the networks to begin killing off money-losing situation comedies and other weekly series long before the end of the official TV season. This created a short "second season" that was ideal for made-for-TV movies and docudramas of one to five episodes. And programmers discovered a strong appetite for news and news-as-entertainment in the viewing public. (In 1968 *60 Minutes* debuted and climbed to number one in the ratings in 1974.) Last, but far from least, the networks discovered that docudramas could be lucrative. A modestly successful show such as *The Atlanta Child Murders,* which claimed some 50 million prime-time viewers, generates advertising revenues of about $4.2 million per hour. In many cases the "based on a true story" movies treated the lives of stars like Marilyn Monroe, Rosemary Clooney, and Ann Jillian, or sensational subject matter such as the murder of a *Playboy* centerfold. Docudramas were often among the most watched programs of the week, while documentaries nearly always finished at the bottom of the ratings.

What is different about today's docudramas on TV, compared to their radio and film predecessors? The size of the television audience is one distinction; and Americans' apparent tendency, amid a general decline in educational achievement, to turn to TV for news, commentary, and even history is another. As a uniquely compelling medium, TV does not encourage its viewers to distinguish between fact and fiction. Even well-educated adults can be misled. In a speech during his tenure as governor of New York, Hugh Carey paid tribute to a heroic black American, Jane Pittman. Pittman, however, was the fictional protagonist of CBS's *The Autobiography of Miss Jane Pittman* (1974).

"News Pollution" and Docudrama

A side effect of the docudrama trend is the creeping pollution of "hard" TV news by what TV people call "entertainment values." On

CBS a 1981 documentary, *In Defense of the United States,* opened with a film clip of a simulated nuclear explosion at Omaha, Nebraska; CBS paid $87,000 for the special effects. On ABC's *20/20,* a "recreation" of President Reagan's treatment in a Washington hospital emergency room during the hours following the 1981 attempt on his life aired in 1982. Meanwhile, some local TV stations began opening their 11 P.M. newscasts with stories related to the evening's docudrama.

Even without the deliberate injection of fiction, it is extremely difficult to convey "the facts" on TV. The medium demands that reality be selected, compressed, and reorganized into brief, dramatic film "stories"; no matter how conscientious they are, news and documentary producers seldom do justice to what cannot be shown on film. And they must cater to the presumed tastes of their mass audience. "Talking heads" who explain the complexities of a major story make boring TV. As David Wolper put it,

> The medium is there to get the big audience, and I don't want to waste that. . . . You may want to take the two hours and have two people sit down and discuss the subject. I consider that a crime because you've wasted two hours of time with which I can reach 80 million people.

At the ATAS symposium, Wolper and his fellow docudramatists complained about the scattered criticism of their art. David Susskind defended his colleagues as "men of artistic integrity; these are men you can't corrupt; these are men that won't be rushed." Scriptwriter David Rintels complained that critics were creating "an unfair, and unhealthy, skepticism in the audience's mind." Among the suggested remedies that emerged: The networks should run disclaimers before their docudramas and consider airing panel discussions by specialists afterwards. The genre should be renamed—"theater of fact" and "historical drama" were proposed.

In fact, the networks today do often label their productions "fact-based dramas"; brief messages sometimes inform viewers that events have been dramatized. It is hard to believe that these minor changes have much impact on audience perceptions, but they help. In 1987 Home Box Office (HBO) aired an interesting experiment in Brechtian docudrama called *Conspiracy: The Trial of the Chicago Eight,* in which the cameras occasionally pulled back to show the technicians and equipment surrounding the stage set. And the director spliced in actual documentary footage from the protests at the 1968 Democratic Convention in Chicago that led to the trial. These devices sharply reminded viewers of the break between "docu" and "drama." But there is little reason to suppose that they will or could be widely adopted.

For lack of alternatives, TV critics for the nation's newspapers and magazines must supply the public's chief antidotes to miseducation-by-docudrama. This task involves some extra work, but the critics would best serve their readers by firmly holding docudramatists (and documentary-makers) to the facts, as best they can be determined.

NOTES

1. For a fuller historical treatment, see the chapter on docudramas by Tom W. Hoffer, Robert Musburger, and Richard Nelson in *TV Genres* (Greenwood Press, 1985), edited by Brian Rose and Robert S. Alley.

Chapter 15

A QUESTION OF IMPACT

by Joel Swerdlow

Historian Daniel Boorstin, former Librarian of Congress, has called television "the next great crisis in human consciousness." Such crises attend the birth of every new form of mass communication. Even the written word did not emerge unchallenged. Plato warned that disciples of writing would "generally know nothing; they will be tiresome company, having the shadow of wisdom without the reality." The printing press, too, had its critics. It bred heresy and dissent, some said, and gave common folk dangerous ideas.

Even the critics of television cannot deny that a revolution has occurred. That we have become intimate with our televisions is shown simply by the numbers. Ninety-eight percent of all American homes have at least one television set. It is on more than seven hours each day. Watching television is what Americans do more than anything but work and sleep. Appropriately enough, brain wave studies indicate that children and adults alike lapse into a "predominantly alpha wave state" (which usually precedes sleep) after only 30 seconds of television viewing.[1]

Television has also eclipsed rival media. In 1986 total revenues in the United States from all book sales were $10.4 billion; for commercial television, advertising revenues alone totaled $21.6 billion. Television reshaped radio content and listening patterns and cut per capita movie attendance from twenty-nine in 1946 to four in 1986. It was an accessory to the deaths of big-city afternoon newspapers.

189

Television: The Flickering Image of "Reality"

Now a New Age of television is also emerging. Half the homes in America have at least one videocassette recorder (VCR); half are also wired for cable. Linkage among cable, satellite, VCRs, and computers has helped television permeate our lives more than ever before. This linkage is occurring precisely as the generations that grew up without television are dying off. More than 70 percent of all Americans alive today were born after television became a mass phenomenon. These new generations are accustomed to—even dependent upon—daily rhythms and reality as defined by television.

For all of us—pre-TV as well as children of the New Age— television has long been the prism through which we view reality; indeed, the flickering image has often seemed, or indeed been more real than experience away from the set. We take it for granted. When 18-month-old Jessica McClure was trapped in a well in 1987, live broadcasts of her rescue—during the dinner hour—united the nation in common emotions of tension and then relief. What came next was no surprise. A nationally syndicated television talk originated in her home town, while Jessica lay in a hospital bed watching television.

But what is television's impact on people? How does it affect the way we view the world, our neighbors, and ourselves? How does it change our behavior?

Firm answers are hard to come by. Because television is so pervasive, researchers find it virtually impossible to form control groups for purposes of comparison. Anyone growing up without television is, by definition, "abnormal." Today, scholars seeking to examine the effect of TV on learning, spending habits, voting patterns, perceptions, and a wide variety of behavior must generally be content to contrast "heavy viewers" with "light viewers" rather than viewers with nonviewers.

How TV Affects People

Even so, research into the behavioral implications of television, using statistical modeling, content analysis, galvanic skin tests, brainwave studies, and other techniques, has become a glamor industry in academe. Although the hundreds of published studies tend to shy away from making explicit the relationship of cause to effect, most of the findings are strongly suggestive. The literature is virtually devoid of arguments that television is either powerless or harmless.

Learning

The difficulties in America's classrooms obviously stem from many causes. *Why Johnny Can't Read* appeared in 1955, well before many U.S. homes had TV sets. Family instability, lack of discipline at home and in the schools, and educational fads have all taken their toll. But not even the most sympathetic analyst absolves TV of a major share of the blame.

Scholastic Aptitude Test (SAT) scores declined steadily for the first twenty years after members of the first TV generation began applying to college. Scores stopped dropping in recent years, but no one has seriously challenged a 1977 SAT study which concluded that "extensive viewing contributed to the achievement decline."[2] The key word here is "extensive." Evidence indicates that too much viewing—not simply viewing—is what hurts school performance. Teachers complain about their pupils' passivity, short attention spans, and lack of imagination—characteristics attributable, at least in part, to TV viewing. There is even a new phrase for this phenomenon: microwave mentality. Many young teachers, themselves raised on TV, now arrive in the classroom without basic skills. Television has apparently fostered a new growth industry: the teaching of "remedial" reading and writing in the nation's colleges.

By about age 15, the average American child has spent more time (about 20,000 hours) in front of a television than in the classroom—or doing homework. During the school year, approximately 1.7 million children ages 2 to 11 are still watching TV at midnight on weekdays. Researchers generally agree that heavy viewers comprehend less of what they read than do light viewers. They also confirm that, other things being equal, the more television a child watches, the worse he or she does in school.[3] (The sole exception may be students with low IQs.) "Mentally gifted" grammar-school students show a marked drop in creative abilities after just three weeks of intense television viewing. In a real sense, then, TV watching acts as a major "drag" on learning in America.

In the classroom itself, some types of learning can be helped by TV. Educators seem to agree that certain televised lessons can eliminate the need for repetitious reading drills, can help improve reading skills, and can be useful in teaching vocabulary.[4] Videodiscs and VCRs have been particularly promising for classroom use. The use of scripts from popular TV shows as a teaching tool—a controversial practice known as "scripting"—has reportedly raised average reading levels in some Philadelphia schools by some 20 percent, although it may also, in the process, have legitimized the misinformation inherent in most TV programs.

The most publicized efforts to tap the educational potential of TV remain public television's *Sesame Street* and similar programs that provide instruction in reading and, it is claimed, help preschoolers learn "how to learn." Critics counter that parents are being tricked, that teaching children to read or count at so early an age has no lasting effect—except, perhaps, to get the child "hooked" on television. Educator John Holt worries that *Sesame Street* teaches children that a "right answer" always exists. Other researchers contend that *Sesame Street* has no demonstrable impact upon later school performance.[5] And, while second-graders in the lower half of their classes do benefit from another program, *The Electric Company,* two years of viewing do not seem to help more than one.[6]

Watching television also has an apparent *physical* effect. A recent American Academy of Pediatrics study discovered a direct correlation between TV viewing in early childhood and likelihood of being overweight as a teenager.[7] The explanation: Too much sitting in front of a TV meant too little exercise.

Much of the problem obviously lies with parents who regard TV as a convenient baby sitter or as a child's afterschool sedative; most parents, surveys show, are not good at estimating how much television their children actually watch. Yet the high number of hours the average child (or teenager) devotes to watching TV means that an equivalent amount of time at home is *not* being given over to reading, hobbies, or socializing. The diversion of time from reading is critical. In a complex, technological society, reading becomes more rather than less important.

Politics

Television has transformed, and continues to transform, American politics. Newscasts and commercials are now the prime link between candidate and voter; we have moved from white papers to ten-second sound bites. In races for most offices, the single largest share of campaign expenditures goes to broadcast commercials. Presidential candidates rely on media consultants as they fly from market to market in search of free air time on the local or national news. In the 1988 presidential campaign television viewers watched more pre- and post-nomination debates, which are themselves organized largely to attract media attention, than occurred in the previous 200 years of American history. At presidential nominating conventions, television technicians nominating conventions, television technicians and journalists outnumber delegates.

That TV defines campaign events has become a cliche. "Television," campaign scholar Theodore H. White wrote several years ago, "*is* the political process." To fully appreciate just how much our politics has changed, one must step far back. Writing in the late nineteenth century, scholar James Bryce noted in *The American Commonwealth* that "for three months [during U.S. presidential campaigns] processions, usually with brass bands, flags, badges, crowds of cheering spectators, are the order of the day and night end to end of the country." These processions no longer exist; they have been killed, in large part, by television. "Three people in front of a television is a political rally," one campaign professional recently noted.

Where parties have innovated in recent years—the spread of meaningful primaries and the sponsorship of debates, for example— reforms have been television-oriented. Such reforms have been attempts to survive in a TV-dominated polity and have not negated a simple truth: The rise of televised politics has also coincided with— and contributed to—the weakening of political parties. With access to voters via television, more and more candidates are building their own organizations, resulting in what can be called the "politics of personality," as opposed to the politics of party. National nominating conventions have become, since the advent of television, far more media shows than deliberative bodies. "Television," historian Arthur Schlesinger, Jr., noted in 1986 could have "a conceivably fatal impact on the party system."[8] Thus, the New Age of television brings the danger that we will move from a two-party to a no-party system.

Television's impact on the *governing* process has been similarly significant. Television has helped to centralize power in Washington, D.C., and "television capability" has become a prime prerequisite for the presidency. You cannot govern unless you are good on TV.

Only the president may command free network air time almost at will—for press conferences, for major addresses, for brief announcements during a time of crisis, or for such special events as the signing of the Egypt–Israel peace treaty in 1979. He is the focus of attention on the evening news: There is *always* a story filmed on the White House lawn. Political scientist Michael Cronin points out that television "serves to amplify the President's claim to be the only representative of all the people." Yet the advent of TV has not eliminated the long-term attrition in the opinion polls that all modern presidents have experienced.

The influence of television is just as strong at the other end of Pennsylvania Avenue. Ever since the House and Senate admitted cameras, debate has been sharpened and behavior modified. Former Senate Majority Leader Howard H. Baker, Jr., noted in 1987: "Television discovered the value of conflict and controversy. There's a higher premium on the spectacular now. The players aren't very different, just the stage."

Television has changed some of the rules of the game, especially those that involve legislators' relationships with their constituents. After Lieutenant Colonel Oliver North's televised testimony during the Iran–Contra hearings of 1987 enthralled America, some committee members said that they should have hired a TV consultant to help them use the medium more effectively. Even for less dramatic legislative events, Congress now has a huge audience. Through C–Span, more Americans each day watch Congress than have seen it in person since the first session convened two centuries ago.

Television also plays a defining role at the state and local level. It has permeated even the last bastion of old-fashioned, closed-door politics. In late 1987, when the Chicago City Council voted to replace recently deceased Mayor Harold Washington, television stations stayed on the air live with coverage of proceedings throughout the night.

Diplomacy and the conduct of foreign policy have not escaped television. TV obliterates borders. Jordanians and Israelis watch the same newscasts; East and West Germans can see the same television channels. This does not automatically make their governments more friendly, but it does help redefine relationships. A similar result could come from events such as the recent linkage of Soviet and American leaders in unedited dialogues broadcast live in both nations.

Television's impact is best seen in the new public diplomacy. The media, for example, provided a platform for—and perhaps even made possible—diplomacy which produced the Egyptian-Israeli agreements of 1979. One of the most effective practitioners of public diplomacy is now the Pope, who in 1987 attracted an audience of one billion for one broadcast. Secular leaders, too, regularly use television to appeal directly to the population of other nations. One result of this capacity to communicate is that public opinion—in democracies as well as totalitarian states—becomes an increasingly powerful force in the conduct of foreign relations. On a smaller scale, the new diplomacy is being practiced when the Iraqi and Iranian ambassadors to the United Nations argue on ABC's *Nightline*.

As they adapt to television, candidates and public officials adopt what journalist Martin Schram calls their "video personae." The rules and values according to which such personae evolve must be understood, but we must also remember that the process is not as new as it may seem. Americans, as F. Scott Fitzgerald noted, have long been known as the people who make themselves up as they go along.

Television has been blamed too often for too many of the ills and limitations of our politics. It *is* extremely significant. "Television," a recent study concludes, "clearly and decisively influences the priorities that people attach to various national problems, and the considerations they take into account as they evaluate political leaders or choose between candidates for public office."[9] It is far from all-powerful. Its exact effect on voter behavior and public opinion has yet to be identified. Political commercials, for example, *do* inform voters of the issues, but they seem to have "no effect on voters' images of candidates" according to one in-depth study of such advertisements.[10] There is no demonstrable correlation between TV expenditures and election results, except when the race is close and one candidate heavily outspends the other.

Researchers agree that TV's chief political role is as an "agenda-setter": It does not so much tell people what to think as it tells them what to think *about*. Studies of Watergate and the Vietnam War, for example, indicate that television identified each as a major problem long before the public did. This in no way makes television unique. Newspapers play the same role, and did so long before television existed. What makes television distinctive is its glamor and its reach. As the chief source of news for most Americans, it has enhanced—and exaggerated—the power of the Fourth Estate.[11]

Even extreme, and highly studiable, events such as the Vietnam War and Watergate indicate that television cannot be too far ahead of preexisting public desires, interests and beliefs. Television is a commercial phenomenon; it follows public opinion far more than it leads it.

Behavior

Television affects all kinds of human behavior, but no aspect has been studied more than violence. (On TV, violent incidents occur, on average, five times per hour during prime time and eighteen times per hour during weekend daytime children's shows.) The evidence here is compelling: Children who see a great deal of violence on television are more likely than children who see less to engage in aggressive play, to accept force as a problem-solver, to fear becoming a victim of violence, and to believe that an exaggerated proportion of the society is employed in law enforcement.[12]

These conclusions remain true when held constant for IQ, social status, economic level, and other variables. A 1982 report by the National Institute of Mental Health concluded that "After ten years of research the consensus among most of the research community is that violence on television does lead to aggressive behavior by children and teenagers."[13] The broadcast industry has itself invested millions of dollars in such research but, perhaps predictably, comes up with, at best, a "not proven." An exception was a six-year CBS study conducted in Great Britain during the 1970s that concluded that young men who are heavy TV viewers are 50 percent more likely to commit violent crimes.[14]

Television, of course, may also teach "pro-social" lessons. Significantly, a TV protagonist in a show like *Cosby* displaying positive behavior has more of an impact upon children's subsequent play than does a character encouraging violence. Producers and writers of popular shows readily admit to writing parables in order to "teach America's families and children." Teaching and learning, of course, are not the same thing; it is a matter of scholarly conjecture whether children "generalize" the specific beneficial lessons they have learned—that is, whether it occurs to children to apply such lessons in real-life situations that may vary in their details from the episode portrayed on television.[15] Recent research indicates, however, that television's prime effect is teaching *values* rather than promoting specific behaviors.

Other changes in society are magnifying the impact—good and bad—of programs on children. Over 40 percent of America's parents now say their children are without adult supervision sometime between school and dinnertime. This percentage holds true for all economic categories.[16] What are most of these kids doing?. Watching television.

Television provides the American child's most easily accessible, if not necessarily most accurate, data on sex. Indeed, sex has become television's chief dramatic device. Recent tabulations document a rapid increase in TV's sexual innuendoes and in TV portrayals of prostitution, incest, rape, infidelity, and other deviations from the so-called old morality. In 1978 references to premarital or extramarital sex occurred in 43 percent of all prime-time shows (versus 21 percent in 1977); a mixture of sex and violence could be found in 10 percent of all prime-time programs (versus zero in 1977).[17] On prime-time shows, sexual intercourse was seven times more likely to occur between unmarried couples than between husband and wife. Since the late 1970s, moreover, the amount of sexual content has increased.

It seems reasonable to suppose that all of this has an impact, but how, and on whom? One study indicates a relationship between TV and unwanted teen-age pregnancies: Heavy viewers are more likely to believe that their favorite television heroine would not use birth control.[18] Another survey concludes that television raises adolescents' expectations of "what sex should be like." Heavy viewers seem to marry earlier and have more children. Such data remain tentative and fragmentary, but many countries now use television soap operas to teach birth control; research indicates that these programs have helped change viewer behavior.[19]

The AIDS epidemic has made sexual behavior a life-or-death matter. Health experts, mindful of the media's impact, are working with the television industry to depict fictional characters taking reasonable precautions and to broadcast commercials providing practical advice on how to avoid contagion.

We are also on firm ground with regard to "sexism." The more television most people watch, media scholar George Gerbner concludes, the more sexist their views are.[20] Other studies find that "children's perspectives of males and females generally correspond to the stereotypes found on TV."[21] Heavy viewers are more likely to prefer sexually stereotyped toys and activities.[22] On the positive side, girls who are shown women in "men's roles" on TV are more likely than other girls to endorse those roles as feasible and desirable.

Much of the argument comes down to research that is by necessity based on counting. The argument among those who believe in television's impact usually goes as follows: An average television viewer sees "X" incidents of "Y" every day year after year; such a deluge by necessity has an impact, particularly on children; the burden of proof must be on those who argue that it does not. Thus, a recent study documenting that "a regular viewer of [television] dramas would be likely to see more than 20" acts of drinking per evening explicitly assumes that this contributes to the nation's problem with alcohol abuse.[23]

What about race? From sit-ins to antibusing violence, civil rights activists and their foes have often shaped their protests with television in mind. Fictional portrayals of blacks have presumably had some impact as well. An estimated 130 million Americans watched ABC's up-from-slavery epic, *Roots,* in 1977. *New York Times* editorial writer

Roger Wilkins called the series "the most significant civil rights event since the Selma-to-Montgomery march in 1965."

Yet precisely what effect the portrayal of blacks has had on white TV audiences is difficult to pin down. Young children, especially suburban whites who may have little contact with blacks, believe television *comedies* faithfully depict other races even when this contradicts what their parents have taught them.[24] Researchers also conclude that many children form stereotypical opinions about other groups during preschool years when they are most susceptible to TV's influence. Yet these children do not seem to believe that a television character's race is important.

One other behavioral note: Families that are asked by researchers to forego television for prolonged periods report that their lives are much improved, but nearly all resume watching as soon as the experiment ends. Some psychiatrists now regard heavy TV viewing as an addiction. One woman who watched no TV for a week commented, "it's like being off drugs."

Selling

Television affects behavior on a crucial front—consumption. This is the economic basis of TV's existence. Advertising's share of the Gross National Product has held more or less steady for the past three decades at around 2 percent, but television's share of total ad expenditures—21.8 percent in 1986—has grown year by year.

HOW ARE TELEVISION AUDIENCES MEASURED?

"[O]ne added rating point on a network's annual prime time average would be worth $55 million."

> William S. Rubens
> Vice President, Research
> NBC

Broadcasters sell audiences to advertisers. It is essential, therefore, to know the size and composition of those audiences. Unfortunately, there is little tangible evidence of how many people are using the medium at any point in time. As a result, ways have been devised to document the existence of unseen viewers.

Two independent research firms, W.C. Nielsen and Arbitron, have become the dominant suppliers of audience data, commonly called "ratings." They use one of two techniques to estimate who is watching what. The simplest method for gathering information on TV audiences is to ask a sample of viewers to fill out a "diary." This is a small booklet in which the viewer is asked to report when his or her TV set is turned on, the program to which it is tuned, and who in the household is watching. Diaries are usually kept for a week and then returned to the research company.

Some people, of course, never fill out their diary or fill it out improperly. Despite these sources of error, diaries are the principal means by which most local TV stations (and radio stations) measure ratings. They offer a useful compromise between precision and cost. Nielsen and Arbitron each collect about 100,000 diaries in a single rating period. There are four such "sweep" periods a year. Using any other measuring technique with so many people would be prohibitively expensive.

Television network audiences are measured differently. For many years the Nielsen company placed measuring devices in homes. These black boxes electronically recorded when a TV set was turned on and the channel to which it was tuned. This information was retrieved over telephone lines and used to produce the famous "Nielsens." Unfortunately, old-fashioned meters could not tell who was viewing. As a result, a new generation of "people meters" has been implemented by Nielsen and its competitors. In addition to monitoring TV set activity, these devices have a special button assigned to each family member. When that person is watching TV he or she is supposed to press the button, alerting the meter to his or her presence.

The question of who is watching has become increasingly important because not all audience members are of equal value to advertisers. During prime time many advertisers want to reach middle-income, 25- to 54-year old women because they do most of America's shopping.

Virtually all successful prime-time programs are "aimed" at viewers who are in the two highest viewing quintiles—that is, the two-fifths of the audience who watch the most TV. These people tend to be older, have lower incomes, are more likely to have children at home, and to live in large households.

Makers of products for the elderly—denture cream, Geritol, and headache remedies—buy the network news programs because more than 40 percent of that audience is aged 55 or older. Toy makers and candy companies dominate the weekend morning children's shows. Commercials tucked into soap operas are aimed mostly at housewives aged 25 to 49. Indeed, shows with relatively small audiences are sometimes renewed, while programs with relatively large audiences are cancelled because of the marketable type of viewers they draw.

No matter what kind of measuring device is used, all ratings research is based on sampling; it is too expensive and time consuming to measure everyone. Instead, subsets of larger audiences are studied. While these samples may be quite large—about 4,000 households in national people-meter samples—and carefully selected, they may not perfectly represent the populations from which they are drawn. Consequently, all audience ratings are appropriately labeled "estimates." True audience sizes may be slightly more or less than the estimate.

The introduction of people meters may have ushered in a "Golden Age of Ratings." Certainly, audience estimates are more precise and detailed than they have ever been. In the future, homes with meters may also report on product purchases. This kind of information, referred to as "single source," will allow advertisers to know who is watching television and what kinds of items they are buying.

James Webster

Businesses do not spend those billions for nothing. Long-distance telephone billings across the nation, for example, rose by 14 percent in 1979 (to $1.3 billion) following introduction of AT&T's "reach out and touch someone" campaign. Television commercials may create a demand for hitherto nonexistent products (such as feminine deodorant sprays) and permit manufacturers to bypass retailers and appeal directly to consumers. Even print ads now make increasing use of the logo "as advertised on TV" as if to lend a certain legitimacy, even reality, to the product.[25]

Television advertisements do not *guarantee* sales success, however, and TV is not necessary for some commodities. Seventy percent of all cigarette advertising was on broadcast media in 1970 when the congressional ban went into effect, yet annual cigarette consumption in America rose from 538 billion in 1970 to 630 billion in 1980. The tobacco industry merely increased its advertising budget and pumped the money into other media.[26]

Perceptions

For innumerable TV viewers, "real life" is not as exciting or dramatic as it is "supposed" to be, and as it is on television. This aspect of television's impact is perhaps the most pervasive and least documented. It is seen, in one of its current manifestations, in the *Miami Vice*-izing of America: You must have the radio blaring a certain type of music as you zoom down the highway. Thus, television penetrates psychological rhythms in a way that the viewers involved may have difficulty recognizing—largely because they are not on guard against it. Novelists, such as Jerzy Kosinski, have lately begun exploring the phenomenon. (A *Journal of the American Medical Association* editorial on insanity recommended Kosinski's *Being There* as a "supplement to scientific study.") Truman Capote's *Music for Chameleons* is written in part as a screenplay, while practitioners of the "new journalism" record their impressions in the manner of roving cameras.

Television projects an aura of authenticity. A significant number of people, for example, believe that what they see on TV is real. In 1967, when TV was still a relatively new phenomenon, the National Commission on the Causes and Prevention of Violence discovered that 15 percent of middle-class white teen-agers and 40 percent of poor black teen-agers believed that TV programs "tell about life the way it really is." One recent study using a scale of 1 to 9 found that children in the third through sixth grades gave TV families an overall reality score of 5.97, and TV policemen a 6.89. Furthermore, the study concluded, "real life experience with parallel television content did not diminish the perceived reality of television."[27] In other words, TV images tended to be seen as "truer" than first-hand information.

Such distorted views of reality may affect reality itself. Physicians cite the "television syndrome"—patients expecting doctors to cure and comfort them quickly and at little cost or inconvenience. Owing to the predominance of police and crime programs on TV, surveys now show that many police officers try to act and look like they are "supposed" to. A Rand survey found that much of what real detectives do during a routine investigation—fingerprinting, lineups, and showing mug shots, for example—is usually not employed to capture criminals. Rather, in many cases, such techniques are intended to satisfy public expectations of how police should behave.[28]

Television also teaches that the police coerce witnesses, bribe, plant illegal drugs, lock up suspects without filing charges, and otherwise subvert the Constitution. When a tape of such illegal practices was shown to a class of prelaw students at the University of Massachusetts, most failed to understand why it was worthy of note. The author of this study, Ethan Katsh, a professor of legal studies, further points out that law is based upon abstract principles that on TV "are replaced by a personification of law. The focus of television is invariably on the visual elements of law such as courts, judges, police, lawyers, and criminals. These elements, which are a part of the law, become identified as being all of law."[29]

Believing that their TV images affect both social status and political power, organizations variously representing Vietnam veterans, women, homosexuals, senior citizens, manual workers, racial minorities, the handicapped, and the mentally ill have started to gather proof. Surveys show, for example, that the more people, especially young people, watch television, the more they tend to perceive old people in generally negative and unfavorable terms. A Machinists' union study laments that on prime-time television shows, "prostitutes outnumber machinists . . . and unions are almost invisible." Such imbalances, the Machinists argue, "devalue and harm occupations of crucial need to the economy."[30]

To sum up, there is no longer much doubt that television may engender or reinforce certain perceptions. The big unanswered question is: How strongly do various TV audiences "offset" what they see on the TV screen with perceptions and values drawn from other sources—personal experience, parents, friends, reading, church, and school?

One of the truisms about insights into the impact of television is that they usually move from startling revelation to cliche so rapidly there has been little time for insight of intelligent public policy. To say that television dominates our politics, was until relatively recently to invite charges of exaggeration and intellectual softness; to say the same thing today evokes only yawns.

This is a principal reason why television has been generating new issues before the old issues are resolved. Things like televised violence still demand our attention, while a new litany of phenomena—things like global newscasting and the impact of new audience measurements—will soon demand our attention.

In all this, television is obviously far from all-powerful. Nor is it, as a technology, either good or bad. Yet, as Daniel Boorstin correctly warns, our uncritical embrace of television has created a crisis. Even the imprecise studies now available suggest TV's far-reaching impact. In theory, public opinion could tilt television programs toward more constructive ends; the TV industry, after all, is a captive of audience taste. But even that would hardly lessen the sheer amount of time many people spend in front of the TV set. And there is no evidence, in any event, that Americans are disposed to rise up, en masse, against those responsible for what appears on the air.

This is perhaps the most alarming aspect of television—not the medium itself, but the fact that most Americans refuse to acknowledge its influence, or to take steps to affect its content, or at the very least to control their own viewing habits and those of their children.

NOTES

1. Barry Siegel, "TV's Effect: From Alpha to Z-z-z," *Los Angeles Times*, March 11, 1979.

2. Congressional Budget Office, Congress of the United States, *Educational Achievement: Explanations and Implications of Recent Trends*, Washington, D.C.: U.S. Government Printing Office, 1987.

3. George Comstock et al., *Television and Human Behavior*, New York: Columbia, 1978.

4. Richard T. Hezel, "Public Broadcasting: Can It Teach?" *Journal of Communication*, Summer 1980.

5. Edith Spiegal, "Yes, *Sesame Street* Has Its Detractors," *New York Times*, Aug. 5, 1979.

6. Whatever the impact of specific programs, some scholars speculate that by relying on the information coded in images, TV watchers may be developing hitherto unused portions of their brains. Harvard University researchers in 1979 showed similar groups of children the same story—one version on film with narration, and the other in a picture book. In response to questions afterward, both groups gave generally the same answers. Yet the film viewers based their answers on visual context, while the readers relied more upon verbatim repetitions of the text. One thought process was neither more correct nor more desirable; they were merely different. Other research suggests that the average IQ may be rising because of children's increased capacity to handle spatial, visual problems.

7. *Pediatrics*, vol. 80, No 3, September 1987.

8. Arthur M. Schlesinger, Jr., *The Cycles of American History*, Boston: Houghton Mifflin, 1986.

9. Shanto Iyengar and Donald R. Kinder, *News That Matters*, Chicago: The University of Chicago Press, 1987.

10. Thomas E. Patterson and Robert McClure, *The Unseeing Eye*, New York: Putnam's, 1976.

11. This can have international consequences. The vision of global TV publicity is a temptation to some terrorists and a tool in the hands of others. The 1979–80 story of the Americans taken hostage in Iran is a case in point. In Tehran, the colorful Islamic "student" militants adroitly exploited the American news teams' hunger for "good film." In the United States, the hostages' families and man-in-the-street reactions added a home-town angle. The TV news organizations saw the hostage story as a continuing melodrama and gave it almost unprecedented amounts of air time. On one occasion, the *CBS Evening News* devoted all but 3 minutes of its regular 22-minute broadcast to the crisis. President Carter, some analysts contend, felt impelled by the "saturation" TV coverage to react in dramatic ways, such as leaving the campaign trail and ordering a Navy task force to the Indian Ocean. He, too, discovered that the crisis could be exploited, as his poll ratings went up. The

distinction between what was important and what was just theater was blurred from the day the American diplomats were taken hostage.

12. George A. Comstock and Eli A. Rubenstein, eds., *Television and Social Behavior: Technical Reports to the Surgeon General's Scientific Advisory Committee on Television and Social Behavior,* Rockville, Md.: National Institute of Mental Health, 1972.

13. National Institute of Mental Health, *Television and Behavior: Ten Years of Scientific Progress and Implications for the Eighties,* Volumes I and II, Washington, D.C.: U.S. Government Printing Office, 1982.

14. W.A. Belson, "Television Violence and the Adolescent Boy," paper presented to the British Association for the Advancement of Science, Sept. 6, 1977.

15. F.L. Paulson, "Teaching Cooperation on Television," *Audio-Visual Communications Review,* vol. 22, no. 3, 1974.

16. The Metropolitan Life Survey of The American Teacher, New York: Louis Harris and Associates, 1987.

17. George Gerbner et al., "Media and the Family," White House Conference on Families, 1980.

18. "TV Viewers: Learning and Media Research," Southwest Educational Development Laboratory, Feb., 1980.

19. Center for Population Communications International, 777 United Nations Plaza, New York, N.Y. 10017.

20. George Gerbner and Nancy Signorielli, *Women and Minorities in Television Drama,* Philadelphia, Pa.: Univ. of Pa., 1979.

21. Women on television are generally attractive, under age 40, use sexual guile, and hold primarily "traditional" female occupations. Women are warm, submissive, timid, and emotional; men are ambitious, intellectual, violent, and logical. In authoritative speaking roles, particularly in commercials, men outnumber women by more than three to one.

22. Paul E. McGhee, "Television as a Source of Learning Sex Role Stereotypes," paper presented to the Society for Research in Child Development, 1975.

23. Lawrence Wallack, Warren Breed, and John Cruz, "Alcohol and Prime Time Television," *Journal of Studies on Alcohol,* vol. 48, no. 1, 1987.

24. Findings about television and blacks also generally hold true for Hispanics, Native Americans, and other groups.

25. The power of television is felt most acutely during childhood. The average child sees about 25,000 commercials a year. Studies show that the younger children are, the more likely they are to prefer playing with toys advertised on TV than with friends, and the more likely they are to ask parents to make a specific purchase. When asked "the kinds of goods you call snacks," 78 percent of the children in one survey named TV-advertised junk food.

26. Tobacco executives resisted the broadcast ban only half-heartedly because earlier federal rulings guaranteed air time for antismoking TV com-

mercials. Surveys indicated that these "counter-commercials" were hazardous to healthy cigarette ads.

27. Bradley S. Greenberg and Byron Reeves, "Children and the Perceived Reality of Television," *Journal of Social Issues,* no. 32, 1976.

28. Jan M. Chaiken, *The Criminal Investigation Process,* Santa Monica, Calif.: Rand Corporation, 1975.

29. Ethan Katsh, "Is Television Anti-Law: An Inquiry into the Relationship between Law and Media," unpublished manuscript, 1980.

30. *Television Entertainment Report,* Washington, D.C.: International Association of Machinists and Aerospace Workers, 1980.

Chapter 16

NEWS FROM EVERYWHERE

by Lawrence W. Lichty

By the 1980s the images of history—the icons we hold in our heads—were being recorded live, in color, and in great clarity on videotape. For the first time we saw dramatic incidents repeated hundreds of times in stunning succession—immediately following the event, then in nightly, weekly, year-end, and other periodic summaries. For decades we were told that newsreels were the "eyes and ears of the world" or that TV could show us history "as it happens." Now it was true.

A president was shot, and we relived the assassination again and again. The wedding of an English prince, demonstrations in Poland, a war in the Falkland Islands—all were clearly seen through our "window on the world." Pictures of starving children in Africa shown on a network news broadcast triggered relief efforts that included a rock concert televised worldwide.

During a hijacking in the Middle East, we saw one captor wave his pistol out the aircraft window while newsmen asked questions of the hostage pilot.

We watched while the space shuttle Challenger exploded, while an American president and a Soviet leader debated arms control, and while an anchorman and a presidential contender exchanged verbal blows in what the candidate called "tension city."

For Americans, it was news from far away, amid economic troubles at home, natural disasters, live congressional hearings, and a presidential campaign that began two years before election day.

Television's handling of the "news" more than ever seemed to fit Walter Lippmann's 1922 description of the press as "the beam of a searchlight that moves restlessly about, bringing one episode then another out of darkness into vision."

The News as Show Business

The three television networks competing for audiences for their evening news shows exaggerate this chronic tendency. The news is presented as one melodrama after another—often far more compelling melodramas than those television could offer as regular entertainment. Ronald Reagan's aides made no secret of their belief that the fortieth president could—and should—play to television's need for "visuals" and ignore the newspapers' traditional preoccupation with words. In the 1984 reelection campaign White House officials arranged a "never-ending string of spectacular picture stories" for television and, as Martin Schram concluded in his book, *The Great American Video Game* (William Morrow, 1987), "were unperturbed about the fact that the correspondents were pointing this out as they showed [them]."

The greatest expansion of television news came in the 1980s. Television news is the child of radio news and the theatrical film newsreels of the 1930s. In its basic attitudes it is not the offspring or even a new relative of the newspapers. In their competition for audiences (ratings) that govern advertising revenues, television news executives, both local and national, can never relax. When Walter Cronkite retired as an anchorman in 1981, the question for CBS was: Could his successor, Dan Rather, preside over the news as effectively as Cronkite? Could he draw the viewers? The answer was a tentative—but controversial—yes. All three networks changed their style and on-camera personalities after 1982. *CBS Evening News* has won the vast majority of all "weeks" since then but the race is very tight. Most of the time no more than one rating point (or fewer than one million homes) separates first place from third.

In June 1980, Ted Turner began Cable News Network (CNN) as a twenty-four-hour-a-day service of news, talk, and interviews, with smaller amounts of business, financial, weather, and sports news. By January 1982 cable television was reaching one-third of all U.S. homes and a second cable service—CNN Headline News—challenged both the other networks and all-news radio with a thirty-minute news format round-the-clock. Other cable networks also offered nonstop weather, financial reports, documentaries, and two C–SPAN channels gave live coverage of the House and Senate as well as hearings, speeches, and telephone call-in programs. Since December 1986 a Long Island cable system has been providing continuous local video news.

The networks responded to the competition with additional newscasts before their 7 A.M. morning programs, more daily "feeds" of stories to their affiliated stations, and an all-night news-interview program on CBS. A second satellite news channel and an overnight news hour on NBC both died after about a year.

This surge of broadcast news seems only to confirm the ascendancy of video. Even the one-half of television homes that lack cable service face no shortage of "news." Most of these viewers can watch more than twelve hours a day, including two stretches of three hours in the early morning and evening.

Furthermore, by 1988 CBS was offering in prime time two weekly "magazine" format documentary programs and a new "video verité," called *48 Hours,* which took viewers "inside" a hospital, airport, election campaign, city, and other institutions. (ABC had only one "magazine"—*20/20*—and NBC had none after more than thirty prime-time documentaries in 1987, of which only seven were seen in more than one-tenth of all U.S. households.) On average, such in-depth looks at social and political issues are seen by only 6 percent to 8 percent of all homes—or fewer than 10 percent to 15 percent of all TV sets turned on at the time. The only weekly documentary series were on PBS—*Frontline, Nova,* and *Nature*—but there were a score of series of five to thirteen episodes produced or rebroadcast each year.

In the 1980s, however, many social issues, formerly treated only in documentary form, were presented as drama: battered women, child pornography, birth defects, AIDS, the mentally retarded, aging parents, surrogate mothers, and even incest. Only a year after Reagan and Gorbachev met at an Iceland summit, the negotiations were dramatized on the eve of a second meeting. The networks and syndicated program producers also experimented with new forms of daytime "infotainment" that combined personal advice, controversial discussions, and interviews with well-known politicians, show business personalities, and others caught up in a breaking news story who enjoyed their fifteen minutes of celebrity.

What is striking, of course, is how thin and how much the same all this video news is. On the three network evening news shows, for example, there is about 50 percent duplication of major stories, far more duplication than exists on, say, the front pages of the *San*

Francisco Chronicle and the *St. Louis Post Dispatch,* leaving aside strictly local items.

Network Newspeople as Stars

The half-hour evening news show has room for seventeen or eighteen items in twenty-two minutes (commercials eat up eight minutes). Eight or nine of these items are tape snippets lasting from a few seconds to one and a half minutes; the rest are the anchorman's brief reports written by anonymous network writers from the news dispatches coming in over the studio teletype from Associated Press (AP) and other services. In Washington or the Mideast, the TV correspondent, as NBC's Douglas Kiker put it, is "making little movies," directing a camera crew, scribbling the words he or she will utter to give significance to the film. Television correspondents are not "reporters," in the sense that reporters for the wire services and newspapers are. They have little time for fact finding, and little time on the air to present any facts they do find.

The requirements of TV news do not, therefore, impel ABC, CBS, and NBC to deploy large numbers of information-seekers, although the logistics and technology require a sizable supporting staff. In Washington, locale of 40 percent of CBS News's stories and (not coincidentally) site of its largest bureau, there are 230 CBS News employees. Of these, only 17 are reporters, for both radio and TV— versus 42 Washington reporters for the *New York Times* and 100 for the AP. At all but the very largest market stations, there is no single reporter wise in the ways of municipal government covering the "city hall beat;" stations usually send a reporter and camera crew to cover scheduled events or in reaction to a local newspaper or news service story. There is unlikely to be any coverage unless it is determined in advance that the effort is likely to produce "good tape."

Overseas, CBS has only 23 full-time correspondents, versus 34 for the *New York Times,* 36 for *Time,* 8 for the *Baltimore Sun,* 19 for the Knight–Ridder papers—and about 300 for the AP, whose operatives and those of rival UPI supply most of the news that Dan Rather (like his ABC and NBC counterparts) reads off a teleprompter every weekday evening.

Television, as Jane Bryant Quinn observed, gives us "the faces," the voices, the scenery—albeit in highly selective bits and pieces. The small number, in comparison with so much other programming, of documentary hours draw relatively small audiences but occasionally strike political sparks. At its best, TV provides us with a live view of the great spectacles: space shots, disasters, presidential inaugurations, primary caucuses and elections, political conventions, congressional hearings, and of course, all of the sports specials—the World Series, Super Bowl, the Olympics, and many more. The annual and quadrennial spectacles are predictable but still thrilling. The unpredictable—the revolutions, assassinations, and natural disasters—serve as our mileposts.

Our society seems to be defined not by what is familiar, solid, and evolving, but by what is different and deviant. This is not a radical change. "News" has always helped us define the boundaries of the typical. But as *Newsweek* reported after the January confrontation

---

AND THAT'S THE WAY IT IS

In *The Right Place at the Right Time* (1982), Public Broadcasting System's Canadian-born Robert MacNeil looks back at his globe-trotting days with the BBC and NBC and explains what is distinctive about TV reporting:

In most of the stories television cares to cover there is always "the right bit." The most violent, the most bloody, the most pathetic, the most tragic, the most wonderful, the most awful moment. Getting the effective "bit" [on film] is what television news is all about. It is the bit you always recognize when you've got it and which you will go through just about anything to get because it means success and missing it consistently means you'd better look for a job other than as a TV correspondent.

And to what purpose are thousands of men and women scrambling over the earth, sometimes at great risk, to get that bit? So that millions of people may be distracted or a moment from their own domestic concerns to witness another human being in great distress? To feel what? A moment of compassion? A second of titillation? A wisp of vicarious fear? Does it not ultimately blunt and cheapen all those natural feelings to have them so often artificially stimulated? Does it not make human pity itself a banality? Does that not force competitive television producers to turn the screw a trifle harder each time to make the sensation fresher, to unbanalize it? Yes.

And what is the ultimate purpose of all this activity? The television journalists, like journalists everywhere, want to tell stories. The networks want to sell deodorant.

And that's the way it is.

between Dan Rather and Vice President George Bush: "In television, style overwhelms substance, image replaces information."

Thus, the further expansion of "video," even as it promises greater diffusion of the same news, does not add greatly to the array of information available to the public. Yet "electronic home delivery" has persuaded many analysts that the "news" in print, as it has evolved over the past 150 years in America, is all but dead. James Martin, author of *Future Trends in Telecommunications* (1977), predicts that by the early 1990s, there may be only a "minor intellectual press, a few picture newspapers for low–IQ readers, and some local newspapers," along with a few newsmagazines. Citing the preeminence of television, NBC's anchorman Tom Brokaw has spoken of the young people who "have come to rely on us as their primary and *only* source of news."

How Influential is TV News?

Indeed, the conventional wisdom, widely echoed, is that Americans get most of their news from Brokaw and his colleagues in television. This assertion stems largely from surveys by the Roper Organization since 1959, indicating that TV became preeminent in home entertainment in 1960 and became the primary source of news for adults in 1970. The question Roper has asked his respondents since 1959 is "Where do you usually get most of your news about what's going on in the world today?" In October, 1986, 50 percent specified television, 23 percent specified newspapers, and 16 percent specified TV and newspapers. Respondents were permitted multiple answers. When all were tallied, 66 percent cited TV, 36 percent newspapers, 14 percent radio, 4 percent magazines, and 4 percent "another person."

From all this, it seems clear that most people now think that they get most of their news from TV. As we shall see, this is almost certainly not true, even though presidents, senators, and other politicians (to say nothing of TV journalists and TV critics) have come to act on the assumption that it is true.

Those in the business of figuring out "audience exposure" to advertising messages have developed a number of surveys that give a far clearer picture of what sources Americans draw on for news and information. Simmons Market Research Bureau, based in Manhattan, does annual studies on "exposure" of Americans to various media.

Some 1986 Simmons data:[1]

• About two-thirds of U.S. adults (63 percent) read at least part of some newspaper every day. Thirteen percent of all adults read two or more newspapers a day.
• Only about one-third of U.S. adults watch the early evening network news, and fewer watch a late-night local TV news summary.
• Two-thirds—about the same as see a daily paper—watch one or more of three major news blocks during the day: an early local news show, a network evening news show, or a late night local news summary.
• About 30 percent of U.S. adults read *Time, Newsweek,* or *U.S. News & World Report.* (More than one-fifth of all U.S. adults read *Reader's Digest.*)

Other data suggest that TV is far from a dominant source of news. The number of American adults watching the three weekday network evening newscasts on a given night is very large (55 million), as is the audience for the highest rated *Cosby Show* (47 million). But the audience for TV news fluctuates. It is far more fickle than the audience for newspapers or magazines. Slightly more than half of the nation's TV households watch one of the network evening news programs at least once in the course of a month. But only 2 percent of all 89 million American TV households watches CBS's Dan Rather as often as four or five nights a week, and Rather presides over the nation's most popular network evening news show. The average for households that watch his program at all is five broadcasts per month. Again, only about 15 percent of homes—10 percent of the adults—watch network evening news four or five times a week; and one-third do not watch any network evening news program each week.

In short, the widely accepted notion that Dan Rather and his rivals each command a vast, devoted, nightly following seems far-fetched.

A related assumption, tenaciously held by both television's critics and its champions, is that the visual impact of TV nightly news "turned the American people against the Vietnam war" and, later, pushed Richard M. Nixon out of the White House. Yet there is no empirical evidence that TV news "shapes" mass public opinion—or that any news medium does.[2]

What "the news" probably influences is not how we think but what we think and talk about. Few subjects get much media attention for very long. When they do, politicians and other opinion leaders may feel impelled to react. Even here, direct links between "news coverage" per se and the evolution of political decisions are not easy to establish.

It might be best therefore to think of TV news as a visual "table of contents." Television calls attention to the "news." It lists the topics for discussion. To be sure, it may show us some events; but it provides very few facts. It is better at showing emotion and reactions. But clearly, it does provide the agenda for much that we read or talk about later. Politics serves as a good example. Candidates must now use paid media (mostly TV commercials) to attract the attention of the "free media" and gain news coverage. As election campaigns unfold, the candidate must again use more paid media, often excerpts from news coverage or debates, to become even better known by the electorate. It is a complex process. It is simply not possible to say that we get X amount of our information from one source, Y from another, and Z from a third. The news media are interrelated and interdependent.

Overall, the evening TV news audience is disproportionately older (especially over 65), female (53 percent), and less well educated than are newspaper readers or the population as a whole. Two types of Americans emerge as the keenest viewers of TV news. One happens to see a lot of TV news largely because he or she watches a lot of television: The news is only a small part of the daily fare. This viewer is somewhat more likely to have had only a high school education, to be in a clerical, sales, or service job, and to live in the South. The other, far less common TV news watcher, is the younger, better-educated American adult, a heavy reader of news, who watches a lot of news and information programming on TV but not much else.

Cutting the Cost of Network News

In the 1970s most network affiliates expanded their early evening news broadcasts from 30 minutes to an hour; in larger markets some stations offer two- and even three-hour news shows. These programs often "recycle" much of the same material—sports, weather, and live on-the-scene segments—and thus produce expanded programming with a minimal increase in costs. Local news has become a real profit center, whereas network news expanded into far less lucrative time periods.

The immensely successful CBS show *60 Minutes* may have produced a yearly profit of up to $100 million, and the evening news programs have also been profitable. But these earnings have generally just covered all other network news operations. By the late 1980s it was estimated that each of the network news divisions had budgets of about $300 million—three and a half times higher than just a decade earlier. Beginning in 1987, with the cost of programming rising and the economy stagnant, each tried to cut its news budget to about $250 million. New owners at all three networks, declining network audience shares, and rising costs in news and entertainment programming forced reductions. Each news operation cut about 200 people from a staff of about 1,400. A number of experienced—and therefore more highly paid—correspondents and producers took early retirement or were fired. The networks remain highly profitable, thanks largely to their owned-and-operated stations and their very lucrative daytime programming (which garners more than half of network earnings).

NBC's John Chancellor has noted the change:

> In the 1950s a lot of television organizations were operated by a system of paternal ownership. When CBS was Bill Paley's network and NBC David Sarnoff's network, they held them in the palm of their hands, and there was that link of personal accountability that no longer exists. It has now been replaced by boards of directors who have a fiduciary responsibility under the law not to run risks, and to maximize profits.

In the 1980s the Federal Communications Commission—first under President Carter and increasingly during the Reagan administration—"deregulated" broadcasting. Gone, according to former CBS President Frank Stanton, was "some pretty strong guidance on what the obligations of the licensees were; for a long time license renewals were based on the mix [of information and entertainment] that you had in your schedule."

Even with this leveling, print journalists never match the salaries or celebrity of their well-coiffed counterparts in television. No daily journal comes even close to the "reach" of each of the network evening new programs. Yet there is no clear sign that "video" in its various forms is about to eliminate its less exciting print competition as a source of information.

What seems obvious, although it challenges the common myth, is that most American adults get their "news" from many sources. And judging from the "exposure" data, most of what they get every day still comes about equally from newspapers and television. Further, the research shows that much of what people think and feel about what they read and see is refined and defined in conversations with other people.

Television is dramatic. Newspapers are easy and efficient. Scores of news items can be scanned, selected, put aside, retrieved, pored over, even reread. This process occurs at the reader's convenience, any time, any place. It takes far less time than the 60 to 90 minutes required to sit through the bits and pieces of the evening's local and national TV news shows. New cable services make news, weather, sports, and business reports available at virtually any time, but they are not yet a big factor for a majority of viewers.

In describing the press as a searchlight, Walter Lippmann concluded that:

> Men cannot do the work of the world by this light alone. They cannot govern society by episodes, incidents, and eruptions. It is only when they work by a steady light of their own, that the press, when it is turned upon them reveals a situation intelligible enough for a popular decision. The trouble lies deeper than the press, and so does the remedy. It lies in social organization based on a system of analysis and record. . . .[3]

Books, newspapers, magazines, radio, television, and now even "newer" media provide Americans with an enormous diversity of record and analysis. We can chose, again in Lippmann's phrase, between "the curious trivial as against the dull important."

NOTES

1. The 1986 Simmons report is based on more than 19,000 interviews, but uses smaller samples for certain segments of the 43 volumes of data.

2. See John E. Mueller's *War, Presidents and Public Opinion* (Wiley, 1973). Critic Michael Arlen reminded us in the *New Yorker* (Aug. 16, 1982) that "what a television viewer of the Vietnam war [usually] saw . . . was a nightly, stylized, generally distanced overview of a disjointed conflict which was composed mainly of scenes of helicopters landing, tall grasses blowing in the helicopter wind. American soldiers fanning out across a hillside . . . with now and then (on the soundtrack) a far-off ping or two, and now and then (as a visual grand finale) a column of dark billowing smoke a half a mile away, invariably described as a burning Viet Cong ammo dump."

3. Walter Lippmann, *Public Opinion*, 1922.

Chapter 17

THE NEW ERA

by Stuart N. Brotman

In the film *Network,* anchorman Howard Beale urges his TV audience to open up their windows and shout: "I'm mad as hell, and I'm not going to take it anymore."

Unlike Beale's frustrated viewers in the 1970s, Americans during the 1980s have acquired powerful tools with which to register their dissatisfaction with traditional TV programming and which allow them, in effect, to vote with their pocketbooks. New video technologies hold out the promise of irrigating a wasteland and bringing a vast array of quality television programming into the living room at moderate prices. But skeptics point to the history of conventional TV broadcasting, itself once hailed as the hope of the future. The claims made for any budding technology, they contend, have always been too good to be true.

Many of the new TV technologies, such as cable television and the videocassette recorder (VCR), have in fact been "promising" for years. Until the early 1980s, however, the performance of "new" TV technologies was generally unremarkable, their growth stymied by federal regulation, scarce venture capital, and a public willing to settle for the menu that ABC, CBS, and NBC provided.

All that has changed dramatically. By the end of 1987, a majority of American homes had cable television service, a VCR, or both. Investment in the new TV technologies, both by businesses and consumers, is up sharply; entrepreneurs are now backed by the financial resources of such firms as Coca-Cola, the New York Times Company, Time Inc., Warner Communications, and RJR Nabisco.

And Congress, along with the Federal Communications Commission (FCC), has followed the lead of the federal courts, substantially freeing the cable TV industry from twenty years of sometimes capricious federal regulation.

The Changing TV Landscape

The television landscape, in sum, has rapidly changed. Although the familiar broadcast channels, divided among independent stations and the local affiliates of ABC, CBS, and NBC, are not about to fall into disuse, they now have formidable competition in viewing households that receive a combination of broadcast and cable channels (nearly twenty on the average). Add to that literally thousands of videocassettes available for sale or rental locally, and it becomes apparent how different the television landscape has become.

Let us begin with a brief primer on a few of the new electronic media.

Cable television transmits video signals through a coaxial cable, usually placed under streets or strung on telephone poles. As of 1987, there were about 7,800 cable systems in the United States serving some 20,000 communities. Another 700 franchises have been approved. Channel capacity on cable increased significantly during the 1980s. At the beginning of the decade, two-thirds of all cable systems carried twelve channels or fewer. Today, fewer than one in four have such a limited capacity, and nearly half of all cable systems have thirty channels or more.

Between 1980 and 1987 cable subscribers increased their expenditures from $2.9 billion to $11.8 billion, according to the CableTelevision Advertising Bureau. For a ten- to fifteen-dollar monthly fee, each cable subscriber receives a basic service ("basic cable") consisting of retransmitted broadcast signals from local TV stations plus a variety of satellite-fed special services, such as an all-news channel, an all-sports channel, an all-weather channel, and an all-religion channel. The average of all revenues, including pay services, per subscriber is about twenty-five dollars per month.

A majority of households with basic cable also subscribe to one or more "pay cable" services such as Home Box Office (HBO), a subsidiary of Time Inc., and the Disney Channel. These packaged services typically offer recent Hollywood movies and original entertainment programming that is not available on commercial stations.

Pay cable subscribers nearly quadrupled between 1980 and 1987, and now number over 26 million households.

Communications satellites have revolutionized the transmission of signals to cable systems by dramatically lowering the cost of transmission (previously accomplished by sending video signals

---

WHAT CABLE SUBSCRIBERS GET

Typical newer, metropolitan cable system has as many as 50–60 channels that might include:

OFF THE AIR

3 local network affiliates; more if the system is near two markets

5–7 independent stations, most playing reruns of previous network programming (many sitcoms and crime detective programs)

2–5 PBS stations

BASIC CABLE NETWORKS

general entertainment (USA)

an entertainment channel targeted for women with medical programming on weekends (Lifetime)

an arts channel (Arts and Entertainment)

a national and local channel of all sports

2 channels providing all news, and several channels with wire reports of news, business, and sports

several channels with mostly religious programming

2 channels providing coverage of the U.S. Senate and House of Representatives, with many political speeches, conferences, and hearings

1 or 2 channels with special programming in Spanish or aimed at blacks

a channel with programming for children

specialized networks with documentaries, financial news, how-to-do-it programs, and general education

a channel with nearly all music, including rock, more adult appeal, country music, and country variety

a channel for weather and the transmission of a nearby weather radar

a channel with text and picture stories for children

1 or 2 "shopping" channels for ordering merchandise

ENTERTAINMENT/"SUPER STATIONS"

These include such stations at WTBS Atlanta, WOR New York, WGN-TV Chicago, and KTTV Los Angeles. While cable systems have more than fifty basic services which they can make available to subscribers, only sixteen of these are carried on enough systems to have the potential of reaching a quarter of American homes.

PREMIUM CHANNELS

Subscribers can usually pay a monthly fee to receive one or more of eight channels offering primarily movies, including those specializing in fine arts, classic films, Spanish, Disney, or more sexually oriented fare. The first and largest premium channel, HBO, is subscribed to by one in six American households. More than one-fourth of all American homes subscribe to at least one pay cable service.

LOCAL CHANNELS

Local cable channels often include programming provided by elementary schools, high schools, and libraries, and coverage of city council and other government meetings. Often when not providing live coverage the channels show "bulletin board" announcements from local organizations.

Source: Lawrence W. Lichty, compiled from cable services available to subscribers in Fairfax County, Virginia, and Evanston, Illinois, and typical of most major cable systems with at least fifty channels.

through long-distance telephone lines). Now cable programming can be efficiently networked across the country. Home Box Office led the way in 1975, and today virtually all pay cable services also transmit by satellite to "receive-only" antennas owned by subscribing cable companies.

Home satellite dishes, also known as TVROs (television receive-only antennas) have emerged as competition for cable because of their ability to pick up the same satellite signals that cable systems receive. Although these dishes require careful placement on land (typically a large backyard) and cost several thousand dollars, they have mushroomed in popularity among both wealthy homeowners and those in rural areas where cable service remains unavailable. By the end of 1987, according to *Channels* magazine, there were 1.7 million dish owners nationwide.

The cable industry saw this as a growing threat since TVROs were providing free programming to anyone willing to make a simple investment in a backyard dish antenna. As a consequence, satellite-delivered cable programming companies have scrambled their signals to prevent unauthorized reception, forcing home dish owners to purchase $400 descramblers and subscribe to the services (often at prices in excess of those paid by regular cable subscribers).

Videocassette recorders, a blip in the new media mix less than ten years ago, have emerged to challenge both broadcasting and cable for the loyalty—and dollars—of the American viewing public. Japanese technological advances have reduced the price of a record-and-play-

CABLE TV: SUBSCRIBER HOMES AND PRIME-TIME VIEWERS

	Subscriber Homes	Prime Time Viewing Average Households
ESPN/Sports	41,000,000	571,000
WTBS/Super Station	40,204,000	1,401,000
CNN/News	38,456,000	607,000
USA/Entertainment	37,000,000	699,000
CBN/Religion	34,086,000	245,000
MTV/Music	33,400,000	256,000
Lifetime/Women, health	30,600,000	139,000
Nashville/Country	26,600,000	438,000

Sources: Subscribers reported in *Cablevision* magazine 4 May 1987. Prime time households for 2d quarter of 1988, A. C. Nielsen, reported in *Broadcasting*, 11 July 1988, p. 41.

MOST POPULAR CABLE PROGRAMS

	Rating	Households (Millions)
Award Theater/WTBS	3.6	1.5
Championship Sports/WTBS	3.2	1.3
Primetime Wrestling/USA	3.4	1.3
A.M. Wrestling/USA	3.2	1.2
Prime Movie I/WTBS	2.7	1.1

Source: A. C. Nielsen, Cable series third quarter 1987.

Of the twenty most popular cable programs, five were wrestling or boxing, six were reruns of network programs such as *Andy Griffith, The Munsters,* and *Bonanza,* and three were movies.

back VCR from more than $1,000 to a few hundred dollars, and sales have soared. In 1980, for example, there were less than one million VCRs sold nationally. By 1987 annual unit sales hovered near 12 million, with more than 44 million in American households.

Not surprisingly, as VCR penetration grew, pay cable sales began to flatten out. The cable industry, fueled during the past decade by the pent-up viewer demand for programming not available on the networks or independent stations, felt the impact in its bottom line, and thus began to reassess its overall marketing strategy. By the mid-1980s, local cable companies moved away from trying to sell three or four pay packages per household in favor of increasing the overall number of subscribers to basic cable.

Emphasizing Basics to Generate Profits

Much of this change in strategic direction was based on cable's potential as an advertising medium. Increasing audience size and bolstering its upscale demographics appear to be the necessary build-

---

HOME VIDEO

In 1976 Sony introduced the first consumer videocassette recorder, the Betamax; it cost $1,200. Today good VCRs can be purchased for little more than $300, or, in inflation-adjusted dollars, about one-eighth the cost of the 1976 machine. And no one doubts that the current models are far superior to the early VCRs in terms of sound, length of play, and various options.

By 1986 receipts for rentals and sales of prerecorded tapes (principally movies) for the first time exceeded the figure for movie box-office receipts in the United States. In the 1970s it was difficult to find tape rental stores. Today tapes can be rented from convenience stores, supermarkets, and bookstores, as well as gas stations and even dry cleaners. In some cities one can rent a tape and have it delivered by a pizza delivery service.

VCR ownership is closely associated with movie rentals. Indeed, one-third to one-half of VCR households rent at least one tape per week. Only one in twenty, however, buy tapes. And the bulk of purchases and rentals center around a handful of hits defined by movie theater audiences.

A hit film can generate substantial revenues for moviemakers through video sales, though not through rentals. Once the tape is sold, it becomes the property of the purchaser, whether that be a VCR owner or a video-rental outlet. In 1986 Paramount's *Top Gun* brought in $82 million in theater distribution. The tape, selling for $26.95, sold more than two-and-a-half million copies in its initial marketing effort, raising Paramount's revenues from that source to $40 million. To put that figure in context, $40 million would have placed *Top Gun* among the top 10 grossing movies for the year.

Many movies never make it to the video rental stores. Even though some 200 new titles from 140 different companies are produced every month, many are withheld from the market until conditions are right. The tenth anniversary of the death of Elvis Presley in August 1987 saw a flood of his old films and concert tapes. Sometimes films sit on studio shelves because no one knows who owns them. It is widely agreed that the famous Bob Hope–Bing Crosby *Road to. . . .* films would sell; but Paramount, which produced them, cannot figure our who controls the rights.

The effects of the VCR revolution have been numerous and far-reaching. The very basis of commercial television and the marketing of many familiar products is threatened because viewers tape shows for later viewing and then effectively remove the advertising messages by using the "fast-forward" control on their VCRs. During the major sweeps rating periods (November, February, and May) when the three networks offer their best shows, VCRs are in heavy use; during the summer reruns they sit idle. Only the year-round taping of soap operas breaks up this seasonal routine.

Working women, longtime soap opera fans, tape with a regularity unmatched by other VCR users. They play the tapes back when they get home from work (from 6 PM to 8 PM), but before the start of regular prime time programming. Nielsen surveys show that taped soap operas, more than any other form of programming, are played back within a week of initial recording.

Still, few programs generate any significant share of their audience through tape-delayed viewing. VCR taping reaches a peak during sweep rating weeks when the networks offer mini-series head-to-head. When NBC's *Peter the Great* ran second to *Sins* it won a 17.7 rating, including 9/10 of a point from recording, representing 5 percent of its audience. *Sins* got a 20.7 rating, including 7/10 of a point from recording, about 3 percent of its audience. Only soaps would be higher, sometimes with 8 to 10 percent of their audiences coming from recording.

Taping of specific shows matches the ratings; the higher the ratings, the more taping. If one were to picture all of America's VCRs working at once, one would think of a Thursday night in 1987 with NBC's blockbuster lineup of *The Cosby Show, Family Ties, Cheers, Night Court,* and *L.A. Law.*

Often VCR owners tape on Friday and Saturday nights when they go out, and then watch their favorite programs at some other time. This was particularly the case with *Dallas* in the Spring of 1987, according to Nielsen surveys.

Saturday night is by the far the biggest playback night because it is a popular time to show rental movies. It has been argued that the networks would be well advised to air very attractive programs late Saturday night to tempt viewers who have finished looking at prerecorded tapes and might be roaming the dial for more to watch.

In 1987 sales of VCRs leveled off for the first time. By then, half of American homes had a machine, surpassing the penetration of cable television for the first time. No one knows for sure how high the penetration of VCRs will rise; much depends on the dollar–yen exchange rate. But the influence of home video is just beginning to be fully felt. Home video will continue to transform American life in unexpected ways well into the twenty-first century.

Douglas Gomery

ing blocks that cable will need in order to be a viable competitor against radio and television stations, perhaps even against the networks themselves under a highly optimistic scenario.

With this "back-to-basics" approach, the cable industry has begun to fulfill its own aspirations. In 1980, according to Paul Kagan Associates, Inc., a Carmel, California-based market research firm, total cable advertising revenue was only $58 million; by 1987 the cable industry boasted that it had generated more than $1 billion in advertising revenues, with nearly 90 percent of this total attributable to national cable networks.

Cable television offered an alternative to the conventional advertiser-supported television system with an economic model that relied on cash flow from monthly subscriptions as the primary source of revenue. In theory, at least, a pay system of TV distribution creates substantial incentives to produce new types of programming, quite apart from its enormous number of available channels. Where a network needs an audience of at least 30 million for a "successful" program in terms of ratings, pay TV can turn a profit with an audience of 3 or 4 million. This is because the networks are essentially feeding sparrows by feeding horses; programs are paid for by advertising, with ad revenues depending on the size of the audience.

Cable's "narrowcasting" has fared quite well. MTV (*Music TeleVision*) has had a significant impact on contemporary style through its airing of music videos. It also has attracted sponsors who find MTV an attractive vehicle for reaching teens and young adults with buying power, and with little interest in tuning in to what older people are watching. ESPN, a nearly 'round-the-clock sports network, has provided sports aficionados with a feast of competition and updates of scores. Advertisers seeking viewers of this type—brewers and auto companies, for example—have signed up for enough ad time to put the network in the black, which is becoming the rule rather than the exception among advertiser-supported cable networks.

Competing (and Cooperating) with the Networks

The size and importance of advertising revenues is destined to grow over time; and already, cable has begun to hedge its bets on narrowcasting. Cable executives realize that in order to compete with ABC, CBS and NBC head-on, as well as with the fledgling Fox Broadcasting Company (which only programs on Saturday and Sunday nights on an ad hoc network of independent stations), a multibillion-dollar commitment to original programming will be necessary.

The economics of television production suggest that cable faces an uphill battle. The three networks now spend millions of dollars a year on programming. The starting budget for half-hour situation comedies is now $400,000, and a single episode for an hour-long series is $1.2 million.

"Our future is by far the brightest," says cable entrepreneur R.E. "Ted" Turner, who pioneered the concept of "SuperStations" by making available his Atlanta independent television station, WTBS, to nearly 50 million potential viewers, followed closely by his Cable News Network (CNN), a 24-hour news and feature satellite channel that Turner launched in 1980.

Turner's hyperbole about cable is well known, but so is his ability to prove the skeptics wrong. He is leading the charge within the cable industry to finance more original programming to compete with the networks. Turner argues that cable does not need to spend as much as the broadcast networks for programming, but that it must make more savvy spending decisions. He cites CNN as an example of how careful budgeting can boost a fledgling service into the big time. By employing young, nonunion workers, CNN operates on a budget of $100 million a year, about one-third of that spent by each of the three networks on their news operations.

The image of cable as offering only a pale imitation of network output is one that network executives work into every discussion of alternative TV technologies. "I wish that there was an infinite quantity of good programming available but there isn't," observes Gene Jankowski, president of CBS/Broadcast Group. "Adding signals to the marketplace will not be adding choice."

The initial response of the broadcast industry to the new video technologies was fear. Throughout the 1960s and most of the 1970s the broadcasters lobbied for federal protection in the form of restrictive FCC rules: limits on how many distant signals a cable system could carry, restrictions prohibiting pay cable from airing feature films more than three but less than ten years old, and prohibitions against televising certain sporting events such as the Super Bowl. Traditional broadcasters argued that the networks were running, in effect, a kind of charity enterprise, bringing the great wide world—documentaries, space shots, inaugurals, the World Series—"free of charge" into the homes of all Americans. Cable operators, they contended, would siphon off all of the good programming into the homes of the affluent.

The broadcast industry's preferential treatment began to crumble in 1977 when the U.S. Court of Appeals in Washington, D.C., in the case of *Home Box Office, Inc.* v. *FCC,* overturned most of the FCC's restrictions on what *pay* cable entrepreneurs could offer their customers. The court cited a breach of the First Amendment rights of producers, cablecasters and viewers. In 1980 the FCC scrapped all but two of its restrictions on *basic* cable programming. And in 1984, Congress itself completed the government's dismantling of its regulatory structure for cable through landmark legislation that allowed cable systems, among other things, to set their own rates for basic cable service rather than entrust the communities that granted operating franchises to do so. Despite its protests, cable has been and will remain a business that pays as much attention to the financial ledger as its broadcast counterparts.

Increasingly, it has become difficult to differentiate between broadcasting and cable executives. The three networks are hedging their bets. In recent years, particularly at the local level, they have been heavily involved in purchasing cable systems. (A third of all cable systems are now owned by companies with some sort of broadcast interests.) All three networks also are actively involved in cable programming or in home-video distribution, with indications that bigger deals loom somewhere on the horizon.

Despite significant erosion of network audiences, perhaps the status quo will *remain* the status quo, with the airwaves still dominated by ABC, CBS, and NBC, with cable and home video cast in the role of lucrative ventures on the fringe. Under this scenario, broadcasters may successfully coopt competition by continuing to buy into cable networks and to invest heavily in programming for cable and home video, in effect playing both ends against the middle.

Cable seems destined to struggle with its balancing act, as both a rich, mature industry and as an entrepreneurial industry nimble enough to jump in with a new concept when the time is right. Home shopping is a case in point. In less than three years since it was introduced, cable shopping programs already have exceeded $1 billion in sales.

Now that cable has largely been unleashed in the marketplace, it will have to be more aggressive in fighting off—even preempting—its competition. The seven large telephone companies created by the breakup of AT&T in 1984 see cable as a lucrative extension of their own businesses, especially since many plan on rewiring their own customers with fiber optic lines by the mid-1990s. Fiber optic technology offers the capability of carrying huge volumes of voice and video signals simultaneously, and many in the cable industry fear that it will make their own expensive coaxial cable networks obsolete. Fiber optics could be the great "breakthrough" of the 1990s.

"Pay-per-view" Arrangements

On the programming front, pay subscribers have defected to home video. Some cable systems have stressed harmony by promoting cable and the VCR as integral components of a home entertainment center. Pay programmers seem less friendly and are hoping that pay-per-view (PPV) arrangements (where special programming is ordered in advance or on impulse) can provide a way to lure customers back from the video store. They sense a growing dissatisfaction among many who drive to their local videocassette outlet only to find that the movie they want has already been rented.

With pay-per-view they hope to marry the price and quality of home video with the convenience of painless ordering and delivery. Only one in six cable viewers has the necessary equipment for pay-per-view so far, making it too early to forecast success or failure. Revenues have grown from $8 million in 1982 to $120 million in 1987, according to Goldman, Sachs & Co., which bullishly projects that PPV will be a $400 million annual business by 1990.

Historically, however, those who conjure up projections of market growth in a competitive media environment have often been proved wrong. Frequently, some critical, unknown factor intervenes to upset predictions that one technology will triumph over another: long-playing records versus audiocassettes; radio versus television; television versus motion pictures; advertiser-supported television versus pay television. As the failure to predict the explosive growth of home video rentals demonstrates, the rapid flow of events in the field of electronic media suggests that today's analysts may be skipping too lightly over areas that lead to the unknown.

It is difficult not to invent dispiriting scenarios, given commercial television's own history and the overall performance to date of the alternatives. The new electronic media are making money. They have given us, here and there, a few more real choices than we had before (for example, televised coverage of the United States Senate and House of Representatives). And the VCR has allowed most Americans to schedule their TV viewing around their leisure time, rather than vice versa.

The new video technologies, however, have not yet brought us much closer to the lofty ideal expressed by E.B. White in 1966:

I think television should be the visual counterpart of the literary essay. [It] should arouse our dreams, satisfy our hunger for beauty, take us on journeys, enable us to participate in events, present great drama and music, explore the sea and the sky and the woods and the hills. It should be our Lyceum, our Chautauqua, our Minsky's, and our Camelot.

Chapter 18

DOES PUBLIC TELEVISION HAVE A FUTURE?

by Stuart Alan Shorenstein and Lorna Veraldi

Throughout its history, public broadcasting in America has been a medium in search of a mission.

In the early 1950s noncommercial broadcasters tried to harness the educational potential of the "electronic blackboard." Then in 1967, what had been educational television was revamped and renamed: the new "public" television was heralded as an institution that would preserve and foster America's (and, cynics would add, Britain's) "cultural heritage." Public television has since received lavish praise, pointed criticism, and millions of dollars in public and private money. Yet twenty years later public television is in the throes of an identity crisis, and its options are limited.

From its start public TV has faced serious trouble. It has never found a reliable source of funds. Organizational headaches have plagued the system. Contributing to these woes has been public broadcasting's perceived lack of purpose. The major networks—ABC, CBS, and NBC—are in business to make money. What is public television in business for? Instruction? Culture? Ratings? Survival? There are now more than 300 public TV stations across the United States, all of them autonomous. They are united by no common mission—not, as a 1979 Carnegie Commission report would have it, "to be a civilized voice in a civilized society." Rather, as former *New York Times* critic Les Brown once noted, their only joint purpose seems to be the pursuit of congressionally authorized funds.

Despite attempts to reach out to a diverse and representative clientele, public TV still attracts only a small prime-time audience that remains disproportionately white, college-educated, and affluent. Rather than serving as a showcase and forum for American history, culture, and public debate, public television buys many of its best shows, including some that deal exclusively with American subjects, from producers in England, primarily, but also in Canada, Australia, West Germany, and even Japan. And now, to compound its problems, public broadcasting faces increased competition from cable TV and videocassettes—competition that may ultimately rob it of its audience, its more popular offerings, and its role as the alternative to the commercial networks.

Public TV in the United States

Public television started out at a disadvantage in the United States. In Britain, West Germany, Japan, and Canada, television, like radio broadcasting before it, was initially state-run. People grew accustomed to paying for TV out of their own pockets. By the time advertiser-supported television came along, public TV was already well established, not as an adjunct but as the leader in the medium.

In the United States the story was exactly the reverse. Here, commercial broadcasting was already in full bloom by the time the Federal Communications Commission (FCC) in 1952 set aside 242 stations, mostly in the UHF band, for noncommercial, educational use. The FCC, it should be noted, was doing public television no great favor. Most TV sets were equipped to receive only VHF. There was little popular demand for educational TV. Commercial television was itself a novelty.

The new educational stations, moreover, were run primarily by educators with little or no broadcasting experience. (A few were veterans of educational radio.) By contrast, in Britain when the Independent Television Authority (ITV) was authorized in 1954, many BBC employees moved laterally into the new commercial ITV network. Predictably, few American commercial broadcasters were tempted by the low pay and relative invisibility of educational TV. By 1957 only twenty-one educational broadcasting stations, run primarily by cities and towns, public school systems, or universities, were actually on the air.

With few exceptions, the promise of the electronic blackboard went unfulfilled. There was never enough money to produce good educational programming. Many educators, then as now, were highly skeptical of TV's pedagogic value. By the early 1960s noncommercial TV was in disarray. Fewer than seventy-five educational stations were in operation around the country, and the few programs they shared had to be "bicycled" from one station to the next. Their audiences were small, their programming lackluster.

Public TV got its first transfusion under the Kennedy administration when Congress enacted the 1962 Educational Facilities Act, which authorized up to $32 million in matching funds over five years to support noncommercial broadcasting. That same year, Congress required all TV sets sold after 1964 to be able to pick up UHF as well as VHF channels. The number of noncommercial stations now began to multiply, reaching 107 by 1966, when the Carnegie Corporation, intrigued by the possibility of "networking," impatient with the American system's shortcomings, and inspired by the manifest achievements of the BBC, charged a select commission to look at the future of noncommercial broadcasting.

Carnegie I: A Vision for the Future

It was the era of Lyndon Johnson's Great Society, when publishing a blue-ribbon study was often tantamount to seeing its recommendations enacted into law. Within a month of its release, the Carnegie Commission report ("Carnegie I") had become the nucleus of LBJ's 1967 Public Broadcasting Act. Carnegie I recommended that a national *public* television network—the word *educational* was discarded as unattractive—be set up as an alternative to the commercial networks, for the purpose of providing cultural enrichment and general information, not just instruction. The Commission also strongly recommended that public television should have long-term, politically insulated funding, from a source like Britain's tax on television receivers. The act (minus any long-term funding provision) sailed through Congress.

To oversee operation of the new system, Congress created the private, nonprofit Corporation for Public Broadcasting (CPB) under a board to be appointed by the president and confirmed by the Senate. The main duties of the CPB were to pay for programs and distribute funds, including an annual congressional appropriation, to member stations. In turn, CPB spun off the Public Broadcasting Service (PBS) to link up local stations, creating, in effect, America's "fourth network." The purpose of this complex organizational layout was to insulate public television from White House and congressional interference.

This is the foundation on which public broadcasting, as Americans have come to know it, has grown. It has expanded rapidly. There are now some 320 noncommercial TV stations on the air, reaching 97 percent of U.S. television households. Over roughly twenty years, public broadcasting's annual budget (for TV and radio) has risen from $58 million to $905 million and funding sources have become broadly diversified. (In FY 1986, 15.4 percent came from the federal government, about 33 percent from state and local governments [including state colleges], 22 percent from subscribers, and 15 percent from corporations.)

Public television, however, has had its growing pains. Since its inception, it has been plagued by jurisdictional conflicts among CPB, PBS, and the hundreds of member stations. Was PBS only responsible for the technical job of "networking," or could it select programs too? Was CPB just a funding body, or did it in fact have ultimate control over what went on the air? No one knew. In trying to insulate public broadcasting, Congress inadvertently had created something of a monster.

The "double-hull" buffer between politics and public television proved rather porous in any event. Although Congress declared CPB to be a *private* entity (it is not an agency of the U.S. government), it found itself politically vulnerable as the subject of annual congressional appropriations. Congress also left selection of the corporation's board to the vagaries of partisan politics.[1]

A decade after Carnegie I served as the model for the Public Broadcasting Act, the Carnegie Corporation impaneled a second blue-ribbon commission to take stock of the system that had been created. In a 1979 report ("Carnegie II"), the commission handed down this verdict:

> We find public broadcasting's financial, organizational and creative structure fundamentally flawed. In retrospect, what public broadcasting tried to invent was a truly radical idea: an instrument of mass communication that simultaneously respects the artistry of individuals who create programs, the needs of the public that form the audience, and the forces of political power that supply the resources. . . . Sadly we conclude that the invention did not work, or at least not very well.

The Carnegie Commission did not recommend that the whole effort be scrapped. Instead, it put forward a meticulously crafted reorganization plan that called for increased, long-term, reliable funding. But the commission's ruminations roused little interest in Congress or the White House. The expensive attitudes of the Great Society have given way to "marketplace" solutions. In an era of unconscionably high deficits and budget constraints, the pressure is on to trim spending, not to subsidize expensive "frills." In the years since Carnegie II was issued, public television has not been exempt and in turn has had to look for more of its income from the private sector.

Chronic financial problems have taken their toll in programming. During the late 1960s and early 1970s, critics were rather tolerant of the system's shortcomings. Give it time, they urged. After twenty years public television's overall record remains uneven. This is not to say that there have not been many notable successes. In addition to such acclaimed news and public affairs programs as *The MacNeil/Lehrer Newshour, Wall Street Week, Frontline,* and *Washington Week in Review,* and children's programming like *Sesame Street,* PBS has brought its viewers such remarkable original fare as *South American Journey, The Brain, God and Politics, America by Design, Nature, American Playhouse,* and *A Walk in the 20th Century,* to name just a few.

But America's public TV stations simply do not have the resources to produce a continuous stream of original programming. This is one reason why PBS airs so many imported shows, despite complaints from talented American writers, producers, and actors. Purchasing a series already produced in, say, Great Britain, costs a fraction of what it would cost to produce it in the United States. The low price tag attracts corporations such as Mobil and Exxon, which underwrite almost all of the imported programs shown on public television. Public broadcasters would like to produce more blockbusters like *The Adams Chronicles;* they cannot afford to.

Because none but the biggest public TV stations have the capacity to produce much original programming, local stations have come to depend on the daily PBS network "feeds" for the biggest share of their schedules. These programs are hatched by station executives in the flagship public stations, including WETA in Washington, WGBH in Boston, and WNET in New York. Many of these executives are veterans of foundations, or universities, or cultural institutions; a few are network refugees. Well-educated, if not intellectuals, committed to "uplift," they are responsible for the genteel, upper-middlebrow quality of public TV's typical offerings, a quality that is public television's signature and, arguably, its chief weakness.

> From the very first, [writes critic Benjamin DeMott] the makers of what we've come to know as public TV have behaved as though their prime duty was to coat the land with a film of what can best be described as distinguished philistinism, lifelessly well-meaning, tolerant, earnest, well-scrubbed—and utterly remote from what is most precious and vital in the soul of this nation.

Public television suffers, too, from a certain inevitable timidity. It is quite all right to be an "alternative," but *too much* of an alternative might not sit well among benefactors on Capitol Hill or in the White House or in the local community. Public affairs programs are especially vulnerable.

Perhaps public television's greatest asset is its distribution system—a network of satellite-interconnected stations that can provide simultaneous coverage to 97 percent of the nation's households. Despite this asset, PBS has remained a player on the fringes, boosted by a small, ardent group of supporters, but limited in its ability to create a lasting niche in an ever-changing technological playing field.

PBS will never achieve ratings to match the commercial networks. Its prime-time rating is about 2.7 percent of television households. Even the most popular shows on public TV, such as the periodic *National Geographic* specials, have never reached more than 17.4 percent of television households. (The prime-time rating for a network hit is about twice that.) Yet in a typical week more than half of all U.S. households watch some public TV programming and over the span of a month public TV reaches three-fourths of American households. And if the audience for a typical network show is larger, it should also be noted that few TV programs have remarkably loyal audiences. Many viewers tune in to daily programs such as network news only once each week, and view weekly programs only once a month.

Public broadcasting's failure to achieve "parity" with commercial television is to some degree understandable. It was, first, a late starter. By the time PBS came into existence, Americans had already become conditioned—by radio even before television—to receiving free, mass-appeal programming. Second, public television was created as an alternative. Unlike commercial TV, it deliberately has *not* sought to deliver massive audiences to demanding advertisers. Thus, say PBS

PUBLIC TV'S HIGHEST RATINGS

About 57 percent of all households watch public television each week in 1988—up from 38 percent in the past decade. During the same period the percent of households watching public television each week in prime time has grown from 20 percent to 34 percent. Programs below are ranked according to percentage of homes viewing.

		Homes (percentage)	*Date*
GENERAL			
1	"The Sharks," *National Geographic*	17.4	1/82
2	"The Grizzlies," *National Geographic*	17.0	3/87
3	"Land of the Tiger," *National Geographic*	16.5	1/85
4	"Incredible Machine," *National Geographic*	16.0	10/75
5	*Great Moments with National Geographic*	15.7	3/85
6	*Best of Wild America: The Babies*	14.7	3/87
6	*The Music Man*	14.7	3/85
8	*Live from the Grand Ole Opry*	14.6	3/79
9	*Live from the Grand Ole Opry*	14.2	3/80
10	"Lions of Africa," *National Geographic*	13.8	1/87
DRAMA			
1	*Death of a Princess*	13.8	5/80
2	*The Sailor's Return*	9.8	1/84
3	"Smooth Talk," *American Playhouse*	9.3	2/87
4	*The Scarlet Letter* (Part 1)	8.6	4/79
5	*Lathe of Heaven*	8.5	1/80
6	"Testament," *American Playhouse*	8.1	11/84
7	"Life on the Mississippi," *Great Performances*	7.7	11/80
8	"Flame Trees of Thika," *Masterpiece Theatre*	7.5	1/82
9	"To Serve Them All My Days," *Masterpiece Theatre*	7.3	10/82
9	"Sweeney Todd," *Mystery*	7.3	10/82
9	*The Scarlet Letter* (Part 4)	7.3	4/79
CLASSICAL MUSIC/DANCE			
1	*Classical Ballroom Dancing*	8.9	1/87
2	"Beverly Sills Farewell," *Live from Lincoln Center*	7.9	1/81
3	"Pavarotti/Mehta," *Live from Lincoln Center*	7.8	4/83
4	"Pavarotti Plus!" *Live from Lincoln Center*	7.6	1/86
5	*The Nutcracker*	7.5	12/82
6	"Danny Kaye," *Great Performances*	7.3	9/81
7	*John Curry Skates Peter and the Wolf*	7.2	1/82
7	"Aida," *Live from the Met*	7.2	1/85
9	"Best of Broadway," *Great Performances*	7.0	5/85
9	*Gala of Stars* (Part 2)	7.0	10/83
9	"Sutherland, Horne, Pavarotti," *Live from Lincoln Center*	7.0	3/81

		Homes (percentage)	Date
PUBLIC AFFAIRS			
1	*Shoah* (Part 1)	9.8	4/87
2	"Unauthorized History of the NFL," *Frontline*	9.2	1/83
3	"Roots of War," *Vietnam: A Television History*	8.7	10/83
4	*Hiroshima Remembered*	8.3	8/85
5	"Death of a Porn Queen," *Frontline*	8.2	6/87
6	*Democratic Presidential Debate*	8.0	1/84
7	*Program for Parent Child Sexual Abuse*	7.4	9/84
8	"Memory of Camps," *Frontline*	7.2	5/85
9	"The Real Stuff," *Frontline*	7.1	1/87
10	"Tet 1968," *Vietnam: A Television History*	7.0	11/83
11	"Visions of Star Wars," *Nova/Frontline Special*	6.8	4/86
11	"The First Vietnam War," *Vietnam: A Television History*	6.8	10/83
13	"88 Seconds in Greensboro," *Frontline*	6.7	1/83
14	"The Earthquake is Coming," *Frontline*	6.6	2/87
15	*Shoah* (Part 2)	6.5	4/87

defenders, there is no point in analyzing public TV's record in terms of commercial TV's Nielsen ratings.

Carnegie II: Finding Fundamental Flaws

Public television's dilemma is that if it cannot attract large enough audiences, many of its funding sources—corporations, foundations, and the federal government, not to mention the audience itself—may dry up. If it gears its programming to the ratings game, it will betray the principles on which it was founded (and may not increase its ratings anyway).

Some public television stations have sought a middle ground, like their commercial counterparts, shifting less popular public affairs programming out of prime time or returning to the air commercial retreads like *The Avengers* and *Leave It to Beaver*. But there may be no middle ground. As *Washington Post* television critic Tom Shales wrote in 1980 about the plan by a consortium of public television stations to air reruns of the acclaimed, but cancelled, CBS series *The Paper Chase*, "If we're going to keep blurring the line between commercial and public TV, why have public TV at all?"

Why have public TV at all? With the proliferation of cable services

DAILY PBS PROGRAMS WITH HIGHEST RATINGS

		Cumulative	
	Average Homes	*Day*	*Week*
Mr. Rogers' Neighborhood	2.1%	2.5%	6.9%
Sesame Street	3.0	4.9	12.1
Reading Rainbow	1.9	2.3	6.9
3-2-1 Contact	.9	1.2	3.4
MacNeil/Lehrer Newshour	1.9	3.3	8.4

Source: A. C. Nielsen, PBS Research.

As is shown, the cumulative (or total percentage of different) homes that tune in to a program is much greater for a whole day, or whole week, than during the "average minute" of the program. This indicates that some viewers are watching only parts of the programs, that the audience is increased by presentation of the program several times each day, and that others may only watch one or two days of the week.

For comparison, about 9,700,000 adults watch some part of the MacNeil/Lehrer Newshour each week while about 6,000,000 listeners hear parts of Morning Edition, All Things Considered, and/or Weekend Edition on National Public Radio.

targeting the upscale culture crowd that had once been PBS's exclusive domain (and most loyal contributors), that question is becoming harder to answer. What complicates matters for public television is that the programs that once made it distinctive (and remain its most popular fare)—the concerts, operas, dramas, science and nature shows, and imported specials—are now marketed successfully via cable and video-cassettes. To be sure, PBS has been in the forefront of some of the new technologies. It began telecasting programs to local stations via the Westar satellite in 1978, years before the three networks switched from using landlines. (In fact, CPB must now plan for—and fund—replacement of public television and radio interconnection systems at the end of their useful life in 1992.) In the 1980s CPB has experimented with linking video programming and computers. But technological capability does not in and of itself justify public subsidies for a service that competes with, rather than complements, commercial services.

After twenty years of striving for acceptability, rather than experimenting on the cutting edge, public television is simply one of many alternatives in the media marketplace of the 1980s. Where once its cultural offerings might have made it the only "oasis" in television's vast wasteland, it is now at best the leader of the pack, one choice in a world of choices.

Stations that have in the past produced some of the best of PBS's offerings are finding it harder and harder to compete for the financial support they need to continue. New York's WNET, for one, has announced production cutbacks. Before, WNET was willing to undertake major series production on the strength of partial underwriting

AN ERA OF CHOICE

A look at a typical week's programming on a cable system like that in Manhattan illustrates public television's dilemma. Several public television stations are carried on the system, and they offer the kind of attractive fare that Americans have come to expect from public television.

Currently, about 21 percent of the programs PBS supplies are classified "educational." Another 50 percent are public affairs. Only about .1 percent is sports. The rest, 29 percent, it labels "cultural."

There is drama on PBS—polished British productions that range from a rebroadcast of the popular *Upstairs, Downstairs* to *The Bretts,* a new series on 1920s London actors. There is *Mystery!* featuring Dorothy Sayers' Lord Peter Wimsey. But cable services, like the advertiser supported Arts and Entertainment Network (A&E), offer polished British drama as well—everything from a British production of *The Last of the Mohicans* to a selection of Noel Coward short stories. And even CBS gets into the act with Agatha Christie's *Murder in Three Acts.*

Public television presents a profile of Norman Rockwell on *You Gotta Have Art.* But the pay cable service Bravo offers the French classic *The Mystery of Picasso.* Public television offers a White House tribute to Jerome Kern. Bravo offers the Munich Philharmonic—and A&E *Jazz at the Smithsonian.* Public television presents a program on dance photography, Bravo the Royal Danish Ballet, A&E a tribute to ballerina Makarova. Bravo out-cultures them all with *Stomu Yamashita at Mount Koya,* a sound and light tribute to the founder of Shingon Buddhism!

Nova and other nature programs occupy a big part of the public TV schedule, especially in prime time. But A&E features *Birds of the World.* The Entertainment and Sports Programming Network (ESPN), also advertiser supported, includes animal shows in its schedule, too—during the week in question, for instance, *Struggle to Survive: China's Giant Panda.* Superstation WTBS airs *National Geographic* and Jacques Cousteau specials, PBS staples, as a centerpiece of its programming. And independent Channel 11, a commercial broadcaster, during the week in question has scheduled *National Geographic on Assignment.*

And so it goes. Public TV schedules documentaries and history programs on World War II and Vietnam. So does A&E. WNET airs vintage documentaries from the 1960s and 70s on *Thirteen Revisited.* Pay service Cinemax that same week is showing a 1965 documentary on John F. Kennedy, *Years of Lightning, Day of Drums*. Public TV has its *French Chef* and *Frugal Gourmet*; advertiser supported Lifetime has its *Wok with Yan*. There is even an advertiser supported children's channel, Nickelodeon, that includes programs like *Mr. Wizard* and *Pinwheel* in its schedule—just as public television has its *Sesame Street* and *3-2-1 Contact*. If Nickelodeon also broadcasts *Lassie* reruns, well, so do some public TV stations.

It is no longer speculation to think that programming indistinguishable from standard public TV fare might find commercial support. It has. The question now is whether public TV's well-heeled and well-read contributors might just as well spend their yearly $50 to $100 on a commercial service. But without their contributions for "culture," it is doubtful that public TV could stay in the business of public affairs.

By duplicating the so-called alternative programs of public television, commercial counterparts are successfully filling previous programming voids. Such duplication is flattering. In the short term, it proves that public television serves an important role. At the same time, it contributes to public television's long-term woes by making it an unnecessary vehicle for enrichment programming.

---

commitments and, if necessary, to subsidize network productions if underwriting ultimately fell short of the goal. (For example, WNET began production of its acclaimed series *The Brain* with only half of its $8 million budget in place. Though it won Peabody and DuPont awards, the series cost WNET $1 million of the station's own money. In 1985 alone similar deficits in other series forced WNET to subsidize PBS productions to the tune of $8 to $10 million.) In 1986 WNET announced it would in the future commit to a production only if it had 100 percent of funding in place in advance and would, in the words of WNET president John Jay Iselin, "be a blockbuster."

What forced WNET to announce such a change in policy? According to Iselin, who has since left the station, the media marketplace has become "fiercely competitive." PBS and WNET are competing for viewers in "an era of choice." Specifically, such cable services as Bravo and the Arts and Entertainment Network (A&E) are competing with WNET, while corporations are finding it less important to underwrite public broadcasting productions to boost their public images.

Only about half of all U.S. households have cable TV. Half do not. Cable services are not yet, and may never be, financially able to provide much original programming. They can buy existing material here and abroad, but they lack the resources to produce new dramas, documentaries, or children's programs. Thus, while they compete for public television's audience, they are not a viable alternative. And it is doubtful that any commercial service ultimately could or would offer the kind of public affairs programming that distinguishes public broadcasting. A&E can rerun *Victory at Sea* or any number of old network documentaries, but who will pay to produce the civil-rights history, *Eyes on the Prize?*

In a sense, PBS is now suffering from its own limited successes. Much of the initial interest in cable arts programming was triggered by advertisers' interest in the upscale following attracted by PBS programs. Recently, A&E broadcast a documentary on the Amish people after it generated good audience figures on selected PBS stations. What A&E paid for this rerun would not have covered a fraction of the original production costs.

The problem is not that cable services can or will duplicate the quality public affairs and other programs that are and probably only can be produced noncommercially with funds from the diverse sources available to PBS. It is instead that such services may drain the lifeblood from public broadcasting by luring away its viewers, or that, to compete with such attractive entertainment services, public television will be forced to turn away from production and broadcast of important new public affairs programming and merely duplicate its commercial competition.

Recently public broadcasting stations have experimented with abandoning on-air pledge drives and auctions, which were raising dollars at the expense of losing viewers. With relaxed rules on corporate underwriting, public television finds itself in direct competition with its commercial counterparts at the very time it most desperately needs to distinguish itself.

The implications for future PBS programming are clear. As public TV must compete with commercial purveyors of culture, there is likely to be even less innovation and risk taking and less of the distinction between public and commercial broadcasting that would justify increased tax subsidies for public television. Commercial services may soon be able to outbid PBS for the best programs. Public television could become a second-string market, airing programs only after their commercial potential (and presumably most of their viewer appeal) has been exhausted.

If the new technologies do siphon off PBS's most popular offerings, public television's strategic choices will be even more limited. It could move into programming that is not yet commercially acceptable, becoming the risk taker of the TV industry, the developer of new talent, the bold experimenter. Unfortunately, it is not likely that this kind of TV is going to attract a broad audience, or a broad coalition of corporate or congressional backers.

Seeking a Middle Ground

Another possibility is a return to localism. (WNET, for example, promised increased local service as it announced cutbacks in its network production.) The FCC has largely deregulated commercial television, no longer requiring much of the public service commitment it used to exact from broadcasters at license renewal time. It has announced that it will no longer enforce its controversial fairness doctrine. If the public wants to guarantee unpopular viewpoints access to the mass media, public television seems an appropriate forum for debate of controversial public issues. Perhaps the time is ripe for public television to "begin to apply talent, time and money to innovative programming that celebrates and illuminates the diversity of American culture," as was urged in Carnegie II.

The debate over whether public television should give viewers what they want or what they need has sharpened as public television has become more competitive—and at the same time faced stiffer competition. As it has been forced to solicit viewers for more and more of its financial support, public television has become more ratings conscious. If its prime-time audience skews upscale, those viewers who respond to their public stations' pledge drives are even more upscale. There is real pressure to give this valuable group of viewers what it wants—nature, opera, British drama, ballet—rather than what David Othmer of WHYY in Philadelphia is quoted as calling "castor-oil television"—public affairs and other programming that is "good for people."

In the end none of public television's options seems very promising. In 1987 Congress considered a proposal that would for the first time have guaranteed public broadcasting long-term, reliable funding. The bill would have set up a public broadcasting trust fund from transfer fees on the sale of commercial broadcast stations. The transfer tax, ranging from 2 percent to 5 percent of the sale price or fair market value of a station, would have raised an estimated $360 million a year. Commercial broadcasters, as might be expected, lobbied against the measure; and it was defeated. However, it is likely to be reintroduced. Even if the transfer tax had been imposed, revenues during the first two years would have gone to offset the federal deficit, rather than to support public broadcasting. It is not hard to imagine that Congress might opt to continue using transfer tax revenues for purposes other than public broadcasting. Or, as the National Association of Broadcasters has suggested, Congress could substitute a tax on television receivers as a funding source that is both more palatable to commercial competitors and a more direct means of passing on the costs of public television to the viewer who reaps the benefits.

But even more fundamentally, whether a transfer tax, a tax on television receivers, or another funding measure is implemented, does public television in its present form deserve increased federal support? Such funding might once have made a critical difference in shaping the system. If public television is now to make a case for substantial increases in federal funds, however, it cannot stay where it is. After years of scrambling for dollars, the system seems to have lost its way. Even if Congress is ready to supply fuel for the journey, public television may have no place to go.

NOTES

1. Congress in 1975 enacted a Public Broadcasting Financing Act, which provided for up to $570 million over a five-year period under a matching formula guaranteeing $1 in federal funds for every $2.50 (since reduced to $2) public TV stations could raise in funds from viewers and foundations. By providing for money over a period of years and tying federal outlays to a matching-fund "trigger" mechanism, Congress effectively protected public television from direct financial and political pressure.

Background Books

TELEVISION

Television has replaced the popular novel—and the movies—as America's chief medium of entertainment, and scores of scholars and journalists have attempted to explain this phenomenon. The Library of Congress card catalog contains entries for more than 6,000 works on television. Yet, among them, truly illuminating studies are few.

The best one-volume history is *Tube of Plenty: The Evolution of American Television* (Oxford, 1975, cloth; 1977, paper) by Erik Barnouw, a former Columbia professor of dramatic arts, television, and film. His well-written account is a condensation of his three-volume *A History of Broadcasting in the United States* (1966–70). In addition to providing crisp analyses of TV's evolution and of individual programs, Barnouw presents brief sketches of television's tycoons, including NBC's David Sarnoff and CBS's William S. Paley.

The General: David Sarnoff and the Rise of the Communications Industry (Harper & Row, 1986) by Kenneth Bilby, is an important biography on a founding father of the American television business as we know it today. Sarnoff created the first radio network in the 1920s and then (along with William Paley of CBS) developed network television three decades later. His life story is indeed the very stuff of the "rags-to-riches" dream. *The General* is important reading for anyone interested in the origins of television.

In 1948 William S. Paley, principal owner of CBS, brightened his network's prospects by raiding rival NBC of some of its biggest TV stars—Jack Benny, Red Skelton, and Frank Sinatra. Paley, who also pioneered in radio news with Edward R. Murrow, William Shirer, H.V. Kaltenborn, and Eric Sevareid, gives an often veiled account of his rise in *As It Happened: A Memoir* (Doubleday, 1979). For another view, see *Empire: William S. Paley and the Making of CBS* by Lewis J. Paper (St. Martins, 1987).

Paley touted CBS-TV as "the largest advertising medium in the world." And, indeed, TV's relationship with business is the medium's Big Story. For a complete account of that symbiosis, readers can again turn to Erik Barnouw.

In *The Sponsor: Notes on a Modern Potentate* (Oxford, 1978, cloth; 1979, paper), Barnouw writes that the real message of TV is a commercial one; the result is "a dramaturgy reflecting the demographics of a supermarket."

Most of the TV-viewing public claims to dislike commercials, but there is little doubt among advertisers that they succeed in selling products. As the head of the "Creative Group" that produced AT&T's campaign to promote long-distance telephoning has remarked, "In thirty seconds, everybody notices *everything*." A funny, behind-the-scenes look at the making of those brief "spots" for the telephone company is *Thirty Seconds* (Farrar, 1980) by *New Yorker* television critic Michael J. Arlen.

For six months in 1979, Arlen, the author of two excellent collections of essays on TV, *Living-Room War* (Viking, 1969) and *The View from Highway 1* (Farrar, 1976, cloth; Ballantine, 1977, paper), followed the commercial-makers around. The result is a deadpan, camera-eye view of the people involved in an exotic process. "Basically," says an ad man, "we are targeting people who have already experienced making a long-distance phone call." The commercial's music composer admits that "Reach out and touch someone" was a "*good* line" but, he adds, "it was genius . . . that thought to extend the basic concept to 'Reach out, *reach out,* and touch someone.' "

How television has "touched" the public, or affected the way people behave, is a growing target of scholarly effort. An extensive round-up of twenty-five years of such research is found in *Television and Human Behavior* (Columbia University Press, 1978, cloth and paper) by George Comstock and others. Not surprisingly, there are few firm answers, but a provocative summary that argues the power of TV's influence is provided by Joshua Meyrowitz in *No Sense of Place: The Impact of Electronic Media on Social Behavior* (Oxford, 1985).

One cannot understand television without bearing in mind that it is an industry regulated by a federal agency, the Federal Communications Commission. Lucas A. Powe, Jr.'s *American Broadcasting and the First Amendment* (University of California Press, 1987) reexamines the role of the FCC by evaluating its long-held "public interest" doctrine and makes the classic conservative argument for eliminating this underlying premise for government regulation.

The Reagan administration moved vigorously to take the FCC out of the regulation business. To understand the current rationale for broadcast deregulation, see Stanley M. Besen, Thomas G. Krattenmaker, A Richard Metzger, Jr., and John R. Woodbury's *Misregulating Television* (University of Chicago Press, 1986). Besen and his collaborators use the University of Chicago school of economic theory to argue that the FCC should abandon all regulation except that which is intended to prevent the signals of television stations from interfering with one another. We can see some of the fruits of deregulation in direct selling through television, reduced spending by the networks on news, and the nearly complete domination of children's programs by toy companies.

In sharp contrast to Powe and Besen and others is James L. Baughman's *Television's Guardians: The FCC and the Politics of Programming, 1958–1967* (University of Tennessee Press, 1985). Baughman chronicles the roles of two FCC chairmen, Newton Minow and E. William Henry, and their efforts in the 1960s to impose their strong views of public service responsibility on television stations and networks. Neither fully succeeded but they did leave the legacy of an activist FCC that Reagan's appointee to the FCC chairmanship, Mark Fowler, labored to undo.

The Changing Television Audience in America by Robert T. Bower (Columbia University Press, 1985) is a sequel to the author's 1973 study of television viewers and Gary Steiner's classic *The People Look at Television* (Knopf, 1963). Using a national sample for the 1980 census (as the other two books did for the 1970 and 1960 censuses, respectively), Bower attempts to evaluate audience reactions to television. He concludes that the public's all-embracing love affair with the medium is over. But the Nielsen surveys find that people seem to be watching more, suggesting that it is wise to examine what people do, not what they say.

Television programming has generated a stream of books that recall those that have flooded Hollywood since the 1920s—fawning biographies and promotional tributes to current productions. An exception is *Supertube: The Rise of Television Sports* (Coward—McCann, 1984) by longtime media observer Ron Powers. Powers lays out in clear prose style the gradual merger of professional sports with television's programming needs. During the past three decades, the two have grown closer together, at times even seeming to merge.

There are any number of volumes on the controversial issue of television's impact on children. As comprehensive as any of these is *Children's Understanding of Television,* edited by Jennings Bryant and Daniel R. Anderson (Academic, 1983). This is a collection of thirteen original chapters by leading researchers examining the psychological uses of television by children.

There is no longer a dearth of books that offer ready access to the masses of information available about the television entertainment business. *TV Facts* by Cobbett Steinberg (Facts on File, 1985) is the second edition of a vast compendium of data about prime-time schedules, top-rated programs, major advertisers, and the armies of annual award winners.

One hardly recommends a textbook for light reading. But *Broadcasting in America: A Survey of Electronic Media* by Sydney W. Head and Christopher H. Sterling (Houghton Mifflin, 1987) is a delightful reference tool.

Close students of American television regard it not as an entertainment medium but rather as a business that uses programs to sell advertising. *Television Marketing: Network, Local, and Cable*

(McGraw Hill, 1983) by David Poltrack, head of research at CBS, provides a useful guide to the arcane business of television time sales. Poltrack makes it seem simple and also far removed from any consideration of the quality of entertainment programming or the educational value of news shows.

Television networks set their crucial advertising rates on the basis of what viewers watch during certain months (May, November and February) and thus try to build audiences during these critical "sweeps weeks" with popular mini-series and investigations of sex scandals. The sweeps weeks of 1983–4 are explored in depth by Mark Christensen and Cameron Stauth in *The Sweeps* (Morrow, 1984). The authors were fortunate in choosing one of television's better seasons when Grant Tinker was still in charge of entertainment programming at NBC and *Cheers* was helping that network win huge audiences.

To appreciate the miracles that Tinker wrought, one has only to contrast his performance with Fred Silverman's earlier efforts. *Up the Tube: Prime Time TV and the Silverman Years* (Viking, 1981) by Sally Bedell, examines Silverman's work at NBC in the late 1970s and early 1980s, as well as his triumphs at CBS and ABC where he was known as "the man with the golden gut." By Bedell's account, Silverman and Tinker represent two sides of the same coin.

American History—American Television: Interpreting the Video Past (Ungar Film Library, 1988), edited by John E. O'Connor, is a collection of fourteen original essays that examine the interaction between television and contemporary American life. Of particular interest are the treatment of race relations as reflected in *Amos 'n Andy,* and the radicalism of the 1960s as seen through the Smothers Brothers programs.

There have been literally thousands of programs on American television. But who, save the committed fan, can even name the shows that appeared and then faded away just last season? Fortunately, we have a source, regularly updated, to help us: *The Complete Dictionary of Prime Time Network Television Shows, 1946 to the Present* (Ballantine, 1985), by Tim Brooks and Earle Marsh. The book provides credits and brief descriptions of themes and stories.

To examine basic documents of television history, see Lawrence W. Lichty and Malachi C. Topping's *American Broadcasting* (Hastings House, 1976). One can find original *New York Times* reports on sending signals through the air waves; Sam Goldwyn's account of the early relationship between Hollywood and television, written in 1950; and analyses of the backgrounds of FCC commissioners who served during the early years of broadcasting.

The monthly *Channels* magazine provides interesting analysis of television and newer media trends and its year-end "Field Guide" is especially useful as a statistical source.

Books discussing broadcast coverage of presidential campaigns have followed each inaugural since 1940 as night follows day. But solid analysis, as opposed to extended sermons and jeremiads, has only begun to appear.

Broadcasting and politics have been closely connected since the beginning of radio. In November 1920, KDKA in Pittsburgh, Pa., broadcast the returns of the Harding–Cox election. By 1928, despite a prominent Republican's remark that "We haven't time to monkey around with novelties," Democrats and Republicans were ready to spend a total of more than $1 million for commercial radio time. But not until the mid-1940s did the first detailed examination of radio's impact on politics appear—in *The People's Choice: How the Voter Makes Up His Mind in a Presidential Campaign* by Paul F. Lazarsfeld and others (Columbia University Press, 1944, later editions, 1948–68, cloth and paper).

The case in point was the 1940 reelection of Franklin D. Roosevelt. Lazarsfeld concluded that, although radio broadcasts (like newspapers) were frequently used as a source for concrete information, their overall impact was small. People-to-people communication had greater significance.

At the turn of the century, Chicago newspaperman Finley Peter Dunne created "Mister Dooley," a fictional Irish bartender who voiced the common man's views. "Politics ain'd beanbag," Dooley once said. "Tis a man's game; an' women, childher, an' pro-hybition-ists'd well to keep out iv it."

If Mr. Dooley were tending bar today, writes Martin Schram in *The Great American Video Game* (Morrow, 1987), he might say that "Politics is video games. 'Tis an actor's game—an imagemark'r's an' illusionist's game—an' women, childher, an' politicians'd do well to keep out iv it."

Television had become so important to politics that by 1984, Schram, a *Washington Post* reporter, decided to cover the election campaign by watching news reports and the candidates' ads on TV. Among other things, Schram concluded that the local television news was more influential than the national network programs in presidential primary campaigns.

During the weeks prior to the crucial New Hampshire primary, some 432,000 adults living in the Boston TV market (which encompasses southern New Hampshire) watched one of the local hour-long news shows; only 312,000 stayed tuned to the half-hour NBC news program that followed. And whereas the network news stories on the candidates usually lasted between eighty seconds and two minutes, the local TV reports often ran twice that long.

"Impact studies" in general fall short of providing conclusive evidence on how the mass media—print or broadcast—affect Americans' votes. Even the widely accepted notion that Nixon's wan physical appearance had an adverse effect on voters watching the Kennedy–Nixon debates of 1960 cannot be "conclusively" proven, as Sidney Kraus's book *The Great Debates: Background, Perspective, Effective* (Indiana University Press, 1962; Peter Smith, 1968) demonstrates.

"To trace a change in a political climate . . . straight to the door of television is a task foredoomed to failure," say Kurt Lang and Gladys Engel Lang in *Politics and Television* (Quadrangle, 1968, cloth and paper). Yet "failure to 'prove' the cumulative effects does not mean that political life has been unaffected" by TV. In their view, the effects on late voters of TV broadcasts of early returns had no impact on the outcome of the 1964 election; future elections might be different.

In *The Unseeing Eye: The Myth of Television Power in National Politics* (Putnam's, 1976), Thomas E. Patterson and Robert D. McClure argue that "in almost every instance" the prevailing view of heavy TV influence in the election process is "wrong." They found that the average change on issues for respondents exposed to TV political advertising and news, compared with those not exposed, was small. Yet their statistics show fairly large changes on individual issues.

In *The Main Source* (Sage, 1986), John P. Robinson and Mark R. Levy argue that television is simply a poor medium for conveying *information*. The typical TV news program, the authors point out, crams twenty rapid-fire stories into twenty-two minutes of commercial-interrupted air time. Television watchers sometimes cannot even tell when one news report ends and the next begins. Nor can they go back and review news they missed or did not understand.

"For many viewers, watching the news may produce an experience of having been informed," say Robinson and Levy, "but it is a false sense of knowledge, for it is based only on a vaguely understood jumble of visual and auditory stimuli that leave few traces in long-term memory."

Whatever its effect on the voters, television has clearly transformed the way the candidates approach presidential campaigns. *Nominating a President* (Praeger, 1980), edited by John Foley, Dennis A. Britton, and Eugene G. Everett, Jr., presents a series of frank round-table talks held at Harvard during the 1980 campaign. One speaker, consultant John P. Marttila, claims that most candidates now spend between 65 percent and 70 percent of their money on TV, radio, and newspaper advertising. "The real foundations of modern campaigning," he says, "are survey research and television." He adds that "most candidates around the country circumvent the local party organization."

Hence, the blossoming of television, combined with the proliferation of state primaries, Nelson Polsby observes in *The Consequences of Party Reform* (Oxford, 1983), has given rise to a new group of political campaign operatives, including "fund-raisers by mail and by rock concert, media buyers, advertising experts, public relations specialists, poll analysts, television spot producers. . . ."

Most political scientists have barely considered TV as a factor in the political education of ordinary Americans. Moreover, most media studies published so far have underrated the impact of TV in "setting the agenda" in campaigns. Sidney Kraus and Dennis Davis make a start on closing these gaps in *The Effects of Mass Communication on Political Behavior* (Pennsylvania State University, 1976).

The first scholarly examinations of TV news "content" focused on the 1972 elections. Most calculate the amount of air time devoted to each candidate, the issues, and other aspects of the campaign and analyze news items for "positive," "neutral," or "negative" coloration.

One example can be found in C. Richard Hofstetter's detailed *Bias In The News: Network Television Coverage of the 1972 Election Campaign* (Ohio State University, 1976). Other content analyses by university researchers generally agree with Hofstetter that network news coverage did not deliberately favor McGovern over Nixon or vice versa.

The half-hour (twenty-two-minute) nightly network news show began in 1963. But only recently have writers begun to analyze *how* NBC, CBS, and ABC cover election campaigns. An early example is former NBC correspondent Robert MacNeil's *The People Machine: The Influence of Television on American Politics* (Harper & Row, 1968, cloth and paper). Despite the title, MacNeil concentrates on the networks' 1960 and 1964 campaign broadcast efforts and the competition for profit (ratings) and prestige (for example, drawing the biggest audience on election nights).

General discussion, mostly by broadcast journalists, of the sins and virtues of network (and local) TV news is available in the seven volumes of the periodic Alfred I. duPont–Columbia University Survey of Broadcast Journalism, edited by Marvin Barrett. One of these volumes, *Moments of Truth?* (Crowell, 1975, cloth and paper), is largely devoted to Watergate coverage. For a careful analysis of the same Watergate period, see *The Battle for Public Opinion: the President, the Press, and the Polls During Watergate* (Columbia University Press, 1983), by Kurt Lang and Gladys Engel Lang.

Edwin Diamond, TV critic and professor of political science at New York University, in *The Tin Kazoo: Television, Politics, and the News* (MIT, 1975), discusses both network and local news, with no great admiration for either.

In *News From Nowhere: Television and the News* (Random House, 1973, cloth; 1974, paper), Edward Jay Epstein reports on news operations, primarily at NBC, over a six-month period in 1968. In the first systematic (though flawed) analysis of its kind, he describes how network news is selected; he stresses the importance of limited manpower, budgets, and the competition to attract (and entertain) mass audiences in shaping what we finally see on the evening news.

Media coverage of the surprise 1968 Tet crisis in Vietnam is examined by Peter Braestrup in *Big Story* (Westview, 1977, cloth; Yale, 1982, paper). Braestrup finds that network TV news, far more than print, was "overwhelmed" by the drama of the communist attack and disinclined to modify its first faulty impressions of U.S. military disaster in South Vietnam.

The frustrations of TV newspeople bulk larger than their flaws in Marvin Barrett and Zachary Sklar's *The Eye of the Storm* (Lippincott & Crowell, 1980), another in the duPont–Columbia University series. Again, for a different view—from the inside—Bill Leonard, the former president of CBS News, has written *In the Storm of the Eye: A Lifetime at CBS* (Putnam Publishing Group, 1987). Though often narrow in scope, there are an increasing number of memoirs by newspeople— such as Mike Wallace, Don Hewitt, Av Westin, Dan Rather, Harry Reasoner, and Charles Osgood—that sometimes add interesting pieces to the puzzle. But one of the best analyses has been provided by sociologist Herbert Gans in *Deciding What's News: A Study of CBS Evening News, NBC Nightly News, Newsweek & Time* (Pantheon Books, 1979, cloth; Vintage, 1980, paper). Gans argues that news is about "the economic, political, social, and cultural hierarchies we call nation and society." For the most part, he says, "the news reports on those at or near the top of the hierarchies and on those, particularly at the bottom, who threaten them, to an audience, most of whom are located in the vast middle range between top and bottom."

In Gans's view, "Journalists themselves stand just below the top levels of these hierarchies, and their position affords them a better view of the top than of either the bottom or middle." Their best view is of their own position, Gans says. "When journalists have autonomy, they represent the upper-middle-class professional strata in the hierarchies, and defend them, in their own vision of the good nation and society, against the top, bottom, and middle."

ADVERTISING

Chapter 19

THE RISE OF AMERICAN ADVERTISING

by T.J. Jackson Lears

In older downtowns across America, the casual observer may still happen upon spectral presences from the commercial past. Where there is available space on brick or stone, ancient advertising murals preside over parking lots, littered playgrounds, and construction projects. Often partly obscured by banks and fast-food franchises, some announce products: Uneeda Biscuit, Wilson's Whiskey; others are populated by fading fantastic characters: the Gold Dust Twins, the winsome White Rock Girl. Once part of the landscape of everyday life, these cultural graffiti somehow exert more fascination as they recede from view.

Those advertisements were part of a new visual environment that emerged around the turn of the century, as American corporations began to advertise "brand-name" products to a national market. Advertisers painted brick walls and billboards, caught the gaze of strap-hangers with subway car cards, and bought acres of space in metropolitan newspapers and the new mass-circulation magazines. And they played a major part in the evolution of a new way of life, in which the acquisition of specific goods was, somehow, associated with psychic self-betterment, fulfillment, and happiness.

The earliest advertising agencies sprang up in the 1870s and 1880s. Two- or three-man operations, they were mostly clustered on Park Row in lower Manhattan, in stuffy backstairs rooms that smelled of printer's ink. As the business historian Daniel Pope observes, early advertising agents merely procured "a shadowy, uncertain commodity—advertising space" from publishers and provided it to "businesses whose own products were often equally obscure"—magic elixirs, investment opportunities, or self-help schemes.

Like jobbers and merchants, advertising agents were middlemen, mistrusted by farmers, manufacturers, laborers, and anyone else who believed himself more engaged with the realities of production. Indeed, the agents' work was even less tangible than that of other middlemen: The only commodity they sold was that (sometimes dubious) service; they received commission from the publisher on the value of the space bought by the advertiser.

During the next fifty years, this method of compensation survived; but the agencies themselves were transformed. The more successful firms grew flush with money, moving from Park Row to more elegant mid-town headquarters. Their clients were no longer marginal patent-medicine firms but established corporations selling brand-name products—Camel cigarettes, Dodge automobiles. As the agencies expanded, they became more bureaucratically organized and functionally specialized and provided a widening spectrum of services: advice on the choice of appropriate media, marketing information, and most important, design of the advertisements themselves.

The Rhetoric of Sincerity

The question of designs, and of the strategies that lay behind them, was of particular concern to the first admen. Throughout the early days of the industry, agency spokesmen sought to establish their dignity as part of "the great distributing machinery brought into existence by the era of great combines." Yet they never fully banished the taint of hokum, the sense that their profession, like that of circus impresario P.T. Barnum, merely manufactured appearances to bemuse and bilk the public.

Fearing that they would be lumped with patent-medicine vendors or even with confidence men, members of the fledgling industry—most of whom were from the Midwest, many of them sons of Protestant ministers—resorted to the rhetoric of sincerity. It was a time-honored Protestant tradition. Throughout the nineteenth century, the sincere man had been the antidote to the confidence man—a reminder that morality could somehow be preserved amid the amoral ambiguities of the marketplace.

But achieving sincerity in one's copy was no easy matter. Sincerity required that the advertisement be seamless, that its artifice be concealed, that it seem straightforward and honest. For advertising men, as for other "impression managers," truth was insufficient and sometimes irrelevant. The important job was, in the words of the leading trade journal *Printers' Ink,* "making the Truth 'Sound True'." Sincerity had become at once a moral stance and a tactic of persuasion.

Few advertising spokesmen were willing to acknowledge that ambiguity. As advertising images became more fantastic and surreal during the 1910s and 1920s, many admen clung to nineteenth-century notions of reality, truth, and meaning. Debate over strategies revealed a persistent conflict within the industry.

During the 1890s the trade press had generally been suspicious of the ad that was "too pretty." As one adman wrote in 1895, "It's the great public you are after and they don't give a continental whether you have been to college or not, what they want is facts; if they are reading your ad for amusement in all probability you don't want their trade." The no-frills, informative approach helped aspiring professionals to distance their methods from the sensational tactics of their patent-medicine predecessors.

At the same time admen realized that they faced a novel difficulty. As advertisements for brand-name commodities multiplied, the description of a product's qualities, such as one finds in a Sears catalog, proved an inadequate strategy for selling.

An "Epidemic of Originality"

As early as 1903 a writer in *Judicious Advertising* complained that "there is so much that is exceedingly good, it is harder than ever to know how to devise creations that are 'different' enough to attract attention." By the early twentieth century, slogans, jingles, and trademarks were familiar sights in the advertising landscape—all designed to catch the eye of a busy distracted public. Illustrated advertising, containing virtually no information, aimed at "general publicity" for the product by associating it with attractive girls, healthy children, or prosperous family scenes.

Proponents of fact fought back, first by ridiculing the "epidemic of originality," then by invoking the formula that advertising was "salesmanship-in-print." That phrase was coined by the copywriter

John E. Kennedy in 1904 and popularized by Albert Lasker and Claude Hopkins as "reason-why" copy.

Each piece of reason-why copy contained a vigorous sales argument, crammed with facts and pock-marked with dashes, italics, and exclamation points. For a time this approach threatened to sweep all before it. In December 1906 a prominent trade magazine contained an obituary for "advertising ideas," the puns and pretty girls that bore no relation to the product: They "passed with the notion that advertising is literature or art."

The obituary proved premature. Many advertising men continued to define their task not as "salesmanship in print" but as "the persuasive art." As Clowry Chapman, a legal consultant to ad agencies, argued in 1910, "mental images," not rational arguments, move the prospective buyer to buy.

According to this view, the advertiser's task was not merely to construct product-oriented arguments, but to turn the potential buyer's emotion into money. Fact men fumed. In 1906 one of them wrote an article bewailing the lack of information in American car ads. He noted that one maker claimed "his car is the Car of Destiny. What does that mean? Who could find any meaning in such a fact, even if it were true?"

Troubled by the absence of clear-cut meaning, opponents of "atmosphere" warned that it was time to talk sense to the American people. But automobile advertisers increasingly surrounded their product with emblems of style, status, and personal fulfillment. In 1910 the Chalmers Motor Company revived lagging sales by switching from reason-why to "word painting the auto's seductive joys." The strategy won praise in the trade press. By 1920 the factual auto advertisement had virtually disappeared.

One reason for the decline of factual auto ads was the increasing difficulty of distinguishing one brand of product from another. The problem was not confined to automobiles. Confronted by standardization born of technological advances, advertisers sought to make a particular beer seem "special" (1907) or to establish "that Bread Isn't Just Bread" (1930). Marketing journals urged manufacturers to devise new specialties, new ingredients, new features.

Colgate dental cream provided a model. In 1911 Palmolive Peet spent a huge sum of money on advertising to demonstrate that their toothpaste lay "flat on the brush like a ribbon." The key, as one adman had observed in 1902, was to recognize "the importance of trifles." The search for trifles led to a proliferation of new, improved

Fuel system of the new Ford has been designed for reliability and long service

THE practical value of Ford simplicity of design is especially apparent in the fuel system.

The gasoline tank is built integral with the cowl and is unusually sturdy because it is made of heavy sheet steel, terne plated to prevent rust or corrosion. An additional factor of strength is the fact that it is composed of only two pieces, instead of three or four, and is electrically welded—not soldered.

Because of the location of the tank, the entire flow of gasoline is an even, natural flow—following the natural law of gravity. This is the simplest and most direct way of supplying gasoline to the carburetor without variations in pressure. The gasoline feed pipe of the new Ford *is only 18 inches long* and is easily accessible all the way.

The gasoline passes from the tank to the carburetor through a filter or sediment bulb mounted on the steel dash which separates the gasoline tank from the engine.

The carburetor is specially designed and has been built to deliver many thousands of miles of good service. Since all adjustments are fixed except the needle valve and idler, there is practically nothing to get out of order.

The choke rod on the dash acts as a primer and also as a regulator of your gasoline mixture. The new hot-spot manifold insures complete vaporization of the gasoline before it enters the combustion chamber of the engine.

As a matter of fact, the fuel system of the new Ford is so simple in design and so carefully made that it requires very little service attention.

The filter or sediment bulb should be cleaned at regular intervals and the carburetor screen removed and washed in gasoline. Occasionally the drain plug at the bottom of the carburetor should be removed and the carburetor drained for a few seconds.

Have your Ford dealer look after these little details for you when you have the car oiled and greased. A periodic checking-up costs little, but it has a great deal to do with long life and continuously good performance.

FORD MOTOR COMPANY

A bit dull, a bit stodgy, "reason-why" copy gave the consumer the facts, and almost nothing but.

features, secret ingredients, and fantastic product claims. As product differentiation became more difficult, reason-why copy became less reasonable.

Ultimately, reason-why and atmosphere advertising converged. There had always been potential for irrationality in reason-why. It could include not only sober statements of a product's merits, but also strings of superlatives, inflated sales arguments, and an insistence that the product could transform the buyer's life. In 1925, when corset advertising rejected "the Bolshevik figure," promising an "ideal posture" that would "reflect good breeding and class distinction," advertising analysts found it possible to praise the copy because it appealed to intelligence rather than to emotion. "Romance and reason-why" could coexist in the same advertisement or in different campaigns for the same product.

"Putting Yourself in the Consumer's Place"

But admen were wrestling with challenges even greater than the debate over romance and reason. The trade press, shifting its orientation from the product to its potential buyer, began to advise "Putting Yourself in the Consumer's Place," puzzling out his or her yearnings and anxieties.

The important change in trade press usage from "customers" to "consumers" that began around 1900, reflected a growing awareness that the audience for national advertisements was remote, impersonal, and difficult to visualize. Customers carried on face-to-fact relations with local entrepreneurs; consumers were the target of standardized persuasion sponsored by corporations. The problem for advertisers was how to bring the target into sharper focus. Slowly admen inched toward the "science" of modern marketing. In the process, they increasingly viewed consumers as a manipulable, irrational mass.

Early speculation on consumers combined confident pronouncements about "human nature" with lists of consumer traits. The first composite portrait to emerge was that of a shrewd customer—subject to flattery but suspicious of bombast, capable of cupidity but essentially reasonable.

But as early as the turn of the century, the picture began to change. Some spokesmen, pointing to "the breathless rush and scramble" of twentieth-century life, noted that "men and women take their knowledge, like their lunches, on the run."

This perception called for either brevity or novelty to catch the busy eye. And for some admen, the power of silly or emotional copy stemmed from human nature itself. "You must take [people] as they are," wrote a *Printers' Ink* contributor in 1897, "grown-up children to a great extent . . . tired and bored by too much argument, by diagrams and prosaic common sense." From this perspective, the most effective advertising was aimed at consumers' irrational impulses.

In the emerging conventional wisdom, the typical consumer was especially susceptible to emotional appeals because he was bored much of the time. "His everyday life is pretty dull. Get up—eat—go to work—eat—go to bed," wrote freelance copywriter John Starr Hewitt in 1925. Yet Hewitt also believed that the typical American compensated "for the routine of today by the vision of what his life is to be tomorrow. It is the vision of getting ahead. Everything he buys comes as a partial fulfillment of that vision."

The notion of consumption as compensation was given a further turn by Paul Nystrom, professor of marketing at Columbia University. In *The Economics of Fashion* (1928), Nystrom noted the importance of boredom, "the desire for a change in personality," and among "not a few people in Western nations . . . something that may be called, for want of a better name, *a philosophy of futility*." With the decline of religious faith, Nystrom believed, the "tendency to challenge the purpose of life itself" grew and made superficial consumer choices seem all the more important. This view of the consumer as anomic "mass man" strengthened advertisers' faith in the manipulability of the public.

There remained a rival faith in the consumer as rational individual, making knowledgeable choices. "In 1911 when the consumer buys," *Printers' Ink* asserted, "he does the choosing. He asserts his particular individuality." Advertising made choice possible: "It has *educated* the consumer into being a connoisseur—which apt word means 'one who knows'."

The Psychological Appeal

But the image of the consumer as connoisseur did not strictly conform to the rational economic man of liberal lore. The new model man exercised his sense of self not through labor or civic responsibility, but through consumer choices, often quite trivial ones.

Notions of "consumer individuality" ended up promoting the

strategy of "personal appeal" rather than genuine respect for the diversity of the mass market. By seeming to single out the individual ("Imagine *your* picture here"), the personal appeal sought to create a sense of uniqueness in the consuming self, to make the buyer forget he was part of a mass market, to convince him that he was a conscious, choosing person.

Psychological theory underwrote that indirect approach and reinforced notions of consumer irrationality. Beginning in 1903, when Walter Dill Scott published *The Psychology of Advertising,* admen flocked to psychological lectures, hired psychological consultants, and wondered "Can You Sell Goods to the Unconscious Mind?" The long flirtation between psychology and advertising was consummated in 1925, when John B. Watson dedicated *Behaviorism* to his employer, Stanley Resor of J. Walter Thompson. The vogue of psychology provoked grumblings among no-nonsense business types, but to many advertising men, it held the key to the mysterious mind of the consumer.

The most alluring use of psychology lay in the area of suggestion. Marketing professor Arthur Holmes summarized the conventional view of the process in 1925 when he wrote:

> People unacquainted with psychology assume that men have the power to say "Yes" or "No" to an advertisement. The assumption is only partly correct. A man has the power to decide in the first stage of the game, not in the last . . . if the printed word can seize his attention, hold him chained, drive from his mind all other thoughts except the one "Buy this!," standing at the head of an organized sentiment from which every opposing idea, perception, feeling, instinct, and disposition have been driven out or smothered to death, HE CANNOT SAY "NO!" His will is dead.

Few admen would have uncritically embraced Holmes's inflated view of the power of suggestion, and some, such as Claude Hopkins, lamented "the fearful cost of changing people's habits." But growing numbers of advertising men were confident they could do almost anything with a consumer through unconscious manipulation, and psychological theory bolstered their confidence.

"Science" of Market Research

Besides psychology, the other major effort to understand consumer behavior was the infant "science" of market research. By the

1910s a number of advertisers were trying to base their strategies on information derived from questionnaires; by the 1920s at least a few were convinced that "the research basis of copy" had been established. The rise of market research offered new possibilities for admen such as J. George Frederick to assert their superiority over "the mere 'word-slingers'."

By 1925 Frederick asserted, copy had become "the apex of a solid base of merchandising plan" that included data questions for advertisers as well as research into consumer types and preferences. The marketing approach was compatible with psychology. In the final stage of Frederick's merchandising plan, an analyst used proofs of varied copy to "conduct a carefully guarded test upon consumers (so planned that their unconscious judgment and not their conscious judgment would be obtained)."

The spread of marketing orientation, by revealing the diversity of the audience and its predilections, might have made more advertising men question their tactics. Every few years, a writer in the trade press remarked that most Americans did not employ maids, play golf, or wear evening clothes to dinner; perhaps the working class majority could be represented in national advertisements. But these early calls for "market segmentation" were largely ignored, as advertisements continued to present a homogeneous portrait of the American people.

Justifying this homogeneity, advertising spokesmen revealed some fundamental assumptions about their craft. To critics who charged that "art directors snootify homely products," an agency art director replied that the homely scene had been "touched by the wizardry of the clever artist." He went on to argue that modish clothes and fine furnishings were "the kind our wives yearn for but seldom have enough pin money to buy." One industry magazine reasoned that this sort of "idealism" was "understood by consumers who do not take life too literally" as an inducement to strive for an ever higher standard of living. From this, it was only a short step to the admission that advertisements were primarily marketing fantastic visions rather than products.

Many advertising spokesmen had already taken that step. As early as 1912, a writer in *Judicious Advertising* had proposed that it was "possible through advertising to create mental attitudes toward anything and invest it with a value over and above its intrinsic worth." By the 1920s mention of a product's "intrinsic worth" had virtually disappeared, as advertising spokesmen argued that consumers could "buy" all sorts of ethereal qualities. James Wallen, who started his

THE FORD TOWN SEDAN

VALUE *far above the* PRICE

IN REVIEWING the many advantages of the Ford car, it is particularly interesting to note the relation between value and price.

The low first cost is a point to keep in mind at all times because it means a considerable saving to you in the purchase of a car.

Of even greater importance, however, is the reason for this low price and the manner in which it has been achieved without sacrifice of quality or performance.

Every purchaser shares the benefits of the Ford policy of owning the source of many raw materials—of making thousands of cars a day—of selling at a small margin of profit—of constantly giving greater and greater value through the vast industrial organization that has been built up for the making of this car.

A new degree of excellence has been brought within reach of all the people through the development of new manufacturing machines

and the discovery and working out of new manufacturing methods.

Evidence of this is found in the extremely close limits of measurement maintained in the manufacture of vital parts. Some of these are held true to within a maximum variation of three ten-thousandths of an inch (.0003), reducing friction and wear and resulting in greater reliability, longer life and better performance.

As the quality of workmanship has been increased through the accuracy of the machine, so has the quality of materials been increased. The savings resulting from new manufacturing economies have been put back into the car. Through typical Ford methods, materials once thought too expensive for a low price car have been made available for use in the Ford.

Today, more than ever, it is an outstanding example of high quality at low cost. Were it made in any other way,

under any other policy, it would unquestionably cost you much more than the present price.

The use of the Triplex shatter-proof glass for the windshield is a definite indication of the quality that has been built into the Ford car. So are the four Houdaille hydraulic shock absorbers. The five steel-spoke wheels. The silent, fully enclosed six-brake system. The aluminum pistons. The chrome silicon alloy valves. The simplicity and efficiency of the lubrication, cooling, ignition and fuel systems. The large number of ball and roller bearings. The extensive use of fine steel forgings instead of castings or stampings. The many other mechanical features that count so much in reliability, economy and long life.

All of these are important considerations to every man and woman who is contemplating the purchase of a motor car. All are important reasons why the Ford delivers a value far above the price.

Ford

FORD MOTOR COMPANY
Detroit, Michigan

This ad is on the road to Xanadu. Facts are still packed into the copy, but it is clear that the buyer of the Ford will be getting much more than a reliable means of transportation.

own agency after working with the flamboyant Elbert Hubbard, agreed that "you do not sell a man the tea, but the magic spell which is brewed nowhere else but in a teapot." What made an effective advertisement, in this view, was not the product but the symbolic context that surrounded it.

This was a long way from the older, business-oriented approach to advertising, but many admen embraced the newer perspective. One herald of the new strategy, James Collins, argued in 1901 that advertising had created an "economy of symbolism," in which symbols, not commodities, were exchanged. Within twenty years it was a common view that the product could be subordinated to its symbolic attributes. Face powder, for example, could be sold to both flappers and antiflappers—depending on whether the copy appealed to restless sexual energy or self-conscious sophistication.

The most commonly used symbolic attributes were meant to animate the inanimate commodity with "richer, fuller life." Like many of their contemporaries, advertising strategists were preoccupied by the pursuit of "life" amid a culture that seemed increasingly to deny it. Restless men, they moved from job to job, eager for variety and stimulation. In their preoccupation with escaping ossified forms and capturing movement in design, they resembled artists such as Braque and Picasso. In their reverence for what one copywriter called "the divinity of common things," they resembled Ezra Pound and William Carlos Williams, who sought to reconnect words with things and rescue poetry from the vapors of Victorian abstraction.

The Magic of Imagery

But for admen, the problem of animating the inanimate was specifically commercial: how to make inert commodities resonant with vitality. The trick lay in the imagining.

One avenue to animation involved the imaginative use of language. In the early years, though most admen preached the gospel of simple and direct, there were many calls for "ginger" in copy; ad writers were advised to "pick out the vital words and form them into sentences that posses the breath of life."

By the 1920s a more overtly literary viewpoint emerged, as writers discussed ways of using the "magical powers" of words. One such writer, Richard Surrey, argued that literary metaphor soothed people by assimilating human travails to larger natural processes. Advertising metaphor moved in a different direction: "Machine-made products, turned out by the millions, must be assimilated to the destiny of things not machinelike; must be translated . . . into human terms."

A number of rhetorical devices served that purpose, but perhaps the most striking was the "'I am' vogue," which lasted throughout the early 1920s, personifying commodities, ideas, and technical processes. Progress, electricity, and light joined adding machines, radios, and locomotives in adopting personae and speaking directly to the audience, often with what was thought to be Biblical eloquence. ("Verily I shrink the world. . . . But never am I my own master," intoned one modest radio.)

In visual strategies the movement toward magic and fantasy was even more apparent, but it developed alongside a powerful countercurrent of realism. One approach incorporated the techniques of cartoonists and avant-garde artists; the other sought increasing proficiency in illustration and photography. In either case, the aim was to avoid the wooden and "unreal."

But real life remained an elusive quarry. Even photographs could be full of " 'rubber-stamp' faces and expressions," the advertising art critic W. Livingston Larned complained in 1930. Unless the faces seemed to project spontaneous emotion, the "advertising language" remained unpersuasive.

"What do the faces in your advertising illustration *say?*" asked Larned. "Are they animate with action?" There were realistic ways to escape still life—placing a pat of melting butter on a stack of pancakes, for example—but ultimately the quest for "sparkle" led realists to the borders of fantasy.

While realism persisted, surreal images proliferated. In 1922 the same issue of *Printers' Ink* that contained a commercial art manager's plea for "Real People, Doing Real Things" also presented an ad for Poster Advertising, Inc., with an example of their work: a billboard showing the earth afloat in space, encircled by a gigantic Goodyear Tire, with the slogan "Goodyear means Good Wear." This technique, according to the ad, had "Strength Beauty Dignity."

Surreal attention-getting devices stretched back several decades, but by the 1920s, an infusion of "foreign art ideas" had generated a wider array of nonrepresentational modes. In 1925 the trade press noted that "Futuristic Monstrosities are all the Rage"—distorted figures, vaguely cubist designs in backgrounds and borders. Technical advances also accelerated the movement toward the bizarre. Airbrushing, double exposures, fadeaways, and various means of "doctoring"

When the runners are bunched on the track—and suddenly Chuck, your own superman half-miler, spurts ahead on the finish and wins —have a Camel!

WHEN the swiftest of the lithe half-milers are fighting for the lead. And suddenly your own dauntless champion fairly soars ahead and smashes the tape for a record and for victory—*have a Camel!*

For you'll never find another friend so attuned to your triumphs as Camel. Camel makes every memorable instant brighter, adds of its own effulgent goodness to supreme days. Camels are made of the choicest tobaccos grown—they never disappoint your taste. Camels are the master blend that annihilated cigaretty aftertaste. Regardless of the price you pay, you'll never buy better tobaccos, or blending, or flavor than you get in Camels.

So this year when the old school's men go through for victory after victory — then, jauntily taste the smoke that's the choice of the world's victorious.

Have a Camel!

Into the making of this one cigarette goes all of the ability of the world's largest organization of expert tobacco men. Nothing is too good for Camels. The choicest Turkish and domestic tobaccos. The most skilful blending. The most scientific package. No other cigarette made is like Camels. No better cigarette can be made. Camels are the overwhelming choice of experienced smokers.

Our highest wish, if you do not yet know Camel quality, is that you try them. We invite you to compare Camels with any cigarette made at any price. R. J. Reynolds Tobacco Company

© 1926

By 1936 the consumer was clearly not being sold cigarettes but a way of life— full of leisure, surrounded by friends. A winner's life, if there ever was one.

photographs could all help the advertiser "write a sales message across the human face"—as Pompeiian Massage Cream did when it showed a man's face in a hairnet with the caption "your face is a net . . . it traps the dirt." Like Barnum's hoaxes, these tactics called as much attention to the techniques of illusion as to the article for sale.

The more common means of visual animation were cartoons and allegorical figures. Since the turn of the century, advertisers had enlisted cartoon figures as trademarks—Sunny Jim for Force Food, the Campbell Soup twins. But as cartoonists began to realize that anything could be animated—not merely human figures but trees, butter, buildings, or automobiles—advertisers embraced the more advanced forms of cartoon art.

By the 1920s trade journal writers were praising a host of animated characters: the oat who "experienced the thrill of a lifetime" when he was judged plump enough to be ground into three-minute Oat Flakes, the fairy characters who embodied the vitamins in Comet Rice.

Strategists seeking animation had one other option: to approach the ad as a drama in which the consumer could participate. "Even a casual examination of a few magazines proves that many of the national advertisers are borrowing dramatic appeal from the motion picture," a writer in *Judicious Advertising* noted in 1925. Static compositions could be vitalized by small details: an open box of bonbons in a living room set piece advertising radios; a lighted candelabrum atop a piano in a candle ad. All sought to create the impression that the scene had just been vacated and was about to be occupied by the consumer.

The advertising man thus became a stage manager, charged, as one copywriter put it, with "introducing the thing advertised in a natural, unaffected, casual manner, with no outward signs of the commercial."

By the late 1920s American advertising had acquired the characteristics it would retain for a least six decades—and perhaps will retain for as long as there is a competitive market economy. This "highly organized and professional system of magical inducements and satisfactions," as social critic Raymond Williams described it, has continued to have as its goal the selling of a panoply of goods among which there are frequently few salient differences. Working from the premise of the irrationality of the consumer, this vast fantasy machine employs every conceivable visual gimmick and rhetorical device to turn the public's attention from the product to its symbolic attributes.

In retrospect, perhaps the two most remarkable aspects of the advertising business are, first, how quickly after the emergence of mass media it assumed its shape, and, second, how durable that shape has proven to be. Its perdurability is all the more remarkable when one considers that advertising is the business of manufacturing evanescent appearances.

Expanded Opportunities in the Electronic Media

Not that things have remained unchanged on Madison Avenue since 1930. The rise of color magazines such as *Life, Look,* and *Vogue* allowed advertising artists and photographers to hone their skills, creating scenes of such voluptuousness and sensual ease that readers might *almost* overlook the item being sold.

And, of course, the electronic media—radio and particularly television—have greatly extended advertising's magisterial sway, further complicating and obscuring elusive "reality." Indeed, television seems almost tailor-made for the advertiser's art: Its speed, its shallow but alluring slickness, and its combination of the visual and aural make it the perfect medium for serving up 30-second segments of idealized life.

Television also makes it possible for the advertiser to use the most powerful device of suggestion—repetition. Thanks to endless, hypnotic repetitions, even the most sophisticated consumers find themselves in the thrall of the jingle of the hour, whether they are reaching out, with the help of Ma Bell, to touch someone, or receiving, from a generous Gino's, the precious freedom of choice. Whether it convinces all of the people some of the time or just some of the people some of the time, TV advertising *does* sell goods.

Riding on an extensive media network, advertising began to move beyond the world of commerce and into such areas as government and politics, particularly during the 1960s. Today, of course, the packaging and selling of politicians has become so widespread and professionalized as to seem commonplace. It is now almost inconceivable for a candidate for high office to undertake a campaign without the help of media consultants, acting coaches, and the usual speech (and joke) writers. And, though it is perhaps too easy to say so, one wonders if the outcomes of elections in America will not soon be determined even more strongly by the candidate's image and appearance—his "fatherly reassuring aura" or his "youthful confidence"—than by his current policies or his political record.

Advertising, then, has conquered important new terrain since 1930, and done so with new forms and appeals. But despite outward changes, it remains, at bottom, what it was sixty or more years ago: the business of manufacturing illusions.

To some degree, it remains so because the admen of today, like those of the past, have experienced the same confusions felt by other members of twentieth-century American society. These confusions stem from a contradiction between our democratic ideology, with its emphasis upon individual choice and freedom of expression, and an economic arrangement that encourages, and indeed depends upon, conformity and predictability among both producers (employers as well as employees) and consumers.

Ours is also a society that has traditionally valued spontaneity, risk, and adventure; largely for that reason we cherish the myth of the frontier, where those qualities, we believe, once flourished. Yet most Americans today inhabit an urban or suburban world that is overly regulated, hemmed in by routine, and presided over by scores of specialists and experts. "Adventure" itself has become a commodity, a packaged trip down the Colorado, an organized trek across the Himalayas, a fortnight on a dude ranch. Room for real adventure is limited, if it exists at all.

Advertising men and women have not been immune to these and other contradictions. Many have been, after all, creative and original thinkers, some outstanding artists (René Magritte), photographers (Richard Avedon), and poets (James Dickey and Allen Ginsberg). Yet even the least talented advertising people have recognized that their skills were harnessed to large, impersonal organizations and that the end of their efforts was to convince millions of consumers that they would be happier, even better, human beings if they used Whiz instead of Duz. Given the conditions of their work and of ordinary life, it is not really surprising that generations of advertising men have aimed to transform a prosaic world of commodities into a magical place of escape, illusion, and fantasy—an ephemeral empire of images.

Background Books

ADVERTISING

"To be for or against advertising in these latter years of the twentieth century is about like being for or against weather. Advertising is ubiquitous, incessant, and inescapable." So writes James Playstead Wood in *The Story of Advertising* (Ronald Press, 1958).

Wood's book is among the best of the early, descriptive histories of American advertising. From 1885 to 1905, according to Wood, advertising was brash, bold, vigorous, and fun. The industry tried to reform itself in the period from 1905 to 1914, toning down the more extravagant and misleading claims for products it was touting to the American public. It lent itself to the government's propaganda efforts during World War I and then returned to excesses of reckless salesmanship in the 1920s. Sobered in the depression years of the 1930s, the ad industry, writes Wood, redeemed itself again in World War II.

Stephen Fox carries the story forward in his book, *The Mirror Makers: A History of American Advertising and Its Creators* (Morrow, 1984). Writing about the relationship between advertising and American culture, Fox examines some of the leading personalities of the advertising business and argues that advertising reached its peak of influence in the 1920s and then steadily declined. Over the course of the twentieth century, advertising has been caught between two contrary regulating forces—the government and the industry itself. "When restricted, more or less, to the truth," writes Fox, "advertising lost some of its more powerful, frightening devices. Advertising became less deceptive, the public grew more sophisticated and skeptical. As advertising grew and prospered, it lost influence."

During the 1920s and 1930s advertising took on new scope and maturity; the number of ads, the variety of products advertised, and the available media grew rapidly. This is the "optimum era" for exploring advertising as a reflection of American culture, asserts Roland Marchand in his classic book, *Advertising the American Dream: Making Way for Modernity, 1920–1940* (University of California Press, 1985). The dream was a distorted image. "Ad creators tried to reflect public aspirations rather than contemporary circumstances, to mirror popular fantasies rather than social realities," writes Marchand. After all, "the central purpose of an ad was not to reflect reality but to 'move merchandise.'"

Marchand notes that ad people displayed a "sense of innocent self-assurance about their cultural mission" during this period. "Their excitement at their new maturity and power led them to fill the pages of the trade press with revealing gossip about their techniques, their perceptions of their audience, and their own motives."

Many of the early books about advertising were confessional and personalized defenses of the industry. Advertising pioneers like Claude C. Hopkins, once said to be the highest-paid ad creator in the world, extolled the ad business in books like *Scientific Advertising* (1923) and

My Life in Advertising (1927; both books reprinted by Crain Communications, 1966). Hopkins was the man who persuaded Quaker Oats to change the name "Wheat Berries" to "Puffed Wheat," the cereal "shot from guns," and discovered dental plaque for Pepsodent.

When the 1970s saw a return to the hard-sell marketing practices of the 1950s David Ogilvy, one of the creative leaders of the ad industry, was ecstatic. "The pendulum is swinging back our way—the Hopkins way," said Ogilvy. For more on Ogilvy, there are two of his own books: *Confessions of an Advertising Man* (Atheneum, 1980), and *Ogilvy on Advertising* (Random, 1985).

Advertising people are anything but shy when it comes to defending themselves and explaining what they do. Among the better examples of this genre: Milton H. Biow's *Butting In: An Ad Man Speaks Out* (Doubleday, 1964); Larry Dobrow's *When Advertising Tried Harder: In the Sixties: The Golden Age of American Advertising* (Friendly Press, 1984); Bart Cummings's *Advertising's Benevolent Dictators* (Crain Books, 1984); and Bob Levenson's *Bill Bernbach's Book: A History of the Advertising That Changed the History of Advertising* (Random, 1987). This last describes the "creative revolution" that hit the advertising industry in the late 1950s and early 1960s with Bernbach's "Think Small" ads for Volkswagen and the "We Try Harder" ads for the Avis car rental company.

A different approach that views advertising as an aspect of business history rather than as art or expression of national character can be found in Daniel Pope's *The Making of Modern Advertising* (Basic Books, 1983). Pope describes the making of modern national advertising in the period between the 1880s and the 1920s, noting how ad styles and appeals changed to meet marketing needs and how advertising people's theories about consumer behavior and human nature reflected prevailing business conditions.

Stuart W. Ewen pursues this approach with a more Marxist perspective in *Captains of Consciousness: Advertising and the Social Roots of the Consumer Culture* (McGraw–Hill, 1975), which views advertising as an arm of capitalism bent on selling products and services to the poor that they do not need and can ill afford.

As the titles suggest, Michael Schudson's *Advertising, the Uneasy Persuasion: Its Dubious Impact on American Society* (Basic Books, 1984) and Ivan L. Preston's *The Great American Blow-Up: Puffery in Advertising and Selling* (University of Wisconsin Press, 1975) take a skeptical view of the role and effectiveness of advertising. Schudson uses the phrase "Capitalist Realism" to describe advertising art and argues that, like the art of Socialist Realism, it portrays the ideals and aspirations of the system more than it does reality.

While "new" is the most used word in all of advertising, the industry, in fact, has not changed much in the past half-century. Warren Dygert's *Radio As An Advertising Medium* (McGraw–Hill, 1939), which includes chapters on music in commercials, contests, and commercial testing, offers the quaint prediction that TV advertising is just too expensive to replace radio but concludes "those who are nearest to television are optimistic about the place advertising is to play in this coming field." Two other books offer summaries of radio advertising in several different decades: Ned Midgley's *The Advertising and Business Side of Radio* (Prentice–Hall, 1948) and Leo Bogart's *Strategy in Advertising* (Harcourt, Brace & World, 1967).

A concise and very readable history of broadcasting advertising is presented by Erik Barnouw in *The Sponsor: Notes on a Modern Potentate* (Oxford University Press, 1978). The best recent survey of TV advertising is by CBS researcher David F. Poltrack. His *Television Marketing: Network/Local/Cable* (McGraw–Hill, 1983) covers ratings, network and local programming, and advertising budgets—setting and evaluating them.

The specialized field of political advertising has been one of the most controversial. Since 1928, broadcast advertising has been the single largest category of expense in presidential election campaigns. A thorough introduction to the field can be gained by comparing the more anecdotal *The Spot: The Rise of Political Advertising on Television* (MIT Press, 1984), by Edwin Diamond and Stephen Bates, with the more scholarly but dense *Packaging the Presidency: A History and Criticism of Presidential Campaign Advertising* (Oxford University Press, 1984), by Kathleen Hall Jamieson.

Other books focus attention on specific aspects or historical periods of American advertising. Hal Morgan's *Symbols of America* (Viking, 1986), for example, explores the origins of the more famous corporate symbols: Underwood's Devil, White Owl, Bull Durham, Arm & Hammer, and Procter and Gamble's moon and stars. The enlistment of advertising skills in wartime is examined by Frank W. Fox in *Madison Avenue Goes to War: The Strange Military Career of American Advertising* (Brigham Young University Press, 1975).

Finally, Judith Williamson's *Decoding Advertisements: Ideology and Meaning in Advertising* (M. Boyars, 1978) brings content analysis and neo-Marxist theory to the analysis of advertisements. Like other studies of this ilk, Williamson's finds more meaning and ideology than most readers can detect and more than the creative geniuses of advertising probably intended.

ABOUT THE AUTHORS

Arthur Asa Berger is a professor of broadcast communication arts at San Francisco State University. A 1954 graduate of the University of Massachusetts, he received a doctorate in American Studies from the University of Minnesota in 1965. Among his many books are *L'il Abner: A Study in American Satire* (1970), *Language in Thought and Action* (1974, with S.I. Hayakawa), *Television as an Instrument of Terror* (1978), *Media Analysis Technique* (1982), and *Media U.S.A.* (1988).

Leo Bogart is executive vice-president and general manager of the Newspaper Advertising Bureau. He holds a Ph.D. degree in sociology from the University of Chicago and is a Fellow of the American Psychological Association. A former president of both the American and World Associations for Public Opinion Research, he is the author of *Press and Public* (1981), *Premises for Propaganda* (1976), *Polls and the Awareness of Public Opinion* (1972, 1986), *Strategy in Advertising* (1967, 1984), and *The Age of Television* (1956, 1958, 1973).

David Bordwell is professor of communication arts at the University of Wisconsin–Madison. Born in New York City, he received a B.A. degree from the State University of New York at Albany (1969) and M.A. (1972) and Ph.D. degrees (1974) from the University of Iowa. He is the author of several books, including *Film Art: An Introduction* (with Kristin Thompson, 2nd ed., 1985) and *Narrative in the Fiction Film* (1985).

James Boylan is an associate professor of journalism and director of the Journalism Program at the University of Massachusetts, Amherst.

A native of Iowa, he received his B.A. degree from Cornell College (Iowa) in 1950, and his M.S. degree in journalism (1951) and his Ph.D. degree in history (1971) from Columbia University. He was the founding editor of the *Columbia Journalism Review,* which he edited in 1961–9 and 1976-9. His books include *The World and the 20s* (1973) and *The New Deal Coalition and the Election of 1946* (1981).

Stuart N. Brotman is a Boston-based communications lawyer and management consultant. He received a B.S. degree from Northwestern University (1974), an M.A. degree in communications from the University of Wisconsin–Madison (1975), and a J.D. degree from the University of California, Berkeley (1978). He served as special assistant to President Carter's principal communications policy adviser and is the editor of *The Telecommunications Deregulation Sourcebook* (1987).

Noël Carroll is associate professor of philosophy at Cornell University. Born in Far Rockaway, New York, he received a B.A. degree from Hofstra University (1969) and doctorates from New York University (1976) and the University of Illinois (1980). His essays have appeared in *Daedalus, October, Drama Review,* and *Film Quarterly.*

Philip S. Cook is secretary of the Media Studies Project of The Woodrow Wilson International Center for Scholars. Born in Troy, New York, he received a B.A. degree in American history from Williams College (1951). He has been a newspaper reporter (*Hartford Courant, New York Herald Tribune*), *Newsweek* correspondent, a founding editor of *The Wilson Quarterly,* and managing editor of *Issues in Science and Technology.* He also served on the staffs of the Peace Corps and the Senate Foreign Relations Committee.

Douglas Gomery is professor of communication arts at the University of Maryland. Born in New York City, he received a B.A. degree in economics from Lehigh University (1967) and an M.A. degree in economics (1970) and a Ph.D. degree in communication arts (1975) from the University of Wisconsin–Madison. He is the coauthor of *Film History: Theory and Practice* (with Robert C. Allen, 1985) and author of *The Hollywood Studio System* (1986).

David Harman is professor of education at Teachers College of Columbia University. Born in Jerusalem, he received a B.A. degree from the Hebrew University of Jerusalem (1965) and an Ed.D. degree from Harvard (1971). He is the author of *Adult Illiteracy in the United States* (with Carman St. John Hunter, 1979), *Learning to be Parents: Principles, Programs, and Methods* (with Orville G. Brim, Jr., 1980), and *Illiteracy: A National Dilemma* (1987).

A.E. Dick Howard, a former Wilson Center Fellow, is White Burkett Miller Professor of law and public affairs at the University of Virginia. Born in Richmond, Virginia, he is a graduate of the University of Richmond (1954), and received his law degree from the University of Virginia (1961). He was law clerk to Supreme Court Justice Hugo L. Black and was chief architect of the new Virginia Constitution, which became effective in 1971. His books include *The Road from Runnymede: Magna Carta and Constitutionalism in America* (1974) and *Commentaries on the Constitution of Virginia* (1974).

Steven Lagerfeld is senior editor of *The Wilson Quarterly*. Born in New York City, he received a B.A. degree from Cornell University (1977). Before joining *The Wilson Quarterly* in 1981, he was an editor at *The Public Interest* and a staff member of the Institute for Educational Affairs. His articles have appeared in *Harpers, The Public Interest, Policy Review,* and *The American Spectator.*

T.J. Jackson Lears, a former Wilson Center Fellow, is professor of history at Rutgers University. Born in Annapolis, Maryland, he received his B.A. degree from the University of Virginia (1969), his M.A. degree from the University of North Carolina (1973), and his doctorate from Yale University (1978). He is the author of *No Place of Grace: Antimodernism and the Transformation of American Culture, 1880–1920* (1981), coeditor of *The Culture of Competition* (1983), and is at work on a book about the relationship between American advertising and American culture. This essay is adapted from a longer piece that appeared in *Prospects: An Annual Journal of American Cultural Studies* (1984).

Lawrence W. Lichty is professor of radio/television/film at Northwestern University and a former Wilson Center Fellow. Born in Pasadena, California, he received an A.B. degree from the University of Southern California (1959) and a doctorate from Ohio State University (1963). He is the coauthor (with Malachi C. Topping) of *American Broadcasting* (1975). He has been the director of audience research at National Public Radio and was director of media research for the 1983 PBS series *Vietnam: A Television History.*

Frank D. McConnell is professor of English at the University of California, Santa Barbara, and a former Wilson Center Fellow. Born in Louisville, Kentucky, he received his B.A. degree from the University of Notre Dame (1964) and his doctorate from Yale (1968). He is the author of *The Confessional Imagination: A Reading of Wordsworth's "Prelude"* (1974), *The Spoken Seen: Film and the Romantic Imagination* (1975), *Four Postwar American Novelists: Bellow, Mailer, Barth, and Pynchon* (1977), and two detective novels.

Nathan Reingold is senior historian at the National Museum of American History. Born in New York City, he received his B.A. (1947) and M.A. degrees (1948) from New York University and his Ph.D. degree (1951) from the University of Pennsylvania. He is the coeditor of *Science in America: A Documentary History, 1900–1939* (1982); editor of the unpublished papers and manuscripts of physicist Joseph Henry, first Secretary of the Smithsonian; and is currently working on a history of the research community in the United States since 1940. This essay has been adapted by the editors from a longer paper prepared for a conference on the popularization of science sponsored by the journal *Sociology of the Sciences*.

Stuart Alan Shorenstein is a partner in the New York law firm of Lowenthal, Landau, Fischer and Ziegler and has taught communications law at Hofstra University Law School. He received a B.A. degree from Duke University (1968) and a J.D. degree from New York University (1971).

Joel Swerdlow is program and publications advisor to the Annenberg Washington Program for Communications Policy Studies of Northwestern University. A native of Washington, D.C., he holds a B.A. degree from Syracuse University (1968) and a Ph.D. degree in American politics from Cornell (1974). He is coauthor of *Remote Control: Television and the Manipulation of American Life* (1978, with Frank Mankiewicz), author of the novel *Code Z* (1979), coauthor of *To Heal a Nation: The Vietnam Vet Memorial* (1985, with Jan Scruggs), and editor of *Presidential Debates: 1988 and Beyond* (1987).

Lorna Veraldi is assistant professor in the School of Journalism and Mass Communications at Florida International University, Miami, and is a communications lawyer. She has also practiced law in New York City and has taught at Hofstra University Law School and the University of Utah. She received a B.A. degree from Eastern Montana College (1970), an M.A. degree in communications from the University of Utah (1976), and a J.D. degree from New York Law School (1981).